Female Railway Workers in
World War II

Female Railway Workers in World War II

Susan Major

PEN & SWORD
TRANSPORT

AN IMPRINT OF PEN & SWORD BOOKS LTD.
YORKSHIRE – PHILADELPHIA

First published in Great Britain in 2018 by
Pen & Sword Transport
An imprint of
Pen & Sword Books Ltd
Yorkshire - Philadelphia

Copyright © Susan Major, 2018

ISBN 9781526703088

Typeset in INDIA By Geniies IT & Services Private Limited.

Printed and bound in the UK by TJ International Ltd.

Pen & Sword Books Ltd incorporates the Imprints of Pen & Sword Books
Archaeology, Atlas, Aviation, Battleground, Discovery, Family History,
History, Maritime, Military, Naval, Politics, Railways, Select, Transport, True
Crime, Fiction, Frontline Books, Leo Cooper, Praetorian Press, Seaforth
Publishing, Wharncliffe and White Owl.

For a complete list of Pen & Sword titles please contact

PEN & SWORD BOOKS LIMITED
47 Church Street, Barnsley, South Yorkshire, S70 2AS, England
E-mail: enquiries@pen-and-sword.co.uk
Website: www.pen-and-sword.co.uk

or

PEN AND SWORD BOOKS
1950 Lawrence Rd, Havertown, PA 19083, USA
E-mail: Uspen-and-sword@casematepublishers.com
Website: www.penandswordbooks.com

Contents

List of Illustrations

Preface

During the Second World War many thousands of the men working on the railways in Britain were called up for military service, and many thousands of women were recruited to replace them, to keep this vital service running. There had of course been women already working in some areas of the railway, such as in clerical, cleaning and catering jobs, although before the war even most of those jobs were carried out by men. But in wartime many women were employed in the kind of work which was completely new to females, working as porters and guards, and in maintenance and workshop operations.

As generations die out and families lose a direct connection with the women who did this work, it becomes more important to be able to preserve a record of their experiences, and to share these with a wider audience. This book draws upon a most valuable but underused resource, the National Archive of Railway Oral History (NAROH). Created by the Friends of the National Railway Museum during 2000-2003, with the support of the Heritage Lottery Fund and many volunteers, the project set out to achieve a comprehensive set of interviews representing the railway industry from the 1940s to the end of the century. Under Project Coordinator Joanne Stewardson, volunteers interviewed hundreds of railway workers about their lifetime railway experiences, with over 1,000 hours of recordings, many of which have been transcribed. These recordings deserve a wider audience. Although the collection features mainly male workers, this book has selected material from the small number of women who were interviewed, about their wartime work. The range is not comprehensive, we have no account here from a wartime signalwoman for example, although many were working in this role. But the difference between the voices of these women, recorded assiduously by volunteers, and the voices of women reported in publicity campaigns at the time, is striking.

These women were recorded at the turn of the twenty-first century, by then all at a good age, being born in the first thirty years of the twentieth century. Inevitably they were almost all young women when they experienced railway work for the first time. The timing of the archive project precluded evidence from older women, who would have been no longer with us by the year 2000. We know however from contemporary press and company magazines that there were many older women, with large families, who took undertook railway work during the war.

This book includes evidence from a further resource, in the form of research by Alan Hammond from the Somerset & Dorset Railway. His sterling efforts have produced an invaluable collection of written accounts by a number of S & D women railway workers, now in the National Railway Museum Search Engine archive.

We have to take account of how memories are shaped by the way that a woman decides to make sense of her time during the war, what she chooses to remember and what she would prefer to forget, and the image she wishes to present to the interviewer (almost all of whom were men) about her role at the time. But at the same time this kind of personal testimony is rare and valuable, when matched against the cheery, formulaic phrases reported from women workers in the press under the control of the publicity managers.

Two historians, Helena Wojtczak and Rosa Matheson, have written meticulously researched and authoritative works on the role of women on the railways. Helena was British Rail's first female guard, at 19 in 1978, and her *Railwaywomen* covers women from the 1830s until the turn of the twenty-first century, with a focus on how they struggled for recognition. It is an impressively comprehensive study of the role of women on the railway. In another invaluable work, *The Fair Sex: Women and the Great Western Railway*, Rosa Matheson concentrates on women working for the Great Western Railway, and how they were regarded by management. But apart from these two books, there is little else reflecting women railway workers in Britain and their wartime experiences. Most of the books about women's wartime role focus on the services or industrial work.

This book uses personal accounts, mainly from the National Archive of Railway Oral History, to supplement those two studies, in a contribution to the study of women's work during the Second World War. Using their transcribed voices, it paints a picture of the lives and experiences of a range of women, set in the context of how they were portrayed in official publicity at the time. Some were carrying out what might be regarded as 'women's work', others were quite definitely doing 'men's work'. It covers the 'big four' railway companies during wartime, but not the London Underground.

These are their stories.
Susan Major

Acknowledgements

This book is based on a most valuable research resource – the National Archive of Railway Oral History - created by the Friends of the National Railway Museum. This collection of interviews with railway workers was carried out in 2000–2003, and many were transcribed, which has made my work much easier. Frank Paterson, their President, has also been particularly helpful in commenting on my draft and answering my many questions, drawing upon his extensive range of contacts for answers. It was also particularly inspiring to talk to and correspond with wartime railway worker Betty Forrester and her daughter Ann Arnot, who provided very helpful photographs. Robin Nelson, who carried out a large number of interviews kindly supplied a photograph of Betty from 2002, when the Friends of the NRM recreated her wartime role in Troon with a telegraphy machine. I was also pleased to make contact with Lydia and Vanessa, granddaughters of Irene Barrett-Locke.

I would like to thank Ed Bartholomew, Senior Curator, Railways and Research, at the National Railway Museum (NRM) in York, for his patient and thorough help and advice in accessing the NAROH collection, and his comments. Other members of staff at the NRM Search Engine have been helpful, especially Angelique Bonamy, who led me to the Alan Hammond collection from the Somerset & Dorset Railway. In addition to thanking Alan Hammond, I would also like to thank Steph Gillett, Honorary Curator of the Somerset & Dorset Railway Trust, who kindly sourced photographs for me, and Jasmine Rodgers at the Science Museum. From the National Railway Museum I am grateful to Chris Mossop and Helen Ashby for leading me to historic exhibition material there. I am also indebted to Simon Dixon and Ian Swirles at the University of Leicester Special Collections, who were particularly helpful in locating material.

I would like to thank my publishers, Pen & Sword for their very welcome support over the last three years, especially Kate Bamforth, Janet Brookes and and my commissioning editor, John Scott-Morgan. Thanks also to Barnaby Blacker for his meticulous copy-editing. This was my first focus on women working in wartime and I was very pleased to be able to contact the two specialists who have carried out extensive work on railway women workers, Helena Wojtczak and Rosa Matheson. I am also grateful to Hannah Reeves from Keele

University, who discussed her work on the railway family. A chance meeting with Megan Doole at a railway workshop led me to the picture of the horse ramps at Paddington Station.

Family members have contributed to the book. I'm particularly grateful to our son Edd Major for his hard work in spending many hours transcribing relevant interview tapes, while he was on his travels around the world. Dianne Bates also kindly gave me help in tracking down a reference.

Lastly, as always, the most important person is my husband Ralph, to whom I'm eternally grateful for doing all the things that needed to be done, while I was busy researching these women.

Susan Major

Foreword

In 1939, at the start of the Second World War, Britain's railway companies had almost 600,000 employees and only 4% were female. Within two years this increased substantially, as by 1941 it was 7% and in 1944 it was over 15%.

Dr Susan Major has put together a fascinating story of how it happened and more importantly who the women were and what they did. Much of the material comes from the National Archive of Railway Oral History and she has used extracts from 28 interviews to tell the individual stories. The verbatim transcriptions bring out the personalities of the individuals and you can almost 'hear them speaking'. The reality was often quite different from that portrayed by the company publicity machines!

The range of railway jobs undertaken was impressive and the women generally found the work and their male colleagues congenial. But their recollections bring out the huge differences from current social attitudes and expectations – an underlying naivety in the way that women accepted their lot comes through in many of their stories.

I'm particularly pleased that Susan has collated so much material from NAROH.

I hope this will lead to other authors recognising the rich store of human interest stories which is available in the over 650 individual interviews held in the NRM Archive.

Frank Paterson
President, Friends of the National Railway Museum
Chairman, National Archive of Railway Oral History Steering Group

"I Cannot Offer Them a Delightful Life"

I have to tell women that I cannot offer them a delightful life. They'll have to suffer some inconveniences, but I want them to come forward in the spirit of determination to help us through.[1]

(*Ernest Bevin, 1941*)

On his 57th birthday on 9 March 1941, Ernest Bevin, Minister of Labour, launched a plea for 100,000 women to enrol for war work in Britain, in farms, in factories and on the railways. He and his colleagues were worried about the need to replace the men recruited into war service. But women had the care of their families to think about, and so as an incentive he announced an expansion of nursery centres and a register of childminders. Here women would only have to pay pre-war costs, at 6d. a day, with the government paying an extra 6d. for looking after the children. Bevin explained that he was hoping that this call would encourage those women who were not already in jobs, or registered for war work. Bevin calculated that for every two men away on service, three women would need to be employed, to make up the short-fall of labour. (He revised his opinion on this ratio in 1943, when addressing the Diamond Jubilee Congress of the Women's Co-operative Guild. In a press report headed 'Our Plane Output Beats Germany's', Bevin stated that his own earlier calculations had been upset by 'the marvellous response of the women of Britain'. He admitted that the output of women, instead of being that of three women to two men, was slightly the other way compared to 1939.) At the time there was some confusion following this plea for women to step forward voluntarily, as Bevin was also introducing measures of compulsory conscription for women.[2]

The idea of railway work for women was not new that year. As early as the summer of 1940, agreement had been reached between the railway companies and the National Union of Railwaymen about employing women on the railways in jobs previously done by men. They were to be paid on starting grades, subject to a three-month probationary period, receiving 4s. less than men.[3]

However at this time some of the media were still wary of removing the focus of women from their traditional roles. *Women's Own* magazine argued in April 1941, 'Whether or not we agree with Mr Bevin's plans for sending women to needed jobs (and to be honest we must admit that our sex isn't without members who might learn a lot by having to do a job of work) we all agree that it is home that matters.'[4] But later on, women's magazines were to play a much more active role in helping to persuade women to sign up for wartime roles. They did this by emphasising positive aspects, by helping women to develop a sense of pride in achievements gained, by lobbying for reforms, by giving advice on how to adapt, and by seeking to change the attitudes of other family members who might object to women working.[5]

While thousands of women were considering contributing to the war effort by joining the military services, or working in industry, for the many women who belonged to railway families the decision was not difficult. They might be encouraged and supported by male family members, and their path to employment eased by the men 'putting a word in for them'. Occasionally families might look down on railway work, but for most it was regarded as a solid worthwhile job, naturally perceived to be an absolute necessity to 'keep the trains running'. At the same time, the introduction of female labour, to be speedily trained and installed, caused some shocks to the rigid hierarchy of the railway occupational structure.

The employment of women on the railways was not new in British history. Helena Wojtczak has identified female railway labourers in the 1851 census, and there were many women working as crossing keepers around then, reflecting their historic role in policing turnpike gates. Rosa Matheson found Great Western Railway (GWR) female crossing keepers in the 1870s, and, unusually, at least one female signalwoman in 1890, working for the GWR in Devon, still there in 1913. Wojtczak found a small number of female station 'mistresses', or 'clerks in charge', from the 1830s onwards, and a female railway porter as early as 1871, at Barrow-in-Furness. There are rare examples of women working in booking offices, and in telegraph work from the 1850s onwards.[6] A few women were working as railway clerks for the London & North Western Railway (LNWR) in 1875, when the company employed fifteen women invoice clerks, and station masters were encouraged to use their daughters as booking clerks 'whenever there was a disposition to do so'.[7] A correspondent in the *Southern Railway Magazine* reported that his mother, Miss Robinson, the daughter of a station master, was employed in the booking office at Woodgate (near Bognor Regis) before her marriage in 1863, and there was also a female booking clerk, a Miss White, at Cosham (near Portsmouth) in the 1880s.[8]

Women were working at the LNWR Wolverton Works from the 1830s, but it appears that the GWR was generally resistant to the employment of women in their workshops at this time, although women had been working at the Swindon Works in the early 1870s, first in the trimming shop and later in the laundry. There was a reason for this: Rosa Matheson suggests that Swindon took on women at this point to encourage their fathers to come, as these were the skilled men they needed. The men had been loath to move to Swindon, when there was no employment for their daughters. As a result the upholstery shop there was set up for women, with a separate entrance, to keep them away from the men. The GWR had also considered taking on female clerks in the 1870s, but had serious concerns. These centred not on their capabilities, but on the need to ensure that men and women were not working in the same office, in their eyes a most inappropriate activity. As the company would have had to construct entirely separate offices, the GWR refused to take on women clerks then. It appears that there may have been a class element shaping this, that working class women were acceptable, possibly more controllable, a known phenomenon, whereas middle class women in offices were not. It was not until 1906 that the company took on a small group of female clerks at Paddington Goods Office (although there was a female clerk at the GWR Swindon Works from 1895). The company had very fixed ideas; astonishingly during the early part of the twentieth century they were still restricting the recruitment of men into skilled jobs, by limiting applications to the sons of skilled men only.[9]

Wartime led to a greatly increased demand for labour. Although previously the few women workers had been kept mainly behind the scenes, during the First World War many women were employed in roles which could be viewed by the public, such as goods and passenger porters, parcel porters and ticket collectors, as well as behind-the-scenes work such as carriage cleaners, engine cleaners, clerks and certain workshop grades.[10] Surprisingly, although cleaning might traditionally be thought of as 'women's work', cleaning carriages and engines had been quite definitely a man's job until now, a view taken by the National Union of Railwaymen (NUR), who felt that young boys would be more suitable for this task. Another difficulty was said to be the unsuitability of women's clothing, such as the voluminous skirts, for such tasks, which might involve climbing ladders. Their participation may also have been opposed on the grounds that the role of engine cleaner was traditionally seen as the first step on the ladder to be an engine driver.[11] But wartime necessity changed the rules and many women took on the work of cleaning carriages and engines in place of men.[12] Very few were able to remain however after the war, and it was not until the 1930s that women were allowed to be carriage cleaners again.[13] By the time the First World War ended in 1918, there were nearly 70,000 women in the railway workforce, around 16 per cent of the total.[14] Some came back to heed the call during the Second World War.

By 1939 the employment of women to replace men on the railways was a growing phenomenon in Britain: men were rapidly disappearing and women were starting to be taken on. There were already 26,000 women working, out of a total workforce of nearly 600,000, in traditional female roles such as clerical and secretarial tasks, catering, carriage cleaners and crossing keepers. It has even been suggested that female railway recruitment during the Second World War was a significant factor in winning the war, as volunteer civilians were not mobilised in Germany in the same way.[15] The Railway Clerks Association (RCA) (which eventually became the Transport Salaried Staffs' Association (TSSA) in 1951) highlighted the increasing number of women working in railway offices.[16] Their General Secretary, W. Scott, admitted that he was not asking the Railway Staff National Tribunal for equal pay for these women, although he suggested that many, especially the senior women, would have had a good claim as they were in his words 'exploited and underpaid'.[17] Attitudes in the RCA towards women were more supportive than the National Union of Railwaymen (NUR) however, as women clerks in female salary grades were often better educated and more vocal, possibly looking at railway careers, and taking part in RCA discussions.[18]

In December 1939, after the war had started, the GWR started to consider taking on women porters.[19] Kathleen Hall recalled being one of the first being taken on by GWR as a 'lad porter' at 17, at Stratford-upon-Avon Station.[20] There was a certain lack of confidence by the railway companies in the abilities of women to take on this new task. The plan was to 'give the women a spell in the warehouses, presumably to toughen them up a bit, and then transfer them to station platforms'. Typically the press addressed this move in syndicated newspaper articles, adopting a jaunty tone, orchestrated centrally by the British Railways Executive:

> So we may soon be greeted as we step from the train by the helpful suggestions of another recruit to the trousered regiments in blue, who will perhaps raise a questioning finger in the approved manner and then whisk away one's bags and golf clubs.[21]

Publicity officers and journalists had some difficulty in treating the new women workers straightforwardly, never being able to report on them without including elements of femininity. There were underlying concerns about their abilities, their 'feminine' characteristics, the threat to 'men's' jobs and a refusal to see women as more than 'decorative objects', unless they had 'proved themselves'. Women often featured in press stories which linked them to their husbands' and fathers' roles, or had to demonstrate that they were still carrying out traditional responsibilities, such as looking after a household, large families and elderly relatives, in addition to long hours in their new railway jobs. In a poem published at the end of 1939, the *Daily Herald* decided that access to a porter's tip might make women more willing to subject themselves to what would now be known as 'mansplaining':[22]

> Whenever I have tried
> To give advice to dames,
> They've usually replied
> With silence – or with Names
>
> But at no distant date,
> It's easy to foresee,
> They'll find I carry weight –
> And take a tip from me. (H.R.)

Looking at relationships with a modern perspective, it is quite difficult to comprehend the attitudes to women and their interests and abilities at that time. A wartime view on the role of women in society appeared in a draft 1942 Mass Observation file report by Tom Harrisson, one of the founders of Mass Observation.[23] In *Appeals to Women,* he sets the scene on how the press might persuade women to respond to the manpower crisis, assessing their 'limited horizons':

> As this war gradually moves towards its fourth year, more and more does it become, on the Home Front, a war of women. At first women played the more negative role of keeping the home going and carrying most of the small worries. Now every available female body is required in a war factory or uniform. Never before in our history has the State had to interfere with the lives of so many people so quickly and so drastically, and particularly never before has it had so much to do direct with women. In normal times, most major decisions of personal conduct are determined largely by a husband or father or fiancé, and without anybody having thought about it very much, most of the instructions, directions, legislations are based on this assumption and are addressed by men to men. Talking to women is limited largely to small matters, particularly concerned with the spending of the wage packet. And on the whole it has to be admitted that the majority of women have been content with this situation. The vigorous suffragette movement did not steadily grow, but faded right away once the vote for women had been won, as if the vote was some sort of final triumph.

The idea presented here is that keeping the home going under extremely difficult conditions was seen as a 'negative role', as opposed to male war service.

Harrisson goes on to use evidence collected by the Mass Observation investigators to contrast the attitudes of older women who came in voluntarily – keen and patriotic – with that of the younger conscripts, who were not so positive.[24] He also suggests that women suffered from tiredness, boredom and apathy, and that there were worries about enforced mobility. This is not surprising as these women had households to run and children and elderly relatives to look after, as well as long hours working on the railway.

Women had to play their part in the war effort. Early in 1941 Bevin announced that under the Registration for Employment Order, women in certain age groups must register for war work, with no 'class distinctions and no exceptions', apart from women in the forces and those in nursing. On 19 April 1941 it was the turn of women aged 20 to register, and women aged 21 shortly afterwards.[25] Registration involved an interview, with the noting of family occupations. Women could choose from a range of jobs, for example the women's military services (no use of any 'lethal weapon' without her written consent), civilian defence, or work in industry, often in armaments factories. If they were without family ties then they would be considered 'mobile' and could be asked to work in other parts of the country.[26]

Bevin had also introduced the Essential Work Order (EWO) in March 1941. This tied workers to jobs considered essential for the war effort and prevented employers from sacking workers without permission from the Ministry of Labour. By December 1941, the government had passed the National Service Act (no 2), which legalised the conscription of women into the women's auxiliary services, civil defence and certain industries.[27] At first, only unmarried women and childless widows aged 21-30 were called up, but this was later extended to 19-43. By mid-1943, it was reported that almost 90 per cent of single women and 80 per cent of married women were employed in essential work for the war effort.[28]

The railways were beginning to lose men in great numbers. The Military Training Act in May 1939 applied to single men aged between 20 and 22, requiring them to undertake six months' military training, and around 240,000 registered for service.[29] On 3 September 1939, the National Service (Armed Forces) Act imposed conscription on all males aged between 18 and 41, who had to register for service unless they were medically unfit or in key industries and jobs. The previous year a Schedule of Reserved Occupations had been drawn up, exempting certain key skilled workers from conscription. These included five million men: railway and dockworkers, miners, farmers, agricultural workers, schoolteachers and doctors. The schedule also prescribed age ranges for being 'reserved', which were subject to review, especially in the light of the recruitment of women to fill these occupations. It included, among many more obvious trades, some surprising people, such as architects, bacteriologists, bedding makers, slipper makers, BBC administrative and executive grades, time and motion study experts, chefs de cuisine, typewriter repairers, French polishers, goldsmiths and silversmiths, glass decorators, stained glass fitters, gem polishers, masseurs, bookbinders, statisticians and trade union officials.[30]

Railway workers to be 'reserved' were categorised as executives, managers, inspectors and agents; engine drivers and shed foremen; firemen, engine cleaners and shed workers; linesmen, gangers, signalmen and platelayers; porters, foremen and goods workers; ticket collectors, guards, shunters, examiners and crossing keepers; railway clerks. With the removal of buffet and dining cars from trains, male railway stewards became liable to be called up for military service, and when these cars were introduced again it was women who worked on them.[31]

In preparation for war it was arranged that the undertakings of the main line railway companies and the London Passenger Transport Board should be controlled by the government, in the form of the Railway Executive Committee (REC).[32] The headquarters of the 'big four' railway companies moved out of London. By the end of 1939 staff from the Paddington headquarters of the Great Western Railway (GWR) had been evacuated to a mysterious newly constructed location in the countryside, near Aldermaston, with 'staff special' daily trains bringing in the workers from their home towns.[33] The need to recruit women failed to rise to the top of the agenda for their company magazine however, where the role of women was confined to announcements about Railway Queens (see page 147) and reports of open days at the Swindon Works, when visitors included parties of 'young ladies':

> They are, of course, conducted with the same decorum as other parties, but if glances are more eloquent than words, their interest in men and machines is divided, and more than one dashing apprentice has felt his heart thump against his boiler-suit when those 'lovelies' pass by.[34]

Around this time there were some female GWR railway clerks photographed in the company magazine, working alongside men in temporary offices in railway carriages.[35] Clearly there was a demarcation of roles here, the men had telephones and pens in their hands, the women were working at typewriters.

The staff magazine of the London Midland & Scottish Railway (LMS) featured a monthly page for women during 1939, written by Agnes Neville, as the company felt the need to address the interests of female members of railway families. This was aimed at housewives in traditional roles, with paragraphs for example in January on bargains in the shops, what the Queen was wearing, garden birds and mushrooms (readers were advised how to detect if the latter were poisonous, using a silver spoon in the pan). Later issues included beauty tips, household hints and cooking, especially jam, which featured at great length across several issues. However, unusually, in April 1939, the company also devoted a whole issue to its women workers. It highlighted women working as telephone exchange operators, waiting room inspectresses, an ambulance sister at Wolverton Works, a range of clerical workers in supervisory positions, hotel and laundry workers, company hospital staff at Crewe Works, French polishers at Derby Works, staff uniform and sheet factory workers at Manchester, clerks at Derby Ticket Sorting Office (where all the tickets were returned, sorted and processed), stewardesses on cross-channel steamers, and women ambulance teams.[36] The company was keen to involve female relatives too, and included two competitions restricted to women entrants, one for photography and another for the best household hint. It was suggested that 'in the house and in the garden there are dozens of happy little incidents each day' which might form subjects for a photograph. It may be 'the children, pets, father up to his tricks'. Emphasis was placed on subjects depicting 'happiness at home'.[37]

The London & North Eastern Railway (LNER) had previously employed many women in certain jobs, for example in LNER grain sack depots. This business had passed on to the railway companies in the 1870s, when it was felt that they could do a better job than a private company, looking after the complex business of hiring out sacks for grain carried by rail, making sure they were returned and accounting for their supply. LNER had three million sacks, hired from depots based in Aberdeen, Edinburgh, York and Lincoln.[38] In another setting, a large number of women were employed in the LNER laundry at Colchester. There was a lot to do, as the laundry serviced hotels, refreshment rooms, dormitories, steamships and offices in the Great Eastern and London section of the southern area, cleaning over eight million items each year. Writers in the staff magazine could not however resist making comments about physical appearance: there were around 80 to 100 girls, 'some of them athletic but not one of them unattractive', and 14 men.[39]

By September 1939 LNER was also on a wartime footing, with senior staff moving out to a country mansion near Hitchin, mysteriously known as HQ1.[40] A humorous staff magazine, *The Ballyhoo Review*, was produced weekly by staff for staff, between September 1939 and May 1940, and included comical pen portraits of office staff, of which there were a number of women. For example 'Ladies of the Engineer's Dept' featured in January 1940, where Miss M. Smythe was 'A problem from Ilford, Essex. Saturated with the dogma of neo-sensation. Dynamic and devastating, good company if you can stand the pressure'. Again a Miss Todd was 'Modest, sympathetic, discreet and tactful, the very antithesis of Miss Smythe above! Originally a Londoner but now a village lass. Has a rumoured affection for a "toddy"'.[41]

With wartime shortages developing in 1940, the government was keen to recruit 250,000 women into manufacturing jobs in the iron and steel industry, reducing the long hours being worked by men and freeing them for war service.[42] On the railways, male railway clerks aged 25 to 30 had now been called up, as they were no longer 'reserved', and so there was a growing need to fill their places with women.[43] In April 1940 the REC Staff Committee asked for information from the railway companies about shortages. They wanted to know which areas were affected by problems of recruiting suitable male labour for railway work, which grades, whether the present and future shortages could be met by employing women, and if so in which grades.[44] Many of the men who had been released from the railways for war service had been porters, carriage cleaners and porter signalmen. While some men in the workforce had been able to move up a grade, it left grade 2 porters, goods porters and carriage cleaners in demand (many women were already doing the latter work). There was also a need for ticket collectors, carters, and a range of assistants in railway workshops. There was much discussion however about how this might affect the progression of men when they returned from the war. The situation was getting worse. In July 1940 the GWR reported a serious shortage of guards, which was preventing the running of some trains. They recognised the need to recruit women as ticket collectors, so that men could be released as guards and shunters. The idea of women being recruited as guards was problematic at first, as male guards had spent many years working their way up the hierarchy to achieve this position. Now it was being suggested that women might be brought in to do the job after a few weeks training. However all of the companies started to recruit women in this post in the early 1940s: GWR were the first to do so, with 46 female guards by 1942.[45] GWR had already taken on over 2,000 women, mostly porters (over 1,300), but also van guards and ticket collectors. By the end of 1942 they also had 976 female carriage cleaners.[46]

The Railway Executive Committee (REC) produced a paper outlining the need for a coordinated publicity strategy on behalf of the railway companies, with 'new experiments to meet war-time conditions', including the need to employ women.[47] But this move failed to find much favour with Southern Railway. In October 1940 SR responded, arguing against some of the points in the document, worried that their hard-fought company reputation would be buried in a coordinated campaign.

Certain attitudes to women prevailed in railway staff magazines. In January 1940, *Carry On*, the LMS wartime newsletter, captioned a photograph of women clerks, 'She tells them where to "Get off"' and these women were said to offer an 'added attraction' to passenger enquiries at Euston.[48] In August their views on women were still patronising, with a photo of a woman collecting LMS salvage for the war effort captioned 'Little Gel'.[49] By September 1940, LMS were recruiting women to replace railway porters in London, inspired by the recruitment of women to replace male bus conductors there.[50] As many as

250 women had already been recruited for the Midlands and North, many were married women, the relatives of railwaymen, reinforcing the idea of 'the railway family'.[51] This was a commonly used characteristic, suggesting that the reputation of a woman worker might be 'safer' when displayed in the light of a male relative and/or, rather surprisingly, a large family of dependent children. The new LMS recruits were to be employed at the main goods depots, and would receive eight days training (three days theory and five under the supervision of a male porter). Their work would be the loading and unloading goods up to 75lb, which might include bedsteads, bales of cloth, ploughs, rubber tyres and drums of oil and paint. In a syndicated article about LMS, appearing in many publications and tightly controlled, one woman said:

> It's a bit tough at first, but we've not been long in getting down to the job. Now I wouldn't like to leave it. We get on very well together, and manage to get a lot of fun out of the work as well. Of course it's no film star's job. We've got no time for lipstick or powder, and we haven't got to be afraid of dirtying our hands or faces.[52]

There were plenty of jokes about 'Oh Mrs Porter'. A *Times* article from October 1940, reproduced by some regional newspapers, and proudly highlighted in *Carry On*, waxed lyrically about the new 'lady porters' being employed by LMS, with a patronising sarcasm and a short poem:

> Send me back to London
> As quickly as you can;
> O dear Miss Porter
> What a silly boy I am![53]

By November 1940, the *Manchester Guardian* was offering a first prize of two guineas and second prize of one guinea for a comment (not exceeding 75 words) on the LMS announcement.[54] A report on the winners suggested that the idea of a woman performing what was regarded as a man's job might offend against the idea of chivalry.[55] But it went on to highlight all the industrial work that women had done in the last war, and the subsequent development of women's athletic prowess in, for example, weight-lifting, rowing and swimming. Readers commented on the example set by Russian women in coal mines, on concerns from existing porters that women might not be able to manage the heavy lifting and the need for legislation against extremely heavy luggage, which affected men as well as women. Although women tended to be smaller and lighter than men, this was at a time when women had many hard and heavy jobs in the home, without labour-saving devices to ease their work. New rules limiting the weight of luggage did indeed emerge later.

The first prize went to Emily Tattersall from Windermere, for her poem, with a patriotic view of women rising to the challenge:

> In times of stress the L.M.S.
> Engages women porters
> On Tube trains, too, this duty new
> Is done by Britain's daughters
>
> They cry "All change!" in voices strange
> Farewell, stentorian bellow!
> Henceforth, instead, our steps are sped
> By dulcet tones and mellow.
>
> They'll pull their weight whatever fate
> Shall test how strong their nerve is.
> Where'er they trip may many a tip
> Reward their national service!

The second prize-winner was G.R. Harrop from Marple, a rather more mixed reaction, assuming that women would not be able to cope with heavy loads:

> Hi! Porter, fetch a taxi quick,
> And bring my golfing kit and bags.
> Say! Hurry up there, man, be slick.
> You'll see my name upon the tags.
> Pardon, madam, what did you say?
> What means these strange of strangest clothes?
> That you are porter from today!
> Allow me, miss, you can't lift those.

Poetry was often used in the press to signal strange new practices. In December 1940 the LMS *Carry On* newsletter reproduced a poem by Robbins Millar from the Scottish edition of the *Daily Express*, using the term porteress, which frequently reared its ugly head in the 1940s, a kind of nod to the idea that when a woman was carrying out a man's role it had to be labelled in a 'feminine' way:[56]

The Porteress

> She'll be spry as a sparrow
> At hurling a barrow
> An absolute ace
> At yanking a case

> You'll never get waxy
> She'll find you a taxi
> Respond to your yell
> Like a dashing gazelle;
> And charge no extortions
> For chipping large portions
> In lumps and in chunks
> Off your holiday trunks.

Female GWR workers at Paddington had some surprising duties. There were of course women nurses staffing the casualty clearing stations there at this time, but in 1940 the 'girls' in the refreshment and waiting rooms, open all night, were apparently sometimes asked for needles and cotton, to carry out 'running repairs' for servicemen and their uniforms, and also to act as 'human alarm clocks'.[57]

There were wage differentials. Negotiations with the National Union of Railwaymen (NUR) resulted in an agreement that women in 'men's jobs' would be paid the starting grade equivalent for a man, after a certain length of probationary time at a lower wage. This did not apply however to those in 'women's jobs', such as many of the railway clerks. In effect women railway workers were paid less than men, because their supplementary war advance was lower, and they also worked less overtime because of their family responsibilities. Generally speaking though women were able to earn more in their jobs on the railway than in other work.[58]

By 1941 the number of women railway workers was increasing rapidly. There were various initiatives to encourage employers to take on women at this time, acknowledging the need to allow women to have 'reasonable time to do her shopping at convenient hours', although it is not clear whether this was allowed in practice.[59] The first women porters arrived at Preston in January 1941, wearing an LMS blue armlet in lieu of a uniform, which was due to arrive later. Publicity suggested that many would be relatives of railwaymen.[60] In February 1941 the LMS wrote to the Ministry of Labour to say they considered women between 25 and 40 the most suitable.[61] They focused on the recruitment of women goods porters in particular, in key locations, presenting a typically positive attitude.[62] In Nottingham a foreman was reported as saying, 'Women are always so much alive, and they are a happy crowd...They are very matey, and when one gets a bundle or a parcel she cannot handle herself, she immediately sings out to another woman to come and help.' Officials said they wanted many more women as clerks, goods and passenger porters, electric truck drivers, carriage cleaners, and staff for railway works. For goods porters they especially wanted women of 'good physique', and already had around thirty working in the goods depot. A press report spotlighted two women who had done similar jobs in the last war, one of whom had had fifteen children.[63]

The LMS also needed dining room attendants, preferring 'Nippys' with previous experience. 'Nippys' were waitresses famous at this time for working in the J. Lyons & Co tea shops and cafés in London. Intriguingly they were formerly known by the nickname 'Gladys', but this became seen as rather old-fashioned. Lyons sought to modernise and renamed them Nippys in the mid-1920s, as the waitresses 'nipped' (moved quickly) around the tea shops. In the tea shops Nippys wore a distinctive maid-like uniform with a matching hat, and it had been suggested that, following training, 'unskilled working class women were transformed into teashop debutantes'.[64]

The LNER embarked on a series of features in their staff magazine about a typical day's work by women railway workers. These must have been popular, as they were appearing more frequently by 1943, with a target presumably of the families of railwaymen.[65] Joan Peck, a 'girl clerk', working in the goods office at St Neots, featured in the first profile, describing her duties and timetable, a gentle introduction to women doing 'men's work'.[66] Joan had been recruited as early as April 1940 to replace a man, but didn't come from a railway family (her father was a farmer).

To persuade the public that the new women employees were fit and able to do heavy work, railway company publicity began to paint a picture of them as 'Amazons', as if to make this new practice more acceptable. Campaigns in Gloucester highlighted 'women Amazons' doing tough work well. The LMS employed their first female draywoman there, the daughter of a farmer, delivering goods, with a further two being trained up.[67] At the same time the company was at pains to emphasise that, where necessary, help with large crates was given by the consignee. Many of the new workers had left their own children with relatives, and some had come from faraway places, such as Birmingham and London, when their houses had been bombed. In July 1943 a staff newsletter feature headed 'Amazons of Oldham Road' focused on women working at the LMS Oldham Road Goods Depot.[68] It talked of 'grannies, mothers and 17-year-old girls' moving freight around and supporting food supplies. 'They tackle it with the same enthusiasm they tackle a dirty front door step', recognising that women often carried out dirty manual work at home. Later the LNER described these new women workers as 'Hercules' too, for example the crane workers, goods porters, at the grain warehouse at Marsh Lane in Leeds. They used hydraulic 'jiggers' to haul 4 cwt of flour or sugar between warehouse and wagon, and to barrow the goods, on average five wagons of 70–100 sacks each.[69] At the SR Redbridge Works near Southampton, a railway town, women were making sleepers, each weighing 1½ cwt, to be lifted by two women. It was calculated that each woman there, noted as 'robust matrons', lifted 1,600 'chairs' for the sleepers a day, each weighing 46lbs.[70] At times there were debates about the strength of the new women workers: a *Railway Gazette* correspondent complained at advertisements picturing women lifting a 56lb weight unaided, to which the response was that railway women had dealt regularly with weights of 56lb up to as much as 112lb.[71]

A Cheshire novelist, Beatrice Tunstall, was commissioned to write a feature in the *Chester Chronicle* in February 1941.[72] She described how she had been invited to Chester Station by R.D. Roberts, District Goods and Passenger Manager, to go and see the women working, as part of their publicity campaign. Guided by Mr Frost, Goods Agent, she waxed lyrically about two women goods porters, 'brunettes with clear pale skins, tall... boyishly slim – with an easy grace that bespoke perfect health and fitness'. These women had been working there for around eight weeks, both were married, one from the Doncaster area and the other from London. This confirms a typically high level of mobility following the bombing of homes, with women often travelling to where husbands were stationed. The article described long hours in shifts, with women wearing bib type jean trousers, an overcoat or mackintosh, oilskin leggings and a sou'wester. There were also vacancies for carters for those attracted to work with horses.

There were a few problems. There were reports about women porters being caught pilfering from goods, for example in Brighton and at Exeter.[73] The fact that they were women made these reports stand out, against the many men caught in similar activities. It seems that relatively small amounts of goods were often involved. Six women working at Wolverhampton were convicted of stealing seven packets of tea, worth 5s. and 3d., and each was fined £3.[74] Later the Retail Traders' Committee included some surprising suggestions in their 1944 report on pilfering problems on the railway.[75] Firstly that women new to railway work should not be trained as guards when there were still men working as ticket collectors. Secondly that when footwear was sent by rail, odd pairs should be parcelled together, to make them useless to thieves.

Early 1941 was a watershed moment, with the recognition by railway companies that women recruits were vital across most railway jobs. The GWR was advertising for women, as well as 'men over military age', to be employed as horse carters for railway goods work at Bristol, and for women to drive 2½-ton motor vehicles.[76] In March 1941 for the first time *GWR Magazine* featured a prominent article titled 'Women Porters "Go To It" on the GWR', on how the railway was employing women.[77] It noted that there were now 500 women engaged in the freight depots as porters, replacing men. There was a posed photograph of women at Bristol, where over 250 were now employed, and in May a female station announcer at Paddington featured in the *Magazine*, following 'experiments', and women were pictured loading milk churns at Swindon station.[78]

The LNER advertised for 'ladies of good education and between the ages of 17 and 25' as 'temporary' women clerks at Stanningley in February 1941.[79] By March, women railway porters had already been taken on in Scotland, both passenger and goods porters, at Dundee (East), Dunfermline Upper, Kirkcaldy,

Thornton Junction and Markinch.[80] By April the company had recruited over 2,500 women, working as signalwomen, stablewomen, buffet car attendants, booking and inquiry office clerks, van drivers and ticket collectors.[81] One Manchester woman, Mrs Madeline Parkes, was believed to be the only signalwoman who had done the same job in the previous war.[82] There was also a couple, Mr and Mrs Attwood, who worked different shifts in the same signalbox at Reddish in Manchester.[83]

Significantly there were now moves to restrict the weight of parcels and luggage, because of the number of women employed, to less than 112lbs per package.[84] In May the LNER advertising department, under manager Cecil Dandridge, produced a special poster on behalf of the Railway Executive Committee, urging traders to use smaller packages when sending them by passenger train, because women were now replacing men as porters.[85]

Press features highlighted the need for women as porters at Euston.[86] At that station they were working as 'van girls' (helping to load and unload parcels on delivery and collection rounds around London), platform porters, parcel porters and carriage cleaners. A reporter was taken around by Mr W.E. Clarke of the LMS publicity department, who introduced specially chosen women, all with a happy and lively response to questions. Similarly the LMS were advertising for women at Walsall, urgently wanted as railway goods porters and carters.[87] The company advertised for both 'boys and girls' as railway clerks in Birmingham and Coventry, whereas in Nottingham they wanted just 'boys of good education' for this job, although they were willing to include women in their advertisement for railway carters and porters there.[88] It was only in March 1941 that Southern Railway (SR) raised the issue of female labour in their magazine.[89] In an article entitled 'The Lady Booking Clerk makes her debut', they describe how many 'young ladies' (25 and over) were being recruited as booking clerks to replace men.[90] The Second World War eventually succeeded in changing attitudes about female clerks, a role previously thought to be only a job for men.[91]

Women who featured in the *LNER Magazine* in 1941 were still doing what might be now perceived as 'female' jobs, such as railway hotel receptionist and station announcer.[92] Surprisingly however, it had only now become acceptable to recruit women as train announcers at the larger railway stations, for example 'Miss LMS calling' at Euston.[93] This move was a great success and led to female station announcers being retained after the war.[94] They worked under difficult conditions in the blackout, when they could barely see the trains, working by the light of a handlamp, with the drone of enemy planes overhead. (The *LNER Magazine* pointed out that the correct way to announce a train was to start with the train details and then give the platform, so that passengers knew straightaway if the announcement was about their train.[95])

It was now being suggested that 'there are, in fact, very few jobs on the railway that women are not doing', with the press noting women porters, ticket

collectors, motor van attendants, stable hands, engine cleaners, dining car attendants and even 'callers up', to call up enginemen on early turns.[96]

Public relations attitudes were depressingly clichéd however, with an image
on the front of the *SR Magazine* in May/June 1941 of women painters posed in
a row in their overalls, with paint pot in hand, a little like a row of chorus girls,
and described as a 'delectable dozen'.[97] At the same time however an article on
'Women on the Southern' described the varied jobs, which by now included
train conductors on suburban services around Plymouth.[98]

In June 1941 the LMS newsletter was not only celebrating the role of women
in railway work but also encouraging its readers to recruit even more women for
other kinds of national service (munitions and armed forces), comparing the situation to that in the First World War, when many women worked successfully.[99]
(Surprisingly in 1940 there were 100,000 women working in munitions, compared to the First World War when there were 800,000.)[100] The writer couldn't
resist the feminine perspective once more, commenting on how the clothing
was more streamlined that that worn in the previous war, and the surprising
thought that they were performing railway jobs that 'many believed were too
intricate or too heavy for the feminine sex'.

During the summer of 1941, railway author and British Railways Press
Officer John R. Hind (ex LNER) wrote a syndicated article about the role of
women in keeping the railways moving, which appeared in many papers.[101] He
described an 'army of women', over 10,000 so far. Once again Russia was held up
as an example of women taking on technical roles such as signalling and engine
driving, although work on the footplates in Britain 'had yet to be decided'. The
article featured all forms of transport, for example buses, the Underground and
canals. But as usual it was found necessary to inject a 'feminine angle'. It ended
with:

> At one of the mainline terminus stations a notice on a door reads,
> "Lady Porters – Please Knock". This is one of the rooms for railway-
> women who find time when they can to cook their own meals, and also
> keep up the national handicraft – knitting woollen garments for the
> fighting men.

A further syndicated press article by Mary Ferguson reviewed the women
working in transport services, with 25,000 women working on the railways in
1941, illustrated by a large photo of women painters on the Southern Railway.[102]
Although there were still no women engine drivers or firemen, she suggested
that might happen later, and that no decision had been taken on this.

By July 1941 there were 650 women in Manchester working on the railways,
and the number was growing rapidly.[103] Half were working as goods and passenger porters, and the only jobs they were not doing were driving and firing

and other 'heavy work'. But there was still a great demand for women to work as porters, signalwomen, carters and crane-drivers. The LMS continued their recruitment campaign in Liverpool, still using the term 'portress' at times.[104] As ever, featured workers extolled the advantages of their new work, after jobs in shops and domestic service, pointing out they got better tips from male passengers, one suggesting she made 17s. 6d. in a morning in tips. Some had returned to railway work after doing similar work in the First World War. One talked about having to walk six miles to work every morning as her bicycle had broken.

By August the GWR were employing around 4,000 women in 'male jobs', on top of the 4,000 clerks and typists from before the war. These included around 2,000 goods and passenger porters, 800 waitresses and other hotel and refreshment room staff, 50 dining car attendants, 300 carriage cleaners and a range of other jobs. One woman, Freda Jones, was gently mocked in an article as the 'Pooh Bah' of Pontdolgoch railway station, fulfilling all tasks under the station master, emphasising that she knew how important her role was. There were also 50 railway policewomen, following much demand for these posts. 'The Chief of Police reports that, for mental alertness and conscientious attention to duty, they are the equals of their male colleagues, who it should be said, have readily recognised their abilities.' While some women were already working in the railway workshops in traditional roles, as seamstresses and French polishers, many further jobs there were now replaced by female labour.[105]

In the summer of 1941 the LNER embarked upon a new recruitment campaign, as by now 17,000 of their male workers had left to serve in the forces. Public relations was an important tool in recruitment campaigns and LNER Information Agent George Dow explained how it was used in the company, to preserve goodwill to support vital business. The company recognised that goodwill arose both from the actions of staff generally and from indirect contact via the media. The LNER had appointed a Press Agent as early as 1925 to advise the Advertising Dept, and by 1928 this function had moved to the Chief General Manager's Office, working with an Information Agent there who was very familiar with railway affairs, and offering a 24-hour news service. Whereas other railway companies retained both advertising and PR together within a publicity department, the LNER kept these separate, with the aim of enabling journalists to talk to someone familiar with railway activity, similar to arrangements at the London Passenger Transport Board.[106]

Many women doing 'unfeminine' jobs on the railway started to appear in photographs in the press: an LNER woman worker driving a mechanical barrow at Newcastle Central Station, the first women engine cleaners, and a woman they claimed to be the first in charge of a signalbox, at Warmsworth near Doncaster.[107] The *Daily Mirror,* focusing on a northern LNER station, highlighted the 30,000 women railway workers by now in wartime Britain.[108] The feature included examples such as carriage cleaners (the station master sadly seemed to think they were better than men at this, as they were used to housework), goods porters and women in charge of signal boxes. Problems were highlighted – the need for childcare by relatives, as many workers were married with children, where a crèche might have been useful, and the lack of time available for queuing up to shop for foodstuffs.

In October 1941 the *GWR magazine* featured a woman van guard, once again focusing on physical attributes: 'Our readers will agree that it is a pleasant snapshot, both from the pictorial and the patriotic point of view.'[109] By December there were 120 women working in the LMS road motor department, doing work such as driving cars, lorries and trucks, repairing tyres, and cleaning and examining vehicles.[110] LNER was experimenting with employing women as permanent way labourers, organising twelve women into three gangs, with men of retirement age overseeing each gang. Their work included oiling and cleaning points, whitewashing line levers and other obstacles and keeping the track clear.[111] A permanent way gang of women based near Darlington featured later in their magazine in October 1944, renewing the track. They had their own mess van and wore boy's boots, slacks and old coats, with scarves tied around their heads turban fashion.[112]

By 1942 the idea of women working on the railways was at last seen to be quite normal, reflected in the range of jobs. Whereas many of the women featured in railway jobs appeared to have a working class background, Policewoman PW101 Lewis of Waterloo Station was described as a former Girton girl, music and speech instructress at public school, broadcaster, singer etc, height 6ft 1in, married, favourite study psychology, 'no soft job but loves it'.[113] Often in suburban stations the stationmaster relied totally on women. Reporters suggested again that these were mainly married women whose husbands were serving with the forces, and it seemed that the press felt the need to focus on this angle in particular, as a patriotic display.[114] There were now 40,924 women employed in 'male wages' positions on the railways, together with 27,453 women and girl clerks, of whom around 6,000 had replaced men now in the forces.[115] It was stressed that this was a temporary arrangement, as the Restoration of Pre-War Practices Act 1942 enshrined in law the idea that after the war women would have to give up 'men's jobs' to accommodate returning servicemen.[116]

At this point the press started to feature women who had gained promotion, for example from porter to ticket collector, and from parcel porter to blackout patrol, supervising blackout blinds on the trains.[117] Kathleen M. Chapman of Manchester was one of the youngest woman porter guards, the first at London Road Station in Manchester. She featured in the LNER staff magazine as well as in a broadcast on the BBC Home Service in *At Home Today*. Kathleen had started there at 18 as a letter sorter, then became a porter in 1943.[118] The LNER was now employing 10,000 women doing men's jobs, including engineering work, assisting installers, wiremen and fixers in signal and telegraph gangs, and maintenance workers helping linesmen. They were also painting bridges and working as platelayers and permanent way labourers.[119] Under pressure from railway companies following the employment of thousands of women together with unfit and elderly men, the Ministry of War Transport made an Order restricting the weight of packages sent by passenger trains to 1 cwt, with very limited exceptions.[120]

The *LNER Magazine* continued its series of feature articles about a day in the life of a woman railway worker. By now these were more adventurous, with a porter, a number taker (recording data about rolling stock in goods trains), an assistant purser, a porter guard, a leading engine cleaner and a goods porter.[121] The December issue also included a short feature and photo of women working as hammer drivers at the Gorton shops.[122]

It was only in 1942 that the report of the SR Annual General Meeting in its magazine mentioned the need for female labour, noting that 8,000 women, 7,000 more than pre-war, were 'tackling their new jobs with courage and resource'.[123] The same issue featured 'the only SR woman blacksmith', Mrs Winifred Martins, of Ashford Works, playing an accordion to fellow workers during a break.[124] Women started to play a part in railway parades: four women porters, each representing one of the big four railway companies, went to the Battle for Freedom pageant organised by the *Daily Express* at the Albert Hall on St George's Day 23 April 1942.[125] Each company sent five representatives and the SR included two women in the five. Two men and two women took part in the Contingent of War Workers parading before the king on United Nations Day 14 June 1942.

Now 50,000 women were being employed in railway work to replace men called for service, in addition to women employed in peacetime.[126] The number of women in the LMS wages grades had increased from 4,000 in 1941 to 13,470 in 1942, and there were also 9,246 women clerks, many taking jobs left open by serving men.[127] By August the LMS used the caption 'The Ubiquitous "Eve"' to highlight the 33,333 women now employed by the company.[128] They were advertising now for women porters between the ages of 31 and 45, to work at Derby, 'night duty in turn'. At the Hunslet Lane Goods Depot there was 'great work by women on the railways', with a picture of a women heaving an enormous goods sack.[129] This article proudly stated that 21 per cent of the goods work in Leeds was carried out by these women, with up to 50 per cent at Hunslet Depot. Trade unions in the Crewe area agreed to women doing skilled work on locomotives 'provided the object is to increase output'.[130]

The question about women's abilities to carry heavy loads reared its head again with an intriguing story about rotten kippers. In a report in the *Nottingham Evening Post* in May 1942 a local fishmonger complained that all his kippers were about to be condemned by the government inspector. They had been cured in the north of Scotland but lengthy transport delays before despatch south had led to their deterioration. He alleged that these delays arose from the use of women porters who could not carry heavy weights.[131]

By October 1942 there were over 80,000 railway women.[132] A Railway Executive Committee draft statement in October 1942 suggested the surprisingly wide range of jobs that these women had left: 'Formerly many of these railwaywomen followed other callings. Some were domestic servants, shop assistants, dressmakers, mannequins, manicurists, housewives and veterinary college students.'[133] To highlight the ability of the new female workers to work on all jobs, a press report featured two women passenger railway guards from Dundee, on the Perth-Dundee line and the Dundee-Kirriemuir line.[134] At least one had already spent sixteen months as a porter. In the *Yorkshire Evening Post* in October 1942 women were pictured cleaning the tubes in the smoke-box on an LNER engine.[135] At this time radio played an important propaganda role in reaching a wide audience of listeners, and some LNER women took part in a broadcast with the famous radio personality Wilfred Pickles.[136] This featured crane drivers, degreasers, electric welders, hammer girls, jig borers, shot blasters and rivet heaters, and once again emphasised that many also had families to look after.

Women were urged to join the NUR Women's Guild, as there were now so many, and it was felt that they should be paid the same as men, but in December 1942 war advances still differentiated between men and women.[137] There were many stories of the hardships these women endured, and the companies made great play of the large families of their new workers. Grace Dawson was 39 but the mother of 12 children, working in an LMS railway works in the Midlands.[138] 'On Sundays she does the family "wash"'. One grandmother, after having nine children, had to get up at 3.30am each morning to be at work in the goods yard at 5am, as well as looking after two more children for her daughter-in-law while the latter did war work on a night shift.[139]

During the war a number of films were made by the railway companies and the Ministry of Information to support propaganda campaigns. These showed women doing a wide range of men's jobs, often using named women to bring home the personal reality of the situation. At times the commentaries could not resist contrasting wartime needs with the pre-war role of the woman in the home, once again to emphasise femininity. In a GWR film, 'wives took their husband's place, sweethearts worked and waited, from armchair to autotruck, from babies to barrows, from crochet to crossing keeping, from dusters to driving, throughout the whole of the company's system, they came and carried on the good work... The carriage cleaner soon got busy, and there's not much you can tell a woman about cleaning.'[140] But it was proclaimed that 'woman rose nobly to the occasion'. Three Sheffield LNER women workers also featured in a documentary film about the war by the Army Film Unit much later, in 1945. Scenes were shot at Sheffield Woodburn Junction signalbox, chosen because it had 91 manually operated levers.[141]

In November 1942, the *Manchester Guardian* featured women workers in London railway goods depots, focusing on the wide range of heavy jobs which women were doing, including driving cranes, loading and unloading, checking weights and roping wagons, as number takers, van guards, sheeters and wagon oilers.[142] At one of these depots there were now 600 women out of 1,600 workers, with the first engaged in March 1941. Some were in charge of gangs, which might include men too old for service. Again many of these women had large families to look after at home too. By now the idea of women taking charge was starting to emerge: the *Perthshire Advertiser* in November 1942 featured three women running the Highlandman station on the Gleneagles-Crieff line, at the time believed to be the only Scottish mainline station run entirely by women.[143] Reassuringly to the company, at least two of the three women were from railway families.

Workshop grade staff were needed urgently in railway running sheds, to provide repair services, as railway workshops were focusing on new construction work, and short training courses were set up to meet this demand.[144] There had been some debate as to whether it was better to take in 'green labour', train them and upgrade them as necessary, or to accept trained women. It seems that the scheme was not particularly successful, as the work was heavy and dirty, with poor conditions in the sheds, and there were competing claims in these industrial areas for the recruitment of women. Some shed superintendents were opposed to the employment of women. While the LMS had 1,428 women in their locomotive running sheds in 1942, for example, and the LNER had 350, embarrassingly the GWR had only 45 women, and none of these were employed as engine cleaners.[145]

At the end of the 1942 the SR featured 'railwaywomen and their work' in its magazine, charting the growth in their women railway workers from 1,200 pre-war to 8,200, with a long list of jobs[146] (SR had been employing women in goods work since March 1941[147]). Women were carrying 'chairs' before fixing sleepers to them at the works, there was a stable horsewoman, a crane driver, acetylene welder, oxygen flamecutter, traversing crane drivers, blacksmiths and rivet heaters. Surprisingly it was said that 'many railwaywomen are performing tasks which were believed to be *too intricate and exacting* for them'.[148] In syndicated public relations articles in the press in December 1942, more SR female workers featured, once again emphasising their 'feminine' characteristics, while painting a picture of the heroic background of some of these women.[149] Written about a particular 'south coast station' an article talked of 'trimly uniformed brunette or blonde' porters, and 'feminine charm' invading the railway. The women featured included a first SR Scammell goods delivery van driver and a checker-up in charge of the weigh bridge. Intriguingly the goods station manager suggests that the girls who came from Woolworths were invariably the most reliable and efficient. There was also a female carriage 'pickler' who applied a special cleaning acid to the carriage windows before they went through the washer.

By December the LMS had their first uniformed policewoman, Mrs A.A. Millan, 'the wife of a policeman'. Obviously the company felt the need for safe, familiar ground here. They also devoted a whole page in their wartime news-letter *Carry On* to a photo montage of women doing manual railway jobs.[150] At times clerks were requested to take on unusual duties in overtime. The GWR asked their male and female clerks to help with heavy manual loading and unloading when needed at docks and depots. They did this after their normal day's work on weekdays, and on Saturday afternoons and Sundays, sometimes leaving home at 4am to get in for 5am.[151]

Working conditions at the GWR Swindon Works were extremely poor and unhealthy. The work was hard, it was dirty and airless, invaded by rats, and there were no cloakrooms or lockers.[152] The company recognised the need to recruit women to fill the gaps, but an article about women locomotive builders there suggested that it was difficult to train women in groups because of the way the work was split. They started with limited repetition work, then transferred to processes requiring greater skill. Eventually work was split into less skilled tasks (women) and more intricate work (skilled men). This goes some way to explaining how the descriptor 'intricate' work was used: as something which it was thought that women could not do, when they meant 'skilled', an achievement which might be gained after practice. But the men were protective of their own skills and unwilling at times to see them gained by women. Understandably skills which they had taken a long time to acquire were now being achieved by women very quickly, with the imperatives of war. There were also concerns that men's piece work rates might be reduced by delays caused by the new women's inexperience. At the works the company used women for operations which fed the processes carried out by men who had greater skills, for example walking-crane drivers and traverser drivers, on which 'most women became efficient in a remarkably short time'. They used women for large overhead cranes, for 'shop labour', tool stores, repairing electric motors, wiring, light coppersmith's work, tinsmithing and welding. In the boiler shop they were helping boilermakers, and rivet heating. In the angle iron shop they were assisting with the hydraulic presses. They were operating capstans, driving tractors, coremaking and brass dressing, and work-ing as 'hammer boys' in the forge. They dealt with 'seventy classes of work' as fitters, turners and machinists'. 'Tube preparing is almost entirely undertaken by women, although the work is of quite a heavy nature'. At the same time women were also working in the centralised Stationery and Printing Department, which involved much ladder work, balancing heavy parcels.[153]

By January 1943 it was becoming quite normal to see women working in 'men's jobs' on the railway and there seemed to be a particular public relations exercise to feature them in the newspapers. The British Railways Executive produced a booklet, *Facts about British Railways in Wartime*, which reported that there were now 544,715 men and 105,703 women working on the railways at this time, and that 102,984 railway workers had been released to join HM forces.[154] All the jobs done by women now were described, with various photos.

> The British railwaywoman has adapted herself quickly to new surroundings and work which is very different from her previous occupation, and she has taken her share of night work. In many cases her husband is in the Forces, and she has shown a marked devotion to duty, sometimes in difficult circumstances during and after enemy air activity. She does her turn of duty and goes home to the cares of a house and children. She is making a vitally important contribution to the war effort.

The press were still keen to highlight older, married women with children, such as Mrs Jones, a 52-year-old truck oiler at Chester Station.[155] Similarly to other women workers, she also looked after a child, a husband and an elderly invalid, and on four evenings a week she worked at the local Salvation Army canteen from 7pm till 10. Many newspapers featured such women: the *Western Daily Press* highlighted women ticket collectors and porters, with a group photo, the *Portsmouth Evening News* photographed women working at the Southern Railway forge, the *Scotsman* reported that LNER electric lamp attendant jobs in Scotland were now being done by women, with the first at Queen St Glasgow and Bo'Ness, north west of Edinburgh. At London Victoria women were employed as station announcers.[156]

In Manchester the LMS were recruiting women as railway policewomen.[157] Mrs Phyllis Dixon and Miss Beatrice Whitehurst featured in a press story headlined 'They Travel and Knit – and Detect', travelling on the Chester train out of Victoria, the only two women detectives in the Northern area. They were both 'slight, young and feminine...part of their job is to be indistinguishable from ordinary passengers, so they knit and read on their journey just like any other woman and they dress inconspicuously'. Their work included looking out for civilian and staff pilfering, and interviewing young girls in assault cases. Here 'feminine shrewdness' was described as a big asset.

A GWR public relations exercise in early 1943 profiled women travelling porters.[158] These worked as a 'parcels flying squad', based in centres such as Bristol and Bath, covering around 230 miles on parcels trains during the day. The aim was to facilitate the loading and unloading of parcels, by arranging for these to be positioned near the correct door, to ensure that trains ran on time. Sadly they were described as the 'good fairy' of all calling stations.

LNER press articles continued to feature a range of women, as did their staff magazine.[159] The latter now covered many types of work: a policewoman, engineer's labourer, porter, motor driver, porter signalwoman, travelling train attendant and ticket collector. P.M. Piper was the first LNER policewoman, posted to Liverpool St district in London.[160] Mrs Wileman, engineer's labourer, had been working for the LNER in her role for two years, repairing signal apparatus. Miss Dale's role of porter included helping with the uncoupling of the engine of 'turn-round' trains, dealing with screw-shackles, vacuum brakes and steam heating pipes. Hilda Reidling, motor driver at Maldon East, was also apparently an accomplished dancer, singer and impersonator. Eveline Arnold was one of the first women to take charge of an LNER signalbox in May 1941, working with another woman at the box by 1943. They appeared in a newsreel film about 'Our Day's Work', broadcast to listeners at home and in New Zealand. A travelling train attendant, apparently the only woman in the role, Mary McCluskey, had the job of enforcing blackout rules and sorting out other problems on busy trains in the Manchester area. Similarly in 1943 LMS's *Carry On* newsletter featured many women workers.[161]

Attitudes to women porters by travellers were often favourable, as men seemed to appreciate the basic courtesies offered by the new women.[162] By this time the idea of the woman railway porter had reached some cultural significance. The Standard Motor Company used an image of a young woman railway porter to represent 'adaptability' in a propaganda motif in their consumer press advertising:[163]

THIS ADAPTABILITY

Her day is a hard one, her work heavy and fatiguing. But she shoulders her unaccustomed tasks with a cheerful vigour. And success...

We can't all be women railway porters. But we can still remember their example of willing adaptability... We can all bring something of this spirit to our daily life... So that by our united labour and self-sacrifice the victory will be won, and another glorious chapter in our history written...

In May 1943, to mark the milestone of 16,000 women working on the GWR, the company featured a magazine photo of 22 women, each in their working outfits and holding a placard with their job title on it. As well as the better known jobs these included a lift attendant, acting caller-off, coilwinder and carriage oiler, all 'working for victory'.[164] Similarly the LNER featured a range of their women workers in Scotland in their magazine.[165] They often highlighted married women, usually the wives of men serving in the forces or present or former railwaymen. The new women railway guards were described, usually drawn from other grades, but some recruited from other jobs, such as a cinema usherette and one from domestic service, trained at a three-week course in Edinburgh.

In 1943 there was a discussion between companies and the Railway Executive Committee about allowing female van guards on delivery lorries to use collapsible seats and steps. SR were keen to provide a tail rope and a looped rope to ease climbing, and a half-moon step cut into the tailboard. The REC agreed that railway companies could make their own arrangements for ropes and steps, but should not provide seats.[166]

In July 1943 the Cheltenham press featured the changing roles of LMS and GWR railway women workers in the town. As well as the many women working at stations they were now also being absorbed into civil engineering roles and in engineering depots. The LMS were using women guards on their branch lines locally, whereas the GWR operated long-distance trains, with six woman guards, and it was stated that this was 'a responsible job' in charge of passenger comfort and that in an emergency the driver had to obey the guard. Apart from Violet Ridler, whose account appears in this book, one of the first was 49-year-old Mrs Alice Slack at St James' Station, Cheltenham. The daughter of a railwayman, Alice had also worked in the First World War and her 18-year-old daughter Mavis was a travelling porter.[167]

Although women's work during the war was frequently described as supplementary and temporary, with the 'dilution of labour' concept placing women squarely in the lower divisions of the hierarchy of labour as substitutes, a few subtle changes started to happen, with the press highlighting workplaces entirely managed by women, and women taking greater responsibility. Many of the women who featured in the interviews in this book were single, but the women who most often appeared in newspaper articles at the time were married, with children. The press vied with each other to talk about the women with the most children doing the work, for example the mother of ten children working at Hunslet Lane Goods Depot in Leeds, whose husband was a PoW in Germany, and who said, 'I have plenty to do when I get home at nights'.[168]

The LMS and the LNER had employed women guards for over twelve months, and there were now around 150 in the north of England. But the SR system was mainly electric and it was suggested that this called for a higher level of training and an attribute surprisingly not perceived as suitable for women: owing to the rapid acceleration of electric trains 'a guard needs to be nippy in jumping aboard after blowing his whistle'.[169] The first two SR London terminus woman rail guards started work in July 1943. The first female guard was appointed at Bournemouth at the end of 1943, 21-year-old Mrs M. Bailey, replacing a retiring guard who had worked there for 52 years.[170] Other jobs were regarded as traditionally more acceptable for women: tribute was paid at the end of 1943 to the ladies' waiting room attendants, all widows, most over 60 and some over 70.[171] By now the 10,000 women employed by SR formed 16 per cent of their total staff.[172]

In the GWR engineering department, while women had traditionally been employed as clerks and drawing tracers, they were now being employed in permanent way 'gangs', and as labourers, painters and cleaners, machine operators, and in painting bridges.[173] They also prepared and assembled steel reinforcements for making concrete pot sleepers, and were employed at the creosoting operation, where they worked with plant for fixing chairs to sleepers.

Some were working on tarpaulins. The GWR had a wartime problem with these when wartime changes from vegetable black colouring to bauxite residue, a by-product of the aluminium industry, meant that the traditional black tarpaulins covering open freight vehicles could no longer be used, and reddish-brown sheets were substituted.[174] Workload in the manufacturing and repair of sheets and ropes increased considerably, with many materials no longer available, so cotton and jute were substituted for flax and hemp. It was found that cotton had a liability to bacterial action which limited its life, and special treatment was necessary to prevent rot. Some sheets were reused as blackout material. Many more sewing machines were installed and the demand for more labour led to the recruitment of many more women: in September 1943 the GWR advertised for men and women for railway sheet and tarpaulin repairs at the GWR Sheet works.[175] The company said that 'while 'sewing' is a women's sphere, the work... is very heavy and exacting, but the women are performing their various wartime tasks very ably.'

By October 1943 there were around 110,000 railwaywomen and it was still being suggested that before the war was over they would be in the cabins as engine drivers.[176] E.H. Fowler, Hull stationmaster, claimed that the women guards had to know as much as a peacetime guard on the Scotch Express.[177]

Uniforms were occasionally an issue, for example the wearing of 'slacks' by women clerks. Apparently some members of the Railway Clerks Association had complained about women wearing these on duty, but the Railway Executive Committee (REC) confirmed this was acceptable as it was allowed in the Civil Service. It was suggested that male colleagues only complained because they preferred to see women's legs. There had also been problems over the need for workshop women machine operators to wear protective caps. Comparisons were made with the engineering industry generally, where workwear was provided free of charge, and it was agreed that the railways should provide these caps free of charge.[178] In the north it was reported that battledress was being introduced for women railway workers 'to give the staff a smarter appearance and to save uniform material'.[179]

In 1944 there were widely circulated articles praising the role of women, as by August 1944 there were 135,000 women working for British Railways and London Transport, in 320 different capacities, with 2,000 on the permanent way, 800 having passed signalmen examinations, and 8,500 cleaning engines.[180] Over 13,000 were working in railway workshops, doing jobs such as working steam drop hammers and using oxy-acetylene flames to cut steel plates.[181] In 1944 women were working as fog signallers on the LMS.[182] Railway companies vied to publish photographs of women doing unusual jobs for their sex: May Bullock was photographed welding an engine part for the LMS in February 1944, 'petite' Mary Lawrie from Ardrossan was their only woman blacksmith's striker.[183] Other photos showed fog signallers, passenger guards, women making gauges from drawings to fine limits, and electricians.[184] The LMS promoted a competition 'for women only', to write an essay 'Women on the Railways', although there was no report of the outcome.[185] Sadly there was also a rather silly photo collection of different ways for women to wear the LMS railway hat.[186]

Betty Lambert, whose account follows later, was the first woman signal lamp-man on the LMS, at Evercreech Junction.[187] She looked after a two-mile stretch of line, with sixty signals to service, plus brake van lamps and office, signal box and shunter's cabins oil lights. Margaret Broadbent was the first LMS woman goods horse carter at Manchester London Road Depot.[188] The company was particularly keen to show the unexpected backgrounds of women, especially if they involved glamour, such as a former actress Daphne Goodacre, now an LMS horse van driver, and a former London 'gown modeller', Peggy Monks, featured as their 500th signalwoman in October 1944, at Llanfairfechan.[189] By the end of 1944 the LMS was employing 377 female guards and 623 female signalwomen.[190]

By 1944 the LNER was training women as 'pilots' at Wigan. This was an important and ground-breaking role, as in the event of a breakdown of electronic token signalling they would take charge of the footplate of trains, with drivers working to their instruction.[191]

Women were working in the GWR Central Enquiry Bureau, which handled on average 3,600 enquiries a day, covering all the mainline companies and London Transport, opening from 7am till 11pm daily.[192] With three assistants and 20 clerks they took 1.25 million calls in 1944 alone, and never ceased to function during the war.[193] In 1946 three ladies celebrated their retirement from the enquiry office after thirty years, as they had started in 1916: Mrs E. Lachner, Miss N.E. Smith and Miss K.S. McKay. Their duties involved shift work, with evenings till 10, often during air raids.[194] However, traditional attitudes to women's abilities prevailed in staff magazines, where it was suggested that 'until the early nineteen hundreds, most women were inclined to look on the railway timetable as a mysterious codebook, to which the knowledgeable male alone held the key'.

It was the end of the war and publicity features inevitably started looking back. In a variation on 'my day's work' Signalwoman A.F. Hanson appeared in July 1945, reviewing her three years with the LNER.[195] She paid tribute to all the men who had helped her and noted that 'soon maybe the company will have no further use for the services of their women workers'. Some awards were given: 'Bessie' Barratt received the BEM for her wartime work as Senior Telephone Supervisor at the LNER York Telephone Exchange.[196] Tribute was paid to the LNER women despatch drivers, tasked with carrying vital letters between the evacuated offices of the mainline companies, London termini, HQ and the Railway Clearing House in wartime.[197] A poem appeared in January 1946, by a Glasgow signalman:[198]

> When you came one wintry day,
> The drab old station seemed quite gay,
> Your pleasant smile, your simple grace,
> They literally transformed the place,
> The young lads looked and grinned with glee,
> But older men, like Alf and me,
> Remarked "My Goodness, things look blue,
> What is the railroad coming to?"
> Since then we've seen you work and play,
> With willing hands and smile so gay,
> And when at last you go away,
> We'll miss you.

The SR noted that a number of 'ladies' who had helped them in the war years were now seeking release to 'resume their domestic responsibilities'.[199] In November 1946 there was a concern about the effect on single women without other means of support having to go, whereas some married women might stay, who also had support from husbands. There was a suggestion that a war gratuity should be paid, but disappointingly this was turned down on the grounds that the women would have no difficulty finding other work.[200] There were discussions about how the displacement of temporary female staff should be managed, on the return of men from the forces. It was agreed to operate on the basis on 'last in first out', rather than choosing between single and married women.[201]

There were a few goodbyes illustrated in the company magazines: a farewell dinner for wartime GWR railway women at Port Talbot and Aberavon Town, a group picture of the LNER women from York Carriage & Wagon Works captioned 'Thank You Ladies and Goodbye'.[202] LNER Signalwoman Mrs M. Parkes, of Ashton Park Parade near Ashton-under-Lyne, described service in two wars in a BBC Home Service broadcast on 15 February 1946.[203] The *South Wales Argos* paid tribute to the sixty railwaywomen who had been working around Newport.[204]

Prevailing attitudes to women were reflected in a cartoon in the Southern Railway magazine in May 1945.[205] With a heading 'The women were great', this showed a woman porter struggling with a huge quantity of luggage piled high on a trolley, saying, 'Lummy – I wish I'd stuck to the "Smalls".' A telephone enquiry office clerk at the London Goods Manager's Office was labelled as 'Dial Doris,…the girl with the bedside manner'.[206]

In June 1946 the LMS announced the return of 20,000 of their workers from the forces.[207] During the war there had been 39,000 women working for LMS, around 17 per cent of the total staff.[208] Some jobs were still deemed acceptable for women after the war, for example as carriage cleaners, in the 'flying squad' of LMS cleaners which travelled on forty-eight main line expresses each day.[209] But in late 1946 the number of women employed by the mainline railways had reduced from 95,061 on 30 Sep 1945 to 58,085 on 30 Sep 1946.[210] The following June there were 57,803 women.[211] The GWR confirmed that they were retaining the forty women announcers they had recruited in wartime, and were recruiting more, to be specially trained. They were to be taught to 'avoid local dialects and the sing-songing of announcements'.[212] Ironically, a labour shortage in 1947 led to many women being invited back again.[213]

During the war the railway companies out of necessity focused their efforts on presenting a particular view of women's work on the railway, through articles in staff magazines and newspapers, supported by films and radio broadcasts. The following personal accounts paint a more nuanced picture. For many women the experience of working on the railway changed the way they thought about themselves, and the way their abilities were perceived publicly. Violet Lee described deriving 'a sense of pride for the years of my girlhood on that wonderful engineering structure, the railways'. Mary Hodgson discovered remarkable abilities which were later buried in the face of marriage choices.

Getting in

In the late 1930s when we were returning home, on a trip from Liverpool to St. Anne's, the guard let my brother wave the green flag to start the train off from Lytham station. And from Ansdell and Fairhaven he asked me if I would like to wave the green flag and start the train off, which I did. And that's when my interest in railways began – it was really thanks to that guard, letting me wave the green flag. So after that I thought, 'Well, I'd like a job on the railway.'

(Mary Hodgson, LMS clerk Chesterfield)

For some women, such as Mary Hodgson with her green flag, working for the railways was a long-held ambition, while others just seemed to fall into the work. A large number were members of 'railway families', with fathers, uncles, brothers and other relatives working on the railways. These were able to find out about opportunities and 'put a word in' for them, encouraged by the railway companies themselves. For some it was a passive decision – they went where they were sent. Many, such as Florence Brinklow, had competing family pressures, involving the care of children and elderly or ill relatives, which influenced their decisions. Often chance meetings led to railway work, and that was the case with Joan Cox and Irene Barrett-Locke.

Around 25,000 women were already working for the railway before the war broke out, almost all in clerical jobs, some of which were 'allowed' as women's jobs, albeit paid less than men. By 1941, when Mary Hodgson started, many of the big four railway companies had started to appoint special welfare officers to support their female recruitment drives. These were a new breed of female employees in high positions. When the LMS embarked on their campaign in early 1941 for a range of jobs, including goods porters, they were at pains to say that women would be supplied with overalls and looked after by a welfare officer, with talks about first aid and accidents, and lectures from the chief foreman on railway working, delivery sheets and consignment notes. The GWR appointed a Welfare Supervisor for women and girls in 1941: Miss Emily Brenan, a Cambridge graduate, previously Divisional Welfare Supervisor with the LMS for seven years, was employed to 'deal with all matters affecting the welfare of all grades of women and girls'.[1] In the autumn of 1941, SR appointed a Welfare Supervisor for Women and Girls, Miss Laxton Lloyd, who had moved from the LMS.[2] It was a big job: a year later they appointed an Assistant Welfare Supervisor, Mrs G.M. Beeson, to support her, and an 'indoor assistant', Miss D.V. Martin, formerly a personal clerk to the Audit Accountant.[3]

Some senior male managers felt the need to protect new women staff, to prevent them from being alone, 'safety in numbers', as Mary Woodfield, GWR linesman's assistant recalled. This meant that there were rules about the number of women working, for example Mary Woodfield couldn't start her job as a linesman's assistant until another woman applied, as there had to be two women working together. LMS Clerk Mary Hodgson was told of a rule that there should be two females in her office, as one woman was not supposed to work alone among men, but this appears to have been ignored. Certainly LMS railwaymen were concerned about training 'unaccompanied women' at this time. There were also concerns about young women working at night alone with men.[4]

Ambitions were often thwarted. Doreen Crawford, who later worked as a housekeeper at railway hotels, had intended to follow her father and brother to Glasgow University, but she said, 'I had an aunt in Liverpool who decided that it would be very hard for my mother because my father had died and she persuaded me it would be better to go to domestic science because then I'd probably get married anyway. Of course I never got a chance to get married after that.'

The women below talk about their first steps in joining the railway – family pressures, caring responsibilities, fathers' ambitions and competing options. Some had been hoping to join the services, in a military support role, and some indeed some went on to join up after their railway work. Some were happy to do what might be regarded as 'women's work', such as clerical work, cleaning and catering, although most of these jobs before the war were carried out surprisingly by men. Some were keen to be out in the fresh air as part of a team on the platform. Most seemed to see the work as a job rather than a heroic action to support the war effort, possibly because many had railway work in the family, in the blood. With many, it was a craving for company and outdoor work, and that was why they stayed.

Many had to carry out other duties as well as their railway work. Miss Pemberton was a ticket collector at Chester, whose shift work limited her ability to do other voluntary work, but she went to St John's Ambulance classes and was also a fire-watcher.[5] Parcels clerk Joan Richards had to do overnight relief at Kidderminster Fire Station once a month, and go to work the next morning as usual. Along with many other industrial workers during wartime, apprentice fitter Vera Jones frequently had to work compulsory overtime, which meant a twelve-hour shift from 8 am to 8 pm. Typist Irene Adgie tells of having to work two hours overtime twice a week.

Most women started their railway work having to negotiate a mysterious process, lacking in confidence. There were rules about stockings.

Mary Hodgson, *LMS clerk Chesterfield*

In the late 1930s when we were returning home, on a trip from Liverpool to St. Anne's, the guard let my brother wave the green flag to start the train off from Lytham station. And from Ansdell and Fairhaven he asked me if I would like to wave the green flag and start the train off, which I did. And that's when my interest in railways began – it was really thanks to that guard, letting me wave the green flag. So after that I thought, 'Well, I'd like a job on the railway.'

I had to go there and we saw a Miss Laws. I presented myself for interview. I can remember that one of the things we had to do was sign a paper, to say that we would always wear long stockings at work. In those days they were very very particular about employing female staff. That's why they had this particular lady, a female welfare officer at St Pancras, Derby, Manchester, and I think there was one in Glasgow. They covered a huge area, but they were responsible for the female staff. So I saw the female welfare officer at the Farm Buildings, and we had to sign a form agreeing that we would always wear long stockings at work...they were very very particular about female staff that they employed. But of course later on during the war, we couldn't keep that promise because all clothing was on coupons. You really couldn't afford the coupons to be wearing stockings during the summer, so we let that pass by and we wore bare legs during the summer.

Betty Spiller, *porter then lampman at Evercreech Junction, Somerset & Dorset Joint Railway*

I wanted to join the WAAF, and family were not in favour of that, and my brother was already a junior porter at Evercreech Junction and father with being a shunter, and a vacancy arose. Station master spoke to my father, said would I be interested and they kind of made me interested and shoved me in that direction. So I saw the station master and he says, 'Fine.' There was then one other girl there, whose father was the signalman.

Mary Buist, *LNER passenger guard, Musselburgh*

When war broke out Mary was married with two small children. Her husband was away with the Territorials and Mary was working in a Musselburgh munitions factory while her mother looked after the children. Mary heard about railway work while she was in an air raid shelter.

So when I was there a woman told me about the railway, that they were advertising for people so I had to get a medical, you know to just check my heart and everything and then we had to go to classes with an inspector sort of explaining what the signals were and what you had to do.

Laura Scott, *sawdust bagger, LNER carriage works, York*

Well, I wrote to t' railway...one day an old man came to see me, and I said to him, 'Do they have any work at railway?" He says, 'No, not as yet,' but he said, 'if ever we do we'll let you know,' so he come and told me if I wanted I could go and be a tea lady. But I wasn't a tea lady, I worked in what they called the sawdust hall, emptying bags of sawdust into a thing...off a plank. Well, it was sawdust that had come off the wood. What they'd been using, you see, and they were bagging it.

Marjorie Pateman, *lathe operator, LMS Wolverton works*

Well, then they had this scheme where they trained people, and you had to go somewhere when the labour exchange would send you to, you had to get some employment, so we went to the works, the school, to do the training on the lathes, probably at 16, it was to do with the technical college, which was across the other side. And we learnt to do on these massive lathes, and we had to make tools – calipers and set squares – and then you had to pass the test with those, which we did, I did. And then after that, then you went into the works, and we went onto a big lathe, and cutting the copper shell bands to the size.

When we were 18, we could have gone to the Land Army, or the WAAFs or the ATS, as they used to call them. I never give it much of a thought.

Florence Brinklow , *LNER parcels delivery, Kings Cross*

Florence joined LNER at King's Cross in 1940. She had previously been working in a pipe manufacturing warehouse.

I would have joined the forces. But I lived with my grandma. And she just couldn't get out. So I had to be there with her most of the time, you know. My father, he got killed at Dunkirk, my dad. Left my mum with twelve children. She had a very large family. I was the eldest. And I was always left with my grandma, from a baby.

Irene Barrett-Locke, *refreshments, GWR Paddington*

I got a job with Lyons, the Corner House. That's the big Corner House attached to the Cumberland Hotel. So I became a nippy for a few months. So I had training for that too. And that was fun, for a while. I got very bored with that, and I thought I'd go back to the buffet 'cos I missed it. And then I met one of the men who knew me there, and he said, 'D'you know what? They're asking for a girl to be a stewardess on the trains. Would you like to apply for that? It should be a very nice job, quite well paid too.' So I did, and I got it. That's how it all began. And there again another interview, but of course having worked in the buffet helped a great deal.

Joan Cox, *SR mobile canteen worker, Redhill*

The war came along, I was just 14 that September as war broke out. And my mother was expecting another baby. She did lose it actually. And so she was entitled to be evacuated, so she went with my two sisters and brother.

...and they gave my mother notice to quit. And she went back to Croydon. So I had to go back to Croydon. And it was at the time when the bombing had really started, the doodlebugs and all sorts. But fortunately our home was OK, we was never bombed. Mum went back and I got a job at Creed's, which was a firm that made teleprinters and typewriters before the war. But they were involved in war work when I went there. I went into their canteen and the canteen unfortunately was at the top of this big building. And if there was an air raid or anything you either had to stay up there and suffer it, or go right down through all the machine shops to the basement. And it was quite frightening to me as a young woman.

And I got friendly with one of the men that used to come to the counter. And he said to me one day: 'You know, Joan,' he said, 'my sister's going to open a canteen at Redhill.' Well I'd never heard of the place. Yet I think it's only about twelve or fourteen miles away from Croydon. And I said, 'Oh, yes?' He said, 'You're just the type that she likes.' I said, 'Am I?' He said, 'Yes, I'll tell her if you're interested.' I said, 'Well, anything to get away from this bombing, and night work' – as I was doing in them days.

So I had to apply to the doctor to get a certificate to say that the war work was getting me down. Cos it was wartime, you had to have these things to move around your jobs, it was war work. And this Mrs Flint turned up at my mum's doorstep one day. And of course I was in bed and asleep because I used to do night work. And she said, 'Well, I'll hang on and see her.' Well, when I got up, I got up early obviously, they woke me at two. And we chatted and I really took to the woman. She was friendly and funny. And she'd been married to an Italian before the war and he'd got killed in the bombing in London. So she was widowed and had remarried. And she was telling us all this and she said that she was hoping to get the canteen started in about a week. So I said, 'Well, as soon as I can get released from the job I would come along.'

So it took actually a fortnight and she hung on for a fortnight and then we opened up.

Annie Lageu, *LMS shorthand typist, Leeds*

There wasn't much work going, I was too small for a telephonist and I was too late for getting into the transport, the Corporation Transport Offices. I went to the British Legion and they weren't interested because my father had not been in the army, they wouldn't allow him to go because he was needed to repair the wagons.

I applied to the railways and I hadn't got sufficient speed in Pitman's shorthand which you'd got to have and typing, so I was going to night school then, to get some speeds. I was sent for interview for this job in 1935 at the railways at the LMS Leeds District Goods Manager's office. There was a shorthand typist job and a clerk's job and there were two of us and she was the shorthand typist so she got the clerk's job and I got the shorthand typist's job!

To go in the office you had to have Pitman's, and it had to be Pitman's shorthand because ... you didn't take dictation, all the clerks wrote their letters out in Pitman's shorthand and you had to read from their shorthand. It was only the heads of department and the managers who did any dictation.

In 1937 they opened the District Passenger Manager's office in Leeds. Before that it had been controlled from Manchester, and they transferred a lot of men from Manchester to Leeds. They wanted five girls, or women in the typing pool, for the District Manager's Office and I was transferred over with three others. There was supposed to be a senior coming and she was ill, she'd had a big operation so she didn't arrive until quite some months later.

Every so often they had a check-up on how much work you were doing and at that particular time there never was enough work to keep us going and I think a lot of people cheated, but I was quite honest and my figure fell low, so it was reported back to our office and I had to have a special count. So I was a little bit of a bad girl because although I'd done all the work I could, you were supposed to do ten memo-size letters in the hour. And four quarto-size and if you did a stencil or a foolscap you were allowed half an hour for that you see. Well it was mostly little memos that we did and everybody was scratching around for typing, you know, and as I say, I'd been honest and my figures hadn't measured up to what they should have done.

It was a big difference because with this senior not turning up I was senior and yet I was only probably four or five months older than two of the other girls in the office, but I was senior so I was taking shorthand and I was typing for the manager, and of course…whereas we'd all little memos in the Passenger Manager's office, you were doing typing, eight copies of excursions for excursion bills, you know they were distributed in those days.

Christina Pettigrew, *shorthand typist, LMS Glasgow*

College station – I remember it very well. I had to ask for a Mr Mitchell who was –– I think they called him an agent at that time. I was a very frightened raw wee lass, and I knocked at the door marked 'Mr Mitchell', and this young man opened it. And then said, 'Yes?' And I said, 'I've come to see Mr Mitchell.' 'Just come in and sit there.' And that was the man I married…married him later after the war. He went away to the army not long after that, 'cos that was '39, and he was in the army…couple of years before I was called up to the ATS. But that was Tom opening the door for me. So that was the man I married. But, oh, College was a wonderful happy place really. I remember we sat at very very high desks. There was a Mr Brown there and a Mr Smith I think he was called, and a Mr Kennedy. They were the clerks, and I was the shorthand typist. They were something out of Dickens – great big sloping desks that they sat at and then they could lift the desk up and put the things into it, almost like a school desk but they were very high.

Doris Maley *shorthand typist, LMS Broad St, London*

I did a course on shorthand typing at a local college, and decided I would rather like to be a shorthand typist. My aunt worked at Euston, and brought me home the application form, which I filled in. Eventually I took the entrance exam, and became a relief clerk, holiday relief, for a short time. I started in August, and this position finished on the 31st of October when holidays were over. I then went back on the 2nd of January 1930, and from then on I stayed on the railway until I retired, after 38 years.

Maureen Evans, *messenger then clerk, LMS Crewe*

In those days, you had to know somebody who worked for the railway, in order to stand a chance of being an employee of the railway. A lot of competition. A lot of 'who you know, not what you know' about it. And I think there was one or two people…my grandparents kept a pub just down the road from where I lived, called the Spring Tavern. And it was the customers who went in there, a lot of railway people, so there was a lot of 'Well, I'll have a talk with so-and-so, and see if we can get her into the railways.'

I was just told what I was going to be doing. So, when it came to leaving school, I was actually still only 13, cos my birthday was in the Christmas holidays. I became 14 during that period, so I was actually 14 when I had my name put down for the General Offices, you see. So then, because there was not a certainty that I would be employed by the railway, I also had an interview at Rolls-Royce, and I had an interview in an accountant's office too. So I had three jobs, and three job interviews, going at the same time. Eventually I was offered a place in all three places, so I had then to make a decision which I wanted to do. So of course my father again was in command of the situation. And he decided that the railway was best for me because I'd get free passes and a safe, secure job. And all the rest of it. So I then was sent to the Railway Carriage and Wagon Department in Gresty Road, as a junior messenger. And there I had to collect the clock cards in the morning, and check what hours the people were doing.

I arrived at this very dirty-looking place. I had to go up a flight of steps. And I had to cycle, because it was not on the bus route. I had to carry my bike up about, I suppose between 25 and 30 wooden steps. Which were, I suppose, railway sleepers set into the ground. And the office was based just inside of the factory itself, the workshop itself. And so there was three men and myself in the office. I was the chief telephone answerer, chief tea-maker, chief stoker, on the sort of pot-bellied stove in the middle of the office. And it was quite a relaxed office actually, there was no sort of watching what I was doing all the time.

Just filing. The filing consisted of a lot of the labels that were put on the sides of wagons, where they were being despatched from and to, and what type of wagon it would be, and what the cargo would be. And a lot of, I can't remember what they were called now. But there were dockets, you know, to deal with what was going from place to place.

Irene Adgie, *typist, SR Woking and Waterloo*

When I was about 16, my father started making noises about – I should get a job with more prospects. And he mentioned the railway. And being a rather obstinate type, I kept saying 'I'm quite happy where I am.' But without telling him I did apply to the Southern Railway for a job as a clerk.

Woking was a railway town. And there were two main sources of employment. The line-packing works and the railway. I really applied for a job as a clerk, because I didn't feel my skills at shorthand and typing at that time were good enough for me to be a typist. I didn't realise that the railway in those days had very few women clerks. It was a male province. So I had to go for an interview at the Deepdene Hotel at Dorking. And a very kind staff office man told me how to do all the sums on the educational test paper. And he took me to lunch and took me out for a walk round Dorking in the lunchtime. Then I had to go to Tooley Street at London Bridge for a medical. And after that I had a letter to say I'd been accepted, but I had to attend the Staff Office at Woking for another interview. And I was given a shorthand and typing test.

And they appointed me to the typing pool. And I think they must have been very hard up for typists at that time. In fact, when I first went to the typing pool, I was the only member who was not a railway daughter. They were all the daughters of railwaymen. Even the middle-aged women, they all had railway connections.

I was very shy and nervous. But they made me so welcome. And I went home to lunch and my mother said she had never seen me so happy, after the first day at work.

Doreen Dickenson, *goods clerk, LMS Liverpool*

Her father wanted her to take the Civil Service exam.

They cancelled them all, they decided they would review their position. They weren't taking anybody on till they knew who was going to go to the war and what was going to happen. So of course it was Christmas and after Christmas, 1939, 1940. And so I registered at the local labour exchange, and that was down Marsh Lane. And there was a right martinet of a lady who was the manager there. She was known all over Bootle as being 'You get back to work, you don't come here signing on the dole'.

Anyway I was interviewed and they said to me, 'Well, we probably can find an office job for you, or a job in a bank, or something.' 'Oh, that's fine.' ... So I came home after being down there a few weeks. And the lady had said to me, 'We think we've got a job for you in Hunts Bank. How would you like to work in Hunts Bank?' 'Oh, that'd be fine.' 'Right. Well I'll get you the application form. Come in and see me in a couple of days' time.' So I went home. I said to my father, 'The lady says she's got a job in Hunts Bank.' He said, 'Hunts Bank? Well, there's the Midland and the District and the whatever-it-is, but I've never heard of Hunts Bank.' He said, 'Where is it?' I said, 'I don't know. She just said there was a job, I'd have to apply.' When I went back again, I got the application form and suchlike. And she said to me, 'I'm sorry, it isn't Hunts Bank,' she said. 'It's Hunts Bank Buildings, Manchester, where you've got to go for an interview. And it's on the railway. And they'll send you a ticket, a free pass ticket,' …which was a little tiny cardboard piece about one-and-a-half inches just by three-quarters... 'and they'll send you a letter and tell you when they make an appointment for you to go.' So this must have been early January, or Christmas, or something. Cos I got a letter to go for an interview to Hunts Bank about the 15th of January or thereabouts. So I had to get a train from Lime Street about eight o'clock in the morning, to get to Manchester for about nine. I think we went into Victoria.

And we crossed the road. We went into this building. And we all sat around. And I met a girl I was at school with. At least I knew her at school. She wasn't in my form at school. But she always looked a bit scruffy. She was one of those that needed a new ... different type blouse cos her collar and tie weren't always good enough, you know. She didn't get past the interview. I was told that if I was taken on I'd have to pass a medical. I'd also have to pass a written exam and I would be sent to Manchester to take a written exam in English, maths and geography. How did that suit me? 'Yes, alright.' And also if I were taken on at all, they had a system where after about 18 months, before you got your 18 rise, you had to sit an efficiency exam. And that was to do with geography. Probably railway geography. And shorthand, and typing. Would I be prepared to take shorthand and typing? 'Oh yes.' 'Right.'

A month later, it'd be February, I went for the day to take an exam, at Hunts Bank Buildings again, I think. We were shown into a room. It must have been the boardroom, which was the size of a ballroom I should think. The table was, oh, at least, I should think, twenty-odd feet long. And we were packed elbow to elbow all round the table. But the papers they gave out, there were two sets of papers. And they were alternate, so you couldn't copy off the people next to you. And I sat an hour and a half maths, which were problems and percentages and heaven knows what. But fortunately I was used to them. I wouldn't say there was a lot of geometry about it, there was lots of areas and triangles and things. But nothing, you know, heavy geometry. And percentages and all the rest of it.

And then after that we had an IQ test, which was one of those 'turn it over and answer 20 questions', and something-or-other. Or 'fill the words in', or something like that. And then we had the English paper, which was a typical English paper, the same as I'd been used to. It was so many subjects, and write an essay, and correct a few sentences, which was never any problem with the grammar et cetera or the spelling. And then we had a geography ... now the geography I was a bit frightened of, because at school we did not do a lot of American geography. Quite a lot of European and African. And definitely British Isles. Well, my uncle had given me a book many moons ago. And it was rather like one of those things where they gave you a name of a place, and it gave you the county and the river and the population and its industries. And, you know, like Nottingham for lace, and Sheffield for steel.

Well, I thought the questions had been taken out of that book. I just whipped through the lot and thought, 'Ooh, it's just like being...' There was only one place I didn't know, and I'd never heard of it, and I thought it might be German. I was so ignorant. It was Fraserburgh. I never associated it with Edinburgh. And that Fraser was a Scottish name. I'd never been out of Lancashire too much, you know. Anyway, I passed the exam. Week or so later, I got notice to say I'd passed the exam, would I come – here's me ticket, will I go for a medical? So the middle of March, I went for my medical. Well, they tested my eyesight, and they did my blood pressure, and I stood on the scales. And I can't remember much else, except giving a history of what I'd had and what I hadn't had.

Gladys Garlick, *LNER guard London*

Well, with my friend, we were really keen to join the army, you know. To join the forces. And we decided to go down to the recruitment centre. It was in Archway Road there. Holloway. And we went there one Sunday. And it was all open, and there was nobody there. And we sort of called, and knocked, and what have you. Nobody there. So we went down the road and phoned. But we still got nobody. So we didn't join up. And then ... I don't know whether it was my father said, but they were looking for booking clerks. So we went for an interview for that. Well, I'm a bit stupid. You know, I get a bit flustered. And we didn't know what they was going to do. We thought it was just an interview. Anyway, we went there, and we had to take a test. Well, spelling is my worst subject. And they gave us, you know, an oral. They read out and we had to write it. Well, of course my mind just went blank. And so of course I made a mess of that. Then they give us a maths thing. Well, I'm pretty good at maths, you know. Oral maths and everything. So of course I did that like that. But of course I'd failed because of the other, hadn't I? And I could have sat there and written what he'd told me ... you know, afterwards. I was fairly young, cos the other two were older than me, to be in the booking office. I think that didn't help either. You know. And he said he was sorry. He said, 'Well, you know, you're so good at maths.' So I said, 'Well, I was nervous.' But I didn't get it.

Anyway, my dad said, 'Oh well, I think they want a lad porter down at the station.' Bowes Park station, that came under Wood Green, which my father was at. And the station master did the two lots, so he said, 'Oh, I'll have a word with the station master.' So the station master said, 'Oh well, send her along and I'll have a look at her.' And he said, 'Oh, she looks a strong enough lass.' So I started as a lad porter. There was two other lads there beside me. And we did shift work, you know, on the platform. Gradually it ended up that the other two must have been called up, cos they went. And I stayed there until I was 20 and then they said, 'Oh, we're very sorry, but you're 20. You've got to be a senior porter now.' And they moved me to Grange Park.

Mary Woodfield, *linesman's assistant, GWR Undy*

Had to look for a job, didn't I. Come back to Undy to look for a job. I'd been courting strong men, and I was engaged. And it was a case of 'go to the labour exchange and find a job'. So I brought my bike home with me anyway. Up to Caldicot I had to come, from Undy, which is a few miles down the road. Because there was the little office, turned into an employment exchange. So of course she said in there, well, there were no jobs to offer, really. That was her words: 'really'. 'But there is one.' Well, I: 'What's that one?' 'There's a job on the railway. But you might not like that. If you'd rather wait for something else...'

So I said, 'Well, what's the job on the railway?' 'Well,' she said, 'I can tell you about it. But I can't start you on it or even tell you when you can start. Because another female must apply as well. Because you've got to be two girls working together. Because you'd be working with men.'

Safety in numbers. That's right. I can appreciate that, kind of thing. So I said, 'Right.' So she said, 'I'll notify you when somebody else applies for a job.' So of course in due course, which was only a couple of weeks, no more than that. And we were not on the phone, so it had to come through the post anyway. And there was only telephone boxes, wasn't it? Hardly anybody had a phone like these days. And so of course I had the message to go up there. Somebody else had applied. So it coincided that she was another girl from the same village, in Undy. And her name was Nancy, her father was a railwayman, he was a guard, I think. So she accepted the job on the railway. And soon as they said it, I accepted it. And so she said, 'Right, you can start next Monday.' So she said, 'I'll be in touch with you.' So of course we both started that same morning.

The first one was Nancy, and she had met up with a driver. And she was expecting a baby. So she wasn't with me. We hardly got to know one another. But anyway, she discovered she was pregnant, and she had twins. I was took on and I started work, on the Monday, like they said I could start. I was in a quandary. Because I was getting married a fortnight after I was took on. So my quandary was writing to the main one...in Newport. To put him in the picture that I would be starting in my maiden name, which was Gunter. And I was getting married then, and I would be changing my name. But the thing was, could I have the fortnight off because I was getting married, and my future husband was in the forces, so of course he come down from Scotland, first to get married. So I had the whole fortnight off while he was off. Had a honeymoon later on. And yes, that was quite alright. But they were quick enough to say you could not start without another girl. But Nancy...she had to be there on her own while I was away.

They were not geared up for women at all. But these two old boys, Harry and Ben, they nursed us. They really, really nursed us. In their minds they thought: 'Fancy girls coming on a job like this.' Because there were shunting yards, wherever you walked there was engines or wagons right back, left, right or centre. And crossing over, if you had to cross over one to another, in their minds I don't think they appreciated it. But they looked after us. Absolutely. As did every railwayman on the railway.

The railways was lovely. I loved every minute of the railway. My father, well, really, he was a lovely tempered man, as well. But when I got home from the labour exchange and he said to me, 'Have you got a job?' you know, kind of thing. This is asking, now, because I mean I was a married woman. It didn't matter to him whether I'd got a job or not. I said, 'Yes dad. What do you think I

got a job on?' And he said, 'Go on, then.' And I said, 'I got a job on the railway.'
Now my father was one for fun. Cos as I say, he entertained a lot in all ways. And
I can see the smile on his face now, as much as say, 'A daughter of mine going
on the railway.' And his first words was, to me: 'Now mind, you join the union.'
And I got my little union badge down there.

Theresa Roberts, *booking clerk, Midsomer Norton and Welton, Somerset &
Dorset Joint Railway*

I was introduced to the S & D by a young man, a near neighbour at Haydon, near
Radstock, who had been at senior school at Mid-Norton where I had attended.
He was working himself on the S & D (he was older than me of course). He
was soon to be going into the forces as were so many other boys and suggested
that I try my luck with S & D as they were looking for office staff. I was already
working for the Co-op locally and had been there for a year or so. Anyway I was
taken on and posted to Mid-Norton and Welton Station, where I stayed for six
years in an otherwise all male environment.

Edith Stretch, *booking office clerk, LMS Hanley*

1937, I was seventeen. I'd been working. I'd got a job in a wholesale grocers, as
a clerical worker. But this is how I found out about the trains, because I used to
go on the train from Hanley to Burslem, to where their place was. But I didn't
want to stay in that thing. Cos I wanted a career. I didn't have very much of one,
did I? I didn't last very long.

From there I went to work on the railway. I did entrance exams for the Civil
Service, for the post office and the railway. It was the LMS railway then. And
they were the first to reply that they'd like to interview me. And I went to Derby,
was interviewed, and that was it.

We were told that they hadn't tried ladies in the booking office before, and
we were experiments. But we managed. We did okay. I think what was really
the start of my working life when I was on the railway, I was quite young, with
a lot of responsibility. Because you were dealing with people. You were dealing
with money. You were dealing with pay cheques. You were dealing with the
telephone. And I think it was such a basic thing that you knew all these things.
And you were on your own. You'd got to be like that. And I think that's what
did me as a real sound basis for everything I did. Because every job I did, I
was either on my own, or just with another. It made you that you were quite
confident. I mean, at such a young age. I can't imagine my granddaughters
being like I was. I mean, they're 20-odd, and they're only just starting to earn
money. They didn't give their money, their wage back and have a shilling back,
if you're lucky.

Vera Jones, *apprentice fitter, LMS Crewe*

When Rolls Royce opened, my father ended up getting a job there, after a long period of unemployment. And then my mother went out to work. And I stopped at home to look after a younger sister and brother. She went out to work because she thought she'd get a bit more money than I did, you see, because she wanted to try and get on, and that, you know. But unfortunately she wasn't well, she was ill, and she had to give it up. So this is when I went into the railway works, after that.

1941, I started into the railway works, September. And I was there till about July 1946. In the railway works. I was employed as an apprentice fitter. And went to work in Nine Shop, what was called Nine Shop then. I had to apply for it. I had to go down to the GO offices that were in the town then. Yes, and pass a medical of course. And I was 16 years of age then, when I started in there. I knew that I would have to get a job. And they were taking women in the works then, you know. And that's why I went to see if I could get a job in there.

Learning the Job

We did a fortnight up at Hatfield, at a school. They taught us about signals and rules and things like that. And then we learnt the road with another guard, you know. There was a bit of a bad feeling by some of the guards cos they thought it made their job look cheap. Well, I suppose in a way it's like my husband working to be a driver. You don't jump straight into it, do you? You have to work your way up to get to be a guard. And they were, some of them were a bit resentful of that. But on the whole they were all very good.

(Gladys Garlick, LNER guard)

Large numbers of women were entering the service. Railway companies realised that they needed to organise special training schemes to help the women learn their new roles speedily. At the same time women relied on the cooperation of experienced male workers to support their training, in what was potentially a sensitive process, when many men had taken years to achieve their positions.

These training schemes recognised the need for both theory and practice in learning a job. The SR set up their training schools for booking clerks at Chislehurst, East Croydon and Clapham Junction. An intensive course lasted four to six weeks, with training in both general and office work, using a model booking office. The clerks were then tested by a final exam. The LNER established staff training schools at Scarborough, Whitley Bay, Harrogate and Hertford, with an intensive four-week training programme in railway routines, covering operating and commercial practice, law and economics. Many of the pupils were women, training as clerical staff. (The school at Watton, Hertford was the former house of Sir Nigel Gresley, LNER steam locomotive engineer). Further LNER residential training centres were set up in Scotland, at Aberdeen and Edinburgh, to train clerks in railway accounts. Again, these intensive courses lasted four weeks, using a model booking and parcels offices, and real money for practice.[1]

The SR had two training schools for guards, at Victoria and at Brighton, where they were taught the rules by a former station master. The company magazine featured twenty women taking the course in July 1943, with six already capable of taking charge of their own train. Their abilities were highly regarded, with recent examination entrants achieving a minimum mark of 93 per cent.[2]

By March 1944 there were 417 signalwomen working for the LMS, and the company newsletter, *Carry On,* featured a signalling class for 'housewives' at Wakefield Central. Again, intensive theory training lasted three months, following by practice in a signal box and an examination. The 'headmaster' had apparently made his own signalling diagram in his spare time and modelled the trains, flagmen and detonators out of Oxo and tobacco tins. He was photographed explaining 'a tricky point' to the women.

Another LMS signalwomen's college was at Leicester, the first one in the Midland Division, with all the women under 23. Staff were apparently amazed by the 'intelligent and experienced questions' which women were asking. When trained, it meant that 18-year-olds were taking charge of signalboxes on their own.[3] At York the LNER signalling classes for women were held in the Engineer's Signalling School, with demonstrations on a miniature electric railway, electric tablets and key token instruments. On average it was said to take three months to train a signalwoman.[4]

By 1943, the LMS driving school at Cleckheaton in Yorkshire had trained around 100 women in a year. These were aged 21-45, from Yorkshire stations, Liverpool and North Wales. Women were taught to drive a variety of vehicles: three-ton lorries, mechanical horses and platform tractors. Uniforms were provided – greatcoats, slacks, leggings and a peaked cap. It was reported that women took two days longer to train but were as good as men once trained.[5]

The Great Western Railway (GWR) Central Enquiry Bureau at Paddington was staffed entirely by women clerks, recruited mainly at 16, and trained in the 'Bureau School'. They had to learn railway geography, how to read a timetable correctly, fares, tickets etc, with question papers set every day to test progress. It took three or four months to get to the practical stage, with a supervisor listening in.[6]

Quite young women found themselves in responsible positions. LMS booking office clerk Edith Stretch, at 17 found herself working with money and wages and dealing with people and a telephone, often on her own. She noted that this gave her confidence later on. 22-year-old Dora Whitfield was moved with others working at Bletchley engine shed, to become hostel supervisor for 100 guards and firemen transferred from the north.[7]

For many of the women however, they learned 'on the job', with support from experienced men. Telegraph operator Berry Forrester recalled the unexpected difficulties she had with Morse Code, which she had been quite comfortable with in the army, but was shocked to find a completely different system on the railway. The railway system combined the Morse Code with polarity reversal. The Morse system worked telegraphically, with the operator holding the transmission key down briefly for a dot and slightly longer for a dash, whereas in the railway system deflecting the instrument needle to the left represented a dash, and to the right a dot. It also adopted two tone sounders. In 2002 the Friends of the National Railway Museum recreated Betty's wartime role in Troon with a telegraphy machine, filming this for their collection.[8] Betty was not provided with a uniform, unlike the platform staff, but she recalls that with her mother they made a sleeved overall from blackout cloth to wear in the office, as the area was grubby from being in the middle of the platforms and having a coal fire in the room.[9]

Some workers, such as LMS goods clerk Doreen Dickenson in Liverpool, had no form of induction or training.

Violet Lee, *GWR passenger guard*

During the interview it was made quite clear to me it was a wartime appointment, and when the men returned from the forces we had to resign. Mr Powell gave me a rule book which I had to carry with me at all times and I was to learn the rules, as I would have to pass an examination. An important safety rule was rule 55. When we stopped for any reason between signal boxes, I had to put the hand-brake on in the guard's van, open the vacuum-brake valve, to stop the train moving off, had to climb down to the ballast and walk back about five hundred yards, and place three detonators ten yards apart on the line and return to the train, and inform the driver you had carried out rule 55. It was carried out with such precision, I can't remember any train smashes! So if a train was coming up on the wrong line and you'd got three detonators on the line, this horrific 'BANG, BANG, BANG', so the train front would know that there was something wrong. And then you, the guard, would return to the van when it was safe to proceed, the driver would inform me with the engine whistle, I had to go back and take the detonators off the line, that's of course if there wasn't a smash, then back to the train, take off the hand-brake, close the vacuum valve, which told the driver the guard was back in the van and he could move off, no two-way radios. There were no radios or train intercom those days.

The Great Western Railway was keen to maintain its boast it was the safest railway in the UK. For my training I was put in the charge of a senior link passenger guard. You can imagine what an elderly gent he looked to me, a mere slip of a 17-year-old girl. To get to the position of senior link passenger guard it would have taken him thirty years. And to pass examinations he moved up through the ranks and medical examinations every two years. I often wondered what he thought at all these young ladies coming to work on the railways. There was seven of us. He was a very smart man, his serge railway suit was always well-pressed, his brass buttons were well-polished with Brasso, his boots shone, and all his equipment was immaculate. I can still see him in my mind's eye now, with his very wide grey wax moustache, which seemed to stretch from ear to ear. He taught me the ropes, what signals controlled what points, and you can have a gantry with anything up to ten main signals...caution signals, covering ten sets of tracks. Then the guard was jointly responsible, with the footplate staff, driver and fireman, that they were obeying the correct signal, head out of the window, no computer monitors while sat in a cosy chair. We had to know the gradients, lengths of station platforms. Some country stations would take about five eights, and the train may consist of about eight or ten eights. What is an eight? It was the number of carriage wheels, two bogies of four wheels, and with your signalling you had to advise the driver to move forward using the signal lamp, ensuring the passengers stepped out onto the platform and not onto the track. Some very small halts were usually about the length of two eights.

Betty Forrester, *clerk/telegraph operator, LNER Thornton Junction*

I started to work as a telegraph operator at Thornton Rail Junction in spring 1944 and that was after three years I had been an instructor in the women's section of the army, and I expected to handle my new job without any trouble, knowing Morse. However on my first day at Thornton I was shocked when I heard the railway Morse, I couldn't read it. The method of transmission was entirely different from the normal dots and dashes sent by wireless in the forces. The rail Morse was a shower of clicks. It seemed to be activated by two small metal poles with different pitches of sound being hit with a metal striker. One pole represented a dot and the other a dash. When Morse is transmitted on air waves, letter B for instance, B for Bob, is a dash and three dots sounding doooo – do – do – do, doooo – do – do – do. But the letter B on railway telegraph would sound as four pings. Thus ping, ping, ping, ping and to confuse matters more, there were six instruments at Thornton office, all clicking at the same time and all twelve poles at different pitches. Every station platform office and all signal boxes had a telegraph instrument for quick communication, but transmission distance was only 60 to 80 miles approximately. Therefore relay stations such as Thornton telegraph office received and forwarded messages in their area and to the next relay office. Each instrument was communal, so on its particular line, whatever was transmitted was audible to all on that line. An operator was alerted when a message was for him, by constant repetition of his call sign. For instance, Thornton's call sign was TY which sounded vaguely like ping-ping- p-- ping-ping, ping-ping- p—ping-ping. And you'd acknowledge by sending K for 'carry on' then R for 'received' at the completion of the message.

The public could also send Post Office telegrams from the telegraph office at Thornton. They cost ten words for a shilling. In fact when I first went to the office, Jimmy, who was a fellow who was retiring and fortunately stayed on for about a fortnight until I mastered the code, told me about the telegrams and he showed me a wee bowl that went out to the platform, and he showed me a drawer where there was forms for the public to write out their message, and two and six pence was the charge. But he said, 'Don't bother,' he says, 'I've been here now five years and nobody sent a telegram yet.' So one day when I was all on my own I heard a constant tapping and I couldn't think where it was coming from and I realised it was from the wee bowl and it was a squad of soldiers sending telegrams and I'd only got two and sixpence worth of change! They were all rushing for their train because I think they had come from abroad, and had maybe landed at Methil and just been given, what, a warrant or something, so I remember one of the NCOs paid for them all.

When I turned up at Thornton station for the first time, the actual office was a room off the stationmaster's office. I could not understand the Morse at all, it was absolutely foreign to me. I was there over a week and I still couldn't read it and I doubted I was going to be a failure at this and no-one was showing it to me or anything, I just had to figure it out for myself. And one day when I was getting off the train and walking up the ramp to the office, I found I was reading it. Maybe I'd been concentrating too hard. I just found I was reading it. We had actually six instruments and five of the instruments I could read easily, but I remember the one to Glasgow I had always great difficulty with it. I think the other five had the T, the dash on the left-hand side and this one was back to front, it was the other way round and I never, never really cottoned on to it you know.

We did two shifts alternately. There was a girl on the other shift and actually I think she did very well because she hadn't done Morse before. We did from half past seven in the morning to two o'clock and then two o'clock till nine. But morning was always very busy, afternoon was more sparse. And every morning of course we got long messages for the signalman. At that time in Scotland the signal boxes had the Morse machines phased out and they had telephones. So we had I think eight telephones, six instruments, and a phone just for the Post Office for telegrams. And then there was a room off the stationmaster's office and the platform inspector had a couple of phones there, and there was always a head clerk, the stationmaster and two lady clerks. So we had a row of hooks on the wall for messages for outside men, like the plumber and the electrician, the ones who looked after the rails et cetera. They looked in every morning to see if there was any messages on their hooks and popped in occasionally throughout the day to see if there was anything for them. And then sometimes of course we had messages. Thornton had myriads of rails, lots and lots of sidings. It wasn't a very big station, there was only an up and down line and the dock in the middle. It was like a letter H and that's what they called the docks, and extra carriages would stand in there. But otherwise there was sheds in the distance and many, many sidings, trucks of coal, trucks of everything and nothing would make me go down in these rails. There was some of the overseers et cetera had huts within the rails and I just stood and shouted till they heard me and came and got their messages

Annie Lageu, *shorthand typist, LMS Leeds*

When you started on the railways, as juniors, you had to go to evening classes twice a week during the winter and then there were exams at the end of it. And one night was for goods work, when you did goods accounting, which we didn't do, but we still had to learn all about it and then of course when I went on the passenger side I had to go to the passenger classes as well.

There was an exam and if you did all right you got a certificate. But you had to pass an exam before you went on the railways and then you had to pass another one at 18, before you got your next rise and that was all on railway work. There was arithmetic, English I think and then Railway Studies. And for the Railway Studies you were supposed to know the line that our area covered going out, of course it finished at Leeds, because beyond there was the East. But ours went to the Diggle Tunnel, and then it went from Normanton, up to Appleby and you had to know the stations that were on that line and they expected you to know something about the different industries. From the geography side, the different industries, the towns were, were involved in, like Luton was hats, Leicester was shoes, Lancashire was cotton, Yorkshire the woollens.

Mary Hodgson, *LMS clerk Chesterfield*

So in April 1941 I started work on the London Midland & Scottish Railway. The first job I had was in the Chief Clerk's Office, principally as the switchboard operator. But in those days there were no extensions to this telephone. So every time anybody needed to speak to the yard foreman or the supervisor on the goods inward side, or on the goods outwards, or on the weighbridge, I had to go running to find them and fetch them to the telephone, because, stupid as it seems, they'd no extension lines. And even some of the offices hadn't got an extension into the Delivery Office. And there was no extension into the Accounts Office upstairs. All you could do is get to the Delivery Office next door and fetch whoever was needed, and for the Accounts Office I had to ring through to the Correspondence Office, and they would go into the Accounts Office and fetch anybody who was needed. Well it seems absolutely ridiculous in this day and age, because there was spare capacity on my switchboard for there to have been telephones in other places.

So I'd 18 shillings a week, plus my free travel, so in effect I was getting about 21 shillings a week. And then when you'd passed your 18 exam, which both males and females had to take this exam. It was a written exam, and along with English and maths, railway geography, knowledge of your local area. So far as females were concerned shorthand and typing. And so far as males were concerned shorthand. And you had to pass that exam just before your 18th birthday. If you didn't pass, you got the sack. But if you did pass, well then, you were kept on. And I was paid then about £70 a year, but out of that you had to pay your own superannuation fund money. The males a job for life, females a job until they got married, unless of course you did something wrong.

Maureen Evans, *messenger then clerk, LMS Crewe*

Well, to be allowed to go into the general offices, which was the next step up, you had to take an exam. If you hadn't matriculated at school, you had to pass this exam, otherwise at the age of 16 you were sent on your way to go and find another job. And I was studying English, maths, shorthand, railway geography. So I was going to night school. I was going to shorthand lessons on a Thursday evening. We worked Saturday morning, I think it was eight till twelve-thirty. Saturday afternoon we'd go to this little old gentleman, a Mr Curtis, who'd taken pupils specially for this examination for the railways. Mr Curtis was a very elderly gentleman. And he'd start off the lesson and after about ten minutes he'd fall fast asleep. My father used to pay good money out of his lowly wages for me to go to Mr Curtis, but he used to fall asleep for about ten minutes or fifteen minutes and then suddenly wake up again and pick up again, ending the sentence he'd just started. So at 16 I passed the exam to go into the General Offices.

Irene Adgie, *typist, SR Woking and Waterloo*

Well, first of all, because I was so inexperienced, I was given mainly letters for the Commercial department, that were standard letters and just had the details filled in. Refunds of money, acknowledgements, that sort of thing. But then I was later given more work doing proper letters, mainly for commercial. And most of the men drafted their letters in shorthand. Very few dictated. In long-hand or shorthand, or both. At that time, male clerks had been expected to know shorthand and typing when they joined the railway.

It was the London Southwest division. Traffic, who had been, of course, evacuated from Waterloo. The commercial work was okay. The head of the department insisted on drafting all his letters in shorthand. Completely. And our supervisor used to tell us that his shorthand was perfect. But none of us could read it. Pitman's, yes. Later on, when I had my own age group, three of us got together and bought a shorthand dictionary and picked out all the mistakes that were in his drafts. But we never had the courage to confront the supervisor with it. I then was sent from Commercial, I tended to sort of dodge about the different departments. Some work for the Rules, some for the Staff Office, but mainly work for the actual Traffic department. The supervisor, she was a tartar, but she was very kind to me. And because she knew I was struggling with short-hand, mainly to get practice for speed, she sent me to a clerk who could read shorthand. And she knew he wouldn't dictate long letters. He would dictate at a speed that would challenge me, but not go too fast. And that was a tremendous help.

Doreen Dickenson, *goods clerk, LMS Liverpool*

And on the 15th of April I started. So I had to report to Waterloo Dock. Now Waterloo Dock is evidently like the headquarters for the goods department. Oh, the funny part about it though, I came here and I told my grandma I was going to get a job on the railway. And do you know what she said? 'Pushing a truck up a platform after the education you've had?' That's the only thought we had that people did, apart from engine drivers, you pushed a truck up a platform. Weren't we naïve? So I thought that was terrific.

When I told my father I was getting a job in the railway, he had the same impression. He said they'll be paying buttons on the railway. Well, they were. They were terribly, grossly underpaid. I mean, no wonder they thought my father was a millionaire cos he was a civil servant. An engine driver got about three pound a week in those days, I should think. Anyway, I got this job. We went to Waterloo Dock. Well, I didn't know Waterloo Dock. …I didn't know the slummy end of Bootle and the docks. But my father had worked down there at Stanley Dock tobacco warehouse. So a couple of days before, we go on the bus, on the tram, whatever it is. And he takes me to where I've got to go, so I know. So I found my way there. I think it was half past nine I had to report. We went into the staff office. They fill a form in and do all the things. And they gave you your free railway pass between the nearest station to your home and Liverpool. The nearest station to my home was Seaforth. Seaforth station wasn't any good for me. It was twenty-five minutes, half an hour's walk from our house. I was better getting the bus and getting off at Bank Hall, as it happened, as I was told my job would be at Canada Dock station, goods station.

And there was a lady there, a girl, 16 like me, who lived in Birkdale. Never been out of Southport, I don't think. Didn't know Liverpool docks or anything. And we had to find our way. They gave us a tram ticket. So we got the tram and we were told to get off at Canada Dock. When we got on the dock road with the dockers, we were told to ask for a Mr Umpleby. Well I'd never heard of that name in my life, before or since. So we remembered it by saying Bumblebee. So we chatted away, Netty and myself, this girl I started with. And we got down to the dock road and we saw a policeman standing at the dock gate. So like two naïve, 16 years of age, we must have been like children, babies. We went up to the policeman and said, 'Do you know where we can find Mr Bum – Mr Umpleby?' He said, 'Never heard of him, love. Who is he?' I said, 'He's the staff clerk at Canada Dock.' Well, Canada Dock was a big dock, and there were big liners up there. And there was big notices like 'Yours truly, Jones Dooley' and all the shipping lines we could see. And we were in a world, I don't know, we just were befogged. So he said, 'Where does he work?' And I said, 'Oh, the LMS railway.' It suddenly dawned on us where we were working. He said, 'Oh, behind you.'

The other side of the dock road was the Canada Dock warehouse, so we went through the yard, the gates. Found somebody who directed us up to the staff office, which was on the first floor. So we were instructed by the chappie. I was put with a Mr Hughes in the Delivery office. And Netty went with a Mr Somebody-or-other in the Forwarding office. And what happened in this office was, the goods used to come in on the ships and were loaded onto engines. And the Dock Board engine carried it from Alexander Dock, and through into the yard. And they went up where they were distributed to wagons which went all over the country. So we had to deal with all the documents that came in. Now in those days, some of the delivery was still done, Cartage office, they called it, and there were horses. Mind you, they were getting lorries, they were up–marketing a little bit. But the carters down there had their big hessian aprons on, full of hay and straw. And they fed the horses and the horses came in and out. But we weren't allowed to go in the Cartage office, because, well, bad language, and the girls weren't supposed to go down there. The little messenger lads had to go there. We had messenger boys. It was a world of its own. It had its own telephone system, its own telegraph system, its own linesmen who came and repaired the telephones.

Well, I'd never met a world like it before. And there were ten of us. Some of them that had started before me and Netty. Now there were ten pretty girls at Canada Dock. And four were blondes and five were brunettes and one was a saucy little redhead. Well you can guess, you know the song, do you? 'There were ten pretty girls on the village green.' Well that's what they used to sing. So of course we were all whistled at by the lads in the yard. And all that kind of thing, you know. Which we were terribly sort of, upmarket. We didn't wave back or anything like that, you ran for your life.

But I had to go up onto the canteen where was a kettle. It was a huge cast-iron thing, about two foot high and eighteen inches across. And it had a brass tap on it which you had to use your handkerchief to turn it on, it was boiling. In fact there was at a time they found a dead rat in there somewhere, when they used to get the water for their tea out of it. And there were rats all over the warehouse. We never really saw any but the young lads who used to do Home Guard duties used to come and shoot them with their rifles. I wasn't there then, I'd gone home for the night. The warehouse was packed with bales of cotton, you know. If you were fat you were like a bale of cotton with the bands off, that's what they used to say on the railway. Full of their own comments, you know.

But for the first week, for the first two or three weeks, I was leaving. 'Oh Dad, I couldn't stand it any longer. Oh, it's dreadful.' I didn't know what I was doing. He'd give me half a job to do. He'd say, 'Get on the phone with Alexander Dock and ask Bill so-and-so, so-and-so' you see. And he'd give me a piece of paper to write down what he said. And I'd have to get on the phone. And I wasn't used to a phone, for the first bit. I was so nervous I could hardly hear what was being said. And I spoke to this Jack. And he said, 'Oh,' he said irritably, 'what's the matter with Dave? Put him on, and I'll talk to him myself.' Cos he was asking me questions about what I was asking him. And I didn't know what I was doing. So all I was doing was getting somebody on the phone so he could talk.

And then he'd go away and he said, 'Can you type?' And I said, 'Only, well, I'm learning.' I'd started to learn to type, you see. And I'd had to type a letter, and ask them to do this, or type and send them back this. You got put with somebody at their desk and you picked it up as you went along. Well, you just learnt the job. And eventually you could help, but there wasn't any training anyway.

But one of the rules was, you got 25 shillings a week, it must have been, when you were 18. And you came from junior to proper sort of female adult standard. And they told us at the time that we wouldn't get our rise when we were 18 unless we passed our efficiency exam. And the efficiency exam was geography, railway geography, and shorthand and typing. So of course I was going to shorthand and typing and suchlike. When we were 18, some people, who say they were 18 in January, and they didn't hold their exam until July, they didn't get the money until they'd passed the exam. And then they got the back-pay from their 18th birthday. But can you see how easy it was to fail people? Cos if they failed then they only got from the date they passed the exam and they had to sit it again six months later. So Netty and I decided that as I was 18 in December and she was 18 in August, we were going to sit the July/August exam, so that we were going to pass it before our birthday. They weren't going to tell us we'd failed so that they didn't pay us the difference. We didn't trust anybody. So we passed our 18 exam in July. And she got her rise when she was 18 in August. And I got my rise when I was 18 in December. And we got a rise to 25 shillings a week. We were very well off, yes. We thought we were, anyway.

We had to go to school. Night classes, privately. They didn't teach us at all. I went to Duckitts in Merton Road, which was an all-day and evening school. A lot of people leaving school went to Duckitts full-time and then they got jobs as shorthand typists. But I only went from, say, seven till nine in the evening, you know, for two or three nights a week. I did quite well with the shorthand. I was doing about 80 in less than no time. And it came up to our efficiency exam, which we were determined to take before our 18th birthday, so that we'd get our rise and they couldn't say we'd failed and postpone it. So, the chappie who was taking it, he stood in front of a class of us. We went to Waterloo Dock for it. And he'd read out whatever it was. And every time he looked up, I looked up. And he looked at me and said, 'Are you getting this down, Miss Ryder?' And I said, 'Yes, I was way ahead, you know ... down as soon as you'd finished speaking.' It was quite easy, really.

But the typing and the shorthand, I never really used again. The idea was in case the boss called you in to take some notes or something. But he had a girl who was his secretary. And we didn't really use it very much. And so I think I can just write 'Dear Sir' now, in shorthand. But the typing, well, we had to do typing because we were in the shipping office.

Gladys Garlick, *guard, LNER London*

I was there till 1943. And one of the inspectors that used to live at Grange Park, he came up one day cos he knew my father. And he said, 'Ooh,' he said, 'how would you like to be a guard?' So I said, 'Ooh, yeah,' I said, 'I really fancy that.' So I went out then to be a guard. I was one of the first two on the LNER.

We did a fortnight up at Hatfield, at a school. They taught us about signals and rules and things like that. And then we learnt the road with another guard, you know. There was a bit of a bad feeling by some of the guards cos they thought it made their job look cheap. Well, I suppose in a way it's like my husband working to be a driver. You don't jump straight into it, do you? You have to work your way up to get to be a guard. And they were, some of them were a bit resentful of that. But on the whole they were all very good.

Gladys had routes to learn. Well, up to Hertford North, and then up to Hatfield. And Welwyn Garden City on the mainline. From Kings Cross, yes. And I was actually stationed at Gordon Hill. There was four of us at Gordon Hill, stationed there.

Edith Stretch, *booking office clerk, LMS Hanley*

Well, we were on our own in one office. We weren't in an office with men. The station master's office was across the road, but he very rarely came in to see us. He knew we were doing alright. We got the work done. We had an auditor occasionally. And he was a great big tall man. When you're an auditor you always go unannounced. And he wanted to look at the books. Course, you're quivering in your boots, in case you've done something wrong. And he looked at me, and I looked at him. And he says, 'Nothing to be afraid of, dear.' I said, 'Alright.' So I gave him everything we'd got. And one of the things that you had to do when you were issuing a ticket. If you had one and a half, you got the ticket for one, you put them in the punch and dated them. But the half, you had to cut a piece out of the bottom, like, with a pair of shears. And it cut a piece out about one inch long and less than a quarter of an inch. And you had to put them in a little tin for when you'd got the monthly return. So you know, you'd got those many tickets to... that money to put there. But you had to make sure that if it was a half you got the piece. And I remember one year it was lost. And one of us had been on holiday. Either Miss Jones or myself. And whoever had done it had put it in the wrong tin. That was it. Everything, it was neat and tidy. I mean, the wages. The foreman used to bring the sheets up. And we'd put them on the big sheets, ready to go. They had to go to Derby to be verified, and then come back. And then we'd make the things out for the station master to fetch them, cos the station master dealt with the bank. He used to go and take the takings up to the bank, and pay them in. And he used to get the money from the bank to pay the wages. Well, he used to sit by me when I put the wages up. And then we used to pay them out to the men.

I'd never used a telephone in my life. But we got the phones, and to ring the signal boxes you did a code. And you'd press a button, it'd go, press one to start it. And one, two, three, four. And that was one signal box. And so you spoke to the signalman. And you'd spoke to the men. And I must say, they were, gentlemen sounds horrible, but they were. They were nice men. And then you'd got passengers that wanted to leave their case in. And you'd go along to the other end of the office and you'd give them a ticket.

It was a good grounding for everything I've done in my life, really. I mean, I got used to being on shift work. I mean, my husband being on shifts, I got used to that. And of course I like my free pass. But if I'd have worked with an office full of people like I have done in other times, because being on your own, you're really, you're responsible to yourself. Because if anything goes wrong, you've only got you to blame. But nothing did go wrong, really.

Working with Men

Men and women. It was very difficult, when you hadn't been used to a lot of men and we didn't have boyfriends like they do today, at 14. They weren't awfully guarded on what they used to say, and it was a bit, you know, embarrassing, well, it was for me, I don't know about the others, but anyway, I fitted in as well as I could, you know. And some were very nice, the older men we found were very nice.

(Marjorie Pateman, lathe operator, LMS Wolverton works)

Conscription had removed many of the young fit men from the railways, leaving behind men who were either older or young boys. Other men were still there because they had been assessed as not fit for military service, in some eyes they were not seen as virile 'real men'. Women such as young Marjorie Pateman had to learn to work with all these men, in the stifling heat and terrible noise of the LMS workshops at Wolverton. But after the end of the war Marjorie married a railwayman, and as a leaving present was awarded the somewhat surprising combination of a chiming clock and a bread knife.

Many of these women, such as GWR linesman's assistant Mary Woodfield, appreciated being 'nursed' by the older men, who guided and supported them in carrying out 'men's work'. Many women were working with men for the first time, quite often much older men, in a setting not designed for women. Even as a booking clerk a woman might be carrying out her job with a totally male workforce. This led to a number of problems, for example female toilets were often just not available, apart from those on the platform, and using those involved special arrangements. In July 1944 a question was asked in Parliament about the 'bad washing and lavatory conditions' at the sidings at Stratford in London. Apparently there were two toilets and six wash basins for the seventy-five women employed there (fifty of whom would be working on a shift together).[1]

There were also protocols to observe, such as being called 'Miss' and 'Mister'. Relationships with these men might prove tricky: women and their fathers in particular debated the kind of language which might be used by their male counterparts at work, and how to deal with it. It has been suggested that signalmen had concerns about working alone with a woman on a dark night in a lonely box, as it might lead to suspicious rumours about what they were up to, and the welfare officers had to play a role in convincing men that this was not a worry.[2]

Women discovered that some of the male groups had well-established strategies to protect their own incomes, such as Maureen Evans' section heads, and Florence Brinklow's driver. These workers were also well aware that the more productive a worker became, the higher the targets that would be set, and this reflects the experiences of women working in wartime factories, as recalled by munitions workers in Croydon.[3] In general however, the women talking about their work often seemed to be conscientious, sometimes more so than their male colleagues, as if they felt the need to prove themselves in an unfamiliar role.

Men gained power from their age, experience and level in the management hierarchy, and at times they might use this to make unwelcome advances. Some women suffered from the kind of sexual harassment which would not be acceptable in the 21st century, but was swept under the carpet in the 1940s, as something that women had to put up with. It seemed normal for typists such as Irene Adgie to share a chair with a male worker when he was checking her work. Some women experienced sexual teasing and had to learn strategies for dealing with it. On occasion women were able to find ways of retaliating when men were troublesome generally, as in the case of Nellie Nelson and her laxative chocolate.

There were pay grievances too and inequalities, and concerns that often women had to leave when they married. Many women were proud of their conscientious abilities and the way they had learned to take responsibility very quickly, but frustrated that this was not recognised by pay. But these women in general liked working with the men, and had positive views about them. They enjoyed their work and the camaraderie, often marrying a male worker.[4]

Nellie Nelson, *LNER porter, York*

We'd an awful parcel foreman. He was a bit of a nuisance, so we cured him one day. You know laxative chocolate you can buy in Boots? Well we bought some of that. We was all on number nine platform and we asked, 'Give you a bit of chocolate Tommy?' 'Aye' and he got some of this and said, 'You're a nuisance you lot I'm having no more chocolate off you lot'.

Laura Scott, *sawdust bagger, LNER carriage works, York*

All men used to shout to you, 'Are you all right, Laura?' and that. There weren't many, but you was up at top of a plank, emptying it down into like, a sawdust hole.

Marjorie Pateman, *lathe operator, LMS Wolverton works*

Wheel shop. Men and women. It was very difficult, when you hadn't been used to a lot of men and we didn't have boyfriends like they do today, at 14. They weren't awfully guarded on what they used to say, and it was a bit, you know, embarrassing, well, it was for me, I don't know about the others, but anyway, I fitted in as well as I could, you know. And some were very nice, the older men we found were very nice. Nearer retiring, they were more nicer to the younger girl, but you just had to get along and you know, take the good with the bad really, you hadn't got a choice had you? I suppose it was just the same for people who went in the forces. The girls had to mix and fit in didn't they?

Oh, they gave me a clock, when I was married, and a bread knife. The knife might have been for bad purposes if I killed my husband, like. [laughs] No, they gave me a chiming clock.

Florence Brinklow, *parcels delivery, LNER Kings Cross*

Ooh, Mr – what was his name? He said to me, 'You're the smartest girl on the station, but you're a cow with your timing.'

Such a lot happened, but I just can't remember half of it, you know. I was on a Scammell and we was coming over, I think it was Waterloo Bridge. And not only was he deaf, he was also half-blind and all, I swear. Cos he used to say to me, 'Can you still see the white line?' Cos we was in the blackout, you see, there was no lighting or nothing. And he used to say to me, 'Can you see the white line?' And I'd say, 'Yes Joe, okay Joe'. Cos I could see the white line. Then I said to him, 'Joe, I can't see the white line.' Bang. He went right into a water butt in the middle of the road. Yeah. Cos we used to have them big water butts, you know.

You got to know quite a few people in the city, you know. [The driver] got the tips on the Friday. He used to say to me, 'I'll go up today,' cos it was Friday. Yeah, they always used to get a drink on the Friday.

Mary Hodgson, *clerk, LMS Chesterfield*

Pre-war the railway had employed women, they must have been in the hotels, as chambermaids. I can remember them working in refreshment rooms, even though they wouldn't have us in the offices, pre-war. There were people who worked in certain facilities on the railway. Well when I went to work at Chesterfield there were already four females there before I got there, so I was number five to arrive, and we had no facilities whatsoever. We'd no toilet, no washbasin, no rest room, we had no facilities whatsoever for the females. But luckily, we had a Chief Clerk, who was a very homely, kindly sort of man. And I think really he took these five females under his wing and looked after them as best he could. The only thing that we did receive, we were each given a key, to one of the toilets, in the ladies' waiting room on the passenger station. That was the only facility we had. So the Chief Clerk said that all five of us, must go to the passenger station together, and we must all wait for each other, and come back together. He wasn't going to have us wandering about on our own. So once in the morning, and once in the afternoon, the five ladies got together and we walked down to the passenger station, to go to the ladies' waiting room. And walk back again. And that, that's the way we were, we were looked after as females working on the railway.

I later became station relief. Because I'd done so many different jobs already, then if anybody was off work for any reason whatsoever, and it was a vital job that had to be done, then I would go and work wherever the clerk hadn't turned up. I know some days I've had as many as three different jobs. Because I would go onto a job, and then later on when somebody else was due on duty, that person didn't turn in, but that job was more important than that one. So I had to transfer to that. And sometimes, I would transfer to a third job. I used to love it, I thought it was extremely interesting.

The females were treated differently to the males. Although I did these different jobs, on an hourly basis or a daily basis or sometimes on a weekly basis, the females didn't get any difference of pay whatsoever. Because on one occasion the Chief Delivery Clerk was involved in a road accident. So his second in command, moved into his chief position. And I moved into the second in command. Now I'd often done that job before. There'd never been any question of a difference of pay, because actually that person would either be off ill, or he would be on holiday, or something would've happened for that second in command of the Delivery Office not to be at work. But if you were only doing it for a short length of time you see you didn't bother. But on this particular occasion when the Chief Delivery Clerk had had a road accident, so he couldn't come to work, second in command did his job, and I was brought from my job to do the second in command of the delivery office. A few days later we got word that the man who had had the accident was going to get compensation from the insurance firm. That meant that because he was going to get money whilst he was off work, the railway were not going to pay him his salary. So the second in command who was doing his job, got what we called DOP which was Difference of Pay: he was going to get extra money, for doing the chief's job. I'm doing second in command; there was no Difference of Pay for me because I was female.

I didn't even get the highest rate of a female's pay, which was when you were 28 years of age. And at this time I'm only about 21, something like that, so there's no difference of pay for me. So I had to be taken off the job, and somebody else put on. And a junior male clerk was put on the job. And paid far more money for doing it than I had ever been paid all the times that I'd done that work. And of course this junior didn't know how to do the work, and he asked me to show him. I must have been feeling like it that morning because I said to him, 'No you've been paid extra money to do the job, you do the work.'

When they needed a relief clerk at Healey on one occasion, they rang up from the Farm and asked me if I would go to Healey, and be relief clerk there. And I went. But I didn't get DOP. So the next time they asked me I said, No I wasn't going. It was the principle of the thing that was all wrong. And that was how the railway treated females in those days. Once the war was over they didn't employ married women. And I'd had to leave the day I'd got married.

Joan Richards, *parcels clerk, GWR Hartlebury*

There were two ladies on the platform, the porters, but nearly all my workmates were male. And my father warned me before I started, he said, 'You'll have to get used to a bit of bad language,' and I said, 'Shall I?' And he said, 'Well, I expect so.' And I always remember the first day something went wrong, and one of the men said, 'Oh, bloody hell!' and then he stopped and he looked at me and he didn't know where to put himself. And I just started to laugh. Anyway, I heard afterwards that he'd seen my father later on, and he said, 'I forgot myself this morning,' he said, 'I swore in front of Joan.' My father says, 'What did she do?' And he says, 'Well, I expected to see her look disgusted, but,' he said, 'she just grinned and walked away.' And he said, 'I don't think you'll have any problem with it.' And after that, well, if they swore, they swore, I didn't take any notice. They were always very decent with me. If they could help they would, they were always very pleasant and no harassment or anything, but the swearing used to make me laugh because sometimes you know, they'd look so guilty afterwards, but I never said anything about it. I got on very well with them.

It was a reserved occupation. So they were men that, I should say in their 30s to 40s mainly, there were one or two young ones, but there were the one lad, you know, he wouldn't have passed for the forces anyway, but he was quite capable of doing the job, and my husband, he did go for his medical, but he was never called up. One or two of them had been for medicals, but because they worked on the railway they weren't called up. But it was a mixed age group sort of thing. But the drivers that came down from the RAF, they were all right, but they weren't so, well, they didn't mind what they said, sort of thing, you know, a bit more rougher really. But the chaps I worked with every day, no complaints whatsoever about them. We had a very good relationship really.

Maureen Evans, *clerk, LMS Crewe*

The section heads, without fail, were all men. So on the end of each desk was the section head, was your desk head and his deputy. All male. And on a Monday and a Tuesday they could be found reading the sports pages and discussing the cricket and discussing the football and the scores and the matches and the politics and everything else. Meandering through the day until it got to about half past four and then they would turn round and say: 'Overtime tonight, everybody, overtime.' You see? So of course we'd been working hard all day in order to try and finish at five o'clock, and these, they all wanted the overtime money, you see. And their money would be quite substantial because they were getting good salaries. But our overtime pay was quite paltry in comparison, we thought, anyway, so this was all part of the ploy to get the overtime money.

Irene Adgie, *typist, SR Woking and Waterloo*

For those of us who were typists, who typed those special notices, we had to go down and check them with one of the men in the office. And there were never enough chairs. So we used to share a chair with a man. And I think the feminists these days would be horrified. They'd probably be having all the men done for harassment. But we used to call it fun.

Irene met her future husband while working in the typing pool. He was down in the control, on the donkey boxes.[5] And he was working alternate at that time. Early and late and every weekend. But when I was doing late turn, he'd come up and see me in the pool. And other times he'd leave a note under my typewriter cover for me. And we could always go out in the evenings when he was doing early turn. But he was living with his widowed mother, who was in her seventies and not at all well. *They married in 1948.*

Doreen Dickenson, *goods clerk, LMS Liverpool*

This elderly gentleman that I was working with. He was a very nice man, really. But he'd been off sick for something like three months. And he was so behind with his filing and his ledger work and whatever-it-is he had to do. And they put me to assist him. Well, what use was I? I didn't know a thing. And I felt as though if you start a job you should know what you're doing, you see? And I felt so awful. And he'd say to me, 'I don't know what they've given me you for. I may as well do the job myself.' Well, that was very encouraging. So he gave me a china jug, or a pot jug which had an advert for Woodbines, or Wills Whiffs, or those sort of things they gave away for advertised tobacco. And he opened a paper with connie-onnie and tea in it, all mixed up like a mixture, spooned it into this jug and said, 'Will you go upstairs and put some hot water on this?' [6] I thought, oh dear. And it came out like treacle and it was black and he said to me, 'Do you want a cup of this?' I said, 'No thank you.' So that was my first day.

Anyway, there was a chappie who worked on a couple of desks, cos we had high desks. And you had foot rails underneath. And you sat on a high stool and it sloped up and all your files were in boxes between you. And if you moved them you could see the fellow opposite. I'd only been there about three weeks or so. And this tall fellow, about 45 or so, probably too old to go in the forces. He'd been in the previous war, you see. About me dad's age. And he came over to me and he said, 'Your name's Ryder, isn't it?' I said yes. He said, 'Are you any relation to Bert Ryder?' So I said, 'I've got an Uncle Albert.' ... Me dad's eldest brother. 'Oh,' he said, 'Well who's your father?' I said, 'Arthur'. 'Oh aye,' he said. 'And there's Bill, isn't there?' So he said, 'Oh my sister was engaged to your Uncle Albert years ago.' He said, 'I could have been related.' Well, now that was a godsend to me, because I could go to him. And I could ask him things. And I didn't mind appearing a fool in front of him. And he would explain. And after I got to know him, I know I must have been a pest in the early stages. But I didn't mind the job then cos I knew what I was doing. He'd explained to me how the system worked, and what we were expected to do, and that was fine. So I stayed there from April 1940, and we went through the Blitz.

And you know the old idea where you start work and they send you for a long stand? You're told to go and get the glass hammer, or something like that. Well, on the railway, they had a saying, 'Go and ask the chief foreman for the key to the tunnel.' Well, I'm sorry, but they didn't get me with that one. 'The key to the tunnel'. Load of rubbish, you see.

But I don't know whether I dare tell you what they did get me with. There were ten girls at Canada Dock. And there was a great long Forwarding Office. And the boss used to sit on a foot-high platform, at a desk at the other end. And in the corner was a glass partition where the switchboard was. And we all had to learn the switchboard. And we all had to take a turn at it and relieve for tea breaks and lunchtime and things like that, you see. So I was relieving on the lunchtime switchboard. And we had two messenger boys. Because we used to have our own telegraph service. And we used to take down telegrams, and they'd run up the yard to the chief foreman with it, you see. And there were two of these little lads sitting there. And a phone call came through for Edna. Now, I'd not been there very long. I didn't know all their second names. There was Edna, and there was Gladys, and there was Mary, she was called the Pride of Lathom cos she was a beautiful-looking girl with lovely curls. That's where she lived. And a telephone call came through from the boyfriend for Edna. And Edna was the boss's typist. Bit older than us. And she was a bit superior, cos she was more like 19 and we were 16, you know. And so I said to the little messenger boy, we had a little private telephone box, and Edna was sat up in the corner, having her lunch near the boss's desk. He was a Welshman with a bald head and red hair. And he sort of looked at you over his glasses, you know, very disapprovingly. 'These youngsters, what they get up to,' you see. And I said to the young lad, I said, 'Will you go and tell Edna she's wanted on the phone. It's her boyfriend. She can come and take it in the private little booth.' So he said, 'Oh, go and tell her yourself. I'm on my lunch.' So I said, 'Well, you've only got to go and shout.' So he said, 'Open the door and give her a shout.' So of course in those days, you didn't call people by their first names across the office. It was always 'Mr This' and 'Mr That'. So I said, 'I don't know her name.' And they started to laugh. I said, 'I can't shout "Edna"'. He said, 'Don't you know her name?' I said, 'No.' 'Oh,' he said, 'her name's Miss Toole.' So I'd heard of O'Toole. But anyway I stood at the office door and shouted 'Miss Toole, you're wanted on the phone.' Well, Edna came with a newspaper in her hand, with a face like fury. And she walked thirty yards, or whatever it is, from that end of the office. And she just said to me, 'You,' she said, 'you ought to have more sense.' And she batted this little lad with the newspaper. I didn't know her name was Edna Dick. Well, I couldn't shout 'Miss Dick' either, could I?

We had our own toilet the men didn't use. I suppose it was probably built in on the warehouse. And it was a bit difficult when we were underneath the arches, cos we had to go through an arch and round the back, and there were toilets round there, which they made over to females, which were probably what the carters used. But it was only bare brick walls, or whitewashed brick walls, and that kind of thing, you know. But I don't know, we just sort of managed alright.

[The goods agent] was one of those fellows. He liked to chat up the girls. He was a dirty old man. Now he had one typist who used to go in to him and he probably sat and talked for ... he'd be three hours doing it, cos he used to chat up people, you see. And he had me in there one day. He just sent for me and wanted to know how I liked ... this was in the old warehouse, before we were blitzed. So I was quite new and naive and knew nothing, you know. Wanted to know how I liked the office. Was I happy at my work, and how I got on, and whatever it is. And if I ever did anything wrong or something, rather than report me to the head office or give me a bad report, wouldn't I sooner he smack my bottom? Now I'm not kidding, this is gospel. And I looked at him. He said, 'I'm sure you'd sooner I smacked you. I'd turn you over my knee and smack your bottom if you were a naughty girl,' and all this. And I got this kind of talk. All of a sudden the phone rings, and it's the chief foreman for the boss. And he said, 'Oh, not at the moment, Andy,' he said. 'I'm busy'. He said, 'Who have you got in there this time?' Or words to that effect. And he must have said who. Five minutes later, the doors bursts open, Andy Campbell says, 'You! Get back to your desk.' And I was dismissed. And he came to me afterwards. He said, 'What was he talking about?' And of course you don't like to say anything, do you? He said, 'Yes, you were in there, and wasting your time, and wasting his time. He's not wasting my bloody time,' he says.

But it seems that after this he did the same with Netty, and he did the same with Gladys. And Gladys as I said was the Pride of Lathom with lovely blonde curly hair. And I think he must have fancied her more than me, because I never went in very much after that. But she did, she went in quite a bit. And she was intimidated by him, in a way. But the girl who was his typist, I think she was used to him, and she was older than us. And I suppose she just dismissed it, whatever it was, you see. But when you talk about harassment or whatever you call it these days, I think we didn't realise, those days, what it was. And of course there was a war on, so the younger fellows had gone away, and the mice thought they would play, you know.

Well you see I had this friend, Bill, and when they said things to me in the yard I'd go and tell him and he'd say, 'Well, you do this or you do that,' and he advised me. And I wasn't intimidated by it. Because every time I went across the yard or went down to the cartage with some invoices or something, they'd shout, 'Hiya, Ginge, are you?' You see. And I'd think, 'Why do they say "Hiya, Ginge, are you?"' So I went to Bill Galley one day and I said, 'Why do they say ...?' 'Oh,' he said, 'Don't you know?' And I said, 'No.' 'Hiya, Ginge, are you Ginge all over?' That's what they wanted to know, whether I was ginger all over. I thought that was dreadful. But the next time they said it, do you know what I said to them? 'If I was a dyed blonde, I could understand you asking silly questions like that.' And marched on. So they never did it any more. I always had to find the answers from somewhere.

Oh, the unions wanted equal pay, didn't they? Do you know how long it took us to get equal pay? Six years. I didn't have equal pay with my husband when I left to have my daughter. Because I'd got another twelve months to go to get the final instalment. And when you got an instalment years ago, when I first started, you see you had Class Five railway clerk. You were fifth or fourth or third. And if you were third then you were getting up on the list. And if you were fourth then you were manager of the office – second, rather, you were manager. Second and first class, I think you were the boss or the agent or something, you see. Then they did away with fifth and made all fifth and fourth amalgamated into fourth-class...citizens, you see. And of course they wanted equal pay. And I didn't want equal pay. I thought if you have equal pay and there's a choice between taking on a man or a woman, they'd take the man on. Because the woman's likely to get married and have children and be a flaming nuisance, you see. So we didn't stand a chance of getting a job if we had to have the same pay as the men. That's the way I looked at it, those days. But the rise between one grade and another was something like three and sixpence a week. You get a grade from a Class Five to a Class Four, you got three and sixpence a week. You might get five bob if you were going up the scale, you know. I mean, the wages were ridiculous.

Doreen went onto the adult rate of pay – 25 shillings. That was as a Class Five clerk. But it was women's grade Class Five clerk. Women's grade, you see. We were the lowest common denominator, if you like. And of course we were doing men's jobs, really. I mean I was sitting at a desk charging out what he'd rated. And anyway, we eventually got equal pay. And so we could do our own rating then, you see. But we didn't have any training. We only picked it up. There were books on the table there, and certain class of goods, you went to look, you looked it up to find out. And it gave you all the places in the country where the train stations were, goods stations were, for that class of travel. And it'd tell you, you know, it's going to Uttoxeter or something or other. Or it's going down to Portsmouth or something. You look it up and it'll give you grades of things, and how much the rate is for that kind of traffic. And you used that. But you had to charge your own things out then. You rated it. We didn't have somebody to charge it out for you, you did it yourself.

Mary Woodfield, *linesman's assistant, GWR Undy*

They were not geared up for women. The only woman was on the platform, tickets and what have you, on Severn Tunnel Station. Because it was something then. Buildings, offices, on the platform, a bar. Didn't call it a restaurant. Ada, this elderly person had run it for years. But Ada had had this doughnut under this glass dome for God knows how long. That was a standing joke. 'Don't ask Ada for a doughnut cos you might get the one under the dome.' We had inspectors, we had everything. And I was the only one I knew on the platform, mind. The only female. But the yard was not geared up for women at all. Which I had to find out anyway. But they told you nothing about it. Simply that you'd be in the yard and you'd be working with a couple of linesmen. But still, I'm game for anything. And I had to have a job. And the idea of being outdoors appealed to me tremendously.

I was an outdoors girl, really I was. I was not one for a factory. But I'd done my duty there, mind. I was a damn good worker in the factory. Because work never bothered me. Even as regards my mother's housework. 'Go upstairs and do the bedrooms.' 'Do this.' 'Time the grate was black-leaded.' You know. And I was the youngest girl. But anyway, to go on the railway. So you were just flung in off the deep end.

This was at Severn Tunnel Junction. And it was in full steam then, busy, the main route from Wales to London. All the different set of lines. There were shunting lines, it was a huge yard. But you got to know there were no toilets for a girl, or anywhere. You were given the key every time, there was a key hanging up for us to go up on the platform. So you just hoped you didn't wet yourself before you got up there. That was the only place to go. Because when you seen the linesmen's shed, the way you had to go in, it was the most despicable sight you ever seen in your life, because they were not geared up for women. Well, it was disgusting. There was a fire, an open little fire in there. You sat, there was a bench one side and there was a bench on the other side. It was a coal fire all the time. And two old men. Old enough to be my grandfathers. Even though I know very well that when you're young everybody seems old.

We weren't supplied with anything then. But in due course we had overalls. Bib and brace. I suppose by that time somebody had asked us our measurements, really. And an overall coat. Mind you, I felt the cat's whiskers in them, because they were brand new anyway.

Theresa Roberts, *booking clerk, Midsomer Norton and Welton, Somerset & Dorset Joint Railway*

It was all very enjoyable and very varied, there just wasn't a dull moment. The station staff were all a very good bunch and very helpful. I remember well one of the porters-cum-shunters Charlie Dowling, he was a very dry Somerset chap who kept us all in fits of laughter with some of his comments. He used to ride a very upright old bicycle, very slowly, he came from Radstock, you see.

Most of the outside staff came to work on bikes, as I did myself for some time, until my father bought me a second-hand Francis-Barnett two-stroke motor cycle, as motor cycles were 'the thing' in our household. Although my brother's motor bike was then under wraps as he had gone with the Royal Air Force. Anyway it took some time to get an allowance of petrol but I suppose railway work was considered essential, so I got some in the end, but it was rationed as was everything else!

Another of the lads at the station (porter-cum-shunter), the opposite turn to Charlie, was Norman Harrison. He was a north country chap who used to come out with some quaint north country sayings, one of which I used a lot when my children were growing up and which I still use today. It is: 'No-one is going to stop a galloping horse to look at that!'

Through popping out to collect tickets when passenger trains stopped we got to know some of the guards and one I remember well, he was a real cheeky chappie and some days, when the train was running in he would call out, 'Ogshot', 'Bagshot' and other less respectable fictitious station names. And sometimes he would call out as the train was running in, 'If there's anyone for here, this is it!' But no one seemed to notice except the station staff!! He didn't care but he got a good laugh. Another of his pronouncements from the guard's van was 'Pouch, run round 'em!' and I never really got to know the origin of this saying. I can only think it was something to do with single line working and shunting of wagons but maybe not, you never knew with Larry. Anyway even after I left the S & D if ever I bumped into this guard at Bath he would call out 'Pouch' and I'd reply, 'Run round 'em,' stupid but fun!

Edith Stretch, *booking office clerk, LMS Hanley*

We called everybody 'Mister' on the railway. It was no Christian names. Even the porters were 'Mister'. I was 'Miss'. Always 'Miss'. Never anything else. Even the station master, who'd got a daughter a bit older than me. We were always 'Miss'.

It was a funny thing, the men that used to relieve you. They were all about the same age as us. And one of them – both of them went in the forces – and one of them came back and he became a vicar. Cos he used to do embroidery and I used to think, that's funny, doing embroidery. But he was making a banner for the Mother's Union at the church he was at. So this is how he became a vicar. I can't remember what happened to the other one. But they were all nice young men.

I like railwaymen, I'm afraid. It's a thing that's in me blood. And it isn't really good for everybody, you know. But no, nobody was nasty.

We were always in contact with signalmen by phones. We'd got to get messages to them and from them and different things. And they were all old enough to be my father. They were lovely men. And one was the same name as my husband. Jack. And he was at a signalbox connected with a mine. And he said to me, he says, 'What do you do when you're on afternoons?' And I said, 'I take my dog for a walk.' 'What kind of a dog have you got?' I said, 'I've got a gorgeous Airedale.' And he says, 'I like Airedales. I'll have to see him one day.' I said, 'Well, come to my home, my mum'll be very pleased to see you.' 'Well, I was thinking if you're on the right shift you could bring him to see me in the signalbox.' I said, 'I'm not allowed on the railway lines. I'd get shot.' 'Well, there's no trains between such-and-such a time and such-and-such a time, cos it's connected with the coal.' So I said, 'Okay.' I said, 'But if I'm on afternoons, I've got to be home by half twelve. So it'll only be just flying visit with me dog. If you want to see me dog.' So anyhow I took my dog. And went up the steps to the signalman. And he was very pleased to see me. And he said, 'Would you like a cup of tea?' I said, 'Not out of that.' Cos railwaymen don't brew tea for a day, they brew it for a lifetime. And I said, 'No thanks.' I said, 'I'll have a look what you do, now I'm here.' And then, I was going to take my dog home. He says, 'Oh well ...' Then he hesitated. Then a young man comes up the steps in, you know, blue overalls, with his billy can. And he was going to make tea. And that's where I met my husband. That was him.

And I married him in 1943. I'd left the railway. I'd gone into munitions.

Vera Jones, apprentice fitter, LMS Crewe

Well, I can honestly say the men that I worked with, they were all very nice to us. They respected us. You never heard them come out with any bad language.

Not unless perhaps one of them hit their thumb, the hammer come in contact with their thumb. And then you'd perhaps hear some Anglo-Saxon. But if you was close to, they would apologise to you. Everyone seemed to get on together. It was like one big happy family. It seemed more of a homely, more a nice experience in a way. You know. Because we just seemed to help one another. And everyone got on well in those days. It was like one big happy family in there.

Doing a Man's Job

Well, the station master came down one day, into the station and he said, 'You come with me.' So we went up the line, and he said, 'You go up that signal.' So I went up the ladder, onto the platform at the top. He shook the signal, and he said, 'Are you alright?' and I said, 'Yes.' So I came down, and he said, 'Well, do you think you could do the lampman's job?' And I said, 'What about Ted?' And he said, 'Oh.' He said, 'He's too young.' So I said, 'Yeah,' and he said, 'Well, we'd better go and see your father.' So off we went to the marshalling yard and saw father, and he said, 'Well, it's up to her whether she does it or not.' When we went home, mother didn't want me to do it. Any rate I did do it.

(Betty Spiller, Evercreech Junction, Somerset & Dorset Joint Railway)

The idea of women coming along and taking over 'men's' railway jobs caused some angry debate in the initial stages of the war. A GWR initiative to take on women porters at the end of 1939 met with some resistance from the National Union of Railwaymen (NUR), unhappy at the new proposals, suggesting that there were men available for these jobs. Some men had been made redundant from their railway work following wartime railway reorganisation and the union felt that they should be given first priority. In 1941, the move to recruit women as LMS goods porters generated some bad feeling amongst the men at Holyhead, supported by the NUR. They argued that thirty casual labourers, engaged on a day-to-day basis, had not been given work for more than three weeks. There were further complaints that the women were working on Sundays. Management defended their recruitment campaign, saying that reductions in Irish traffic following an outbreak of foot-and-mouth disease had reduced the need for these women, but they were being trained in readiness.[1]

An anonymous correspondent in the *Perthshire Advertiser* in March 1941, writing under the name 'Truth', suggested that women were being employed because they were cheap, not because of the lack of men, of whom there were plenty unemployed in the Perth area. He complained that there were many unfilled vacancies for women in canteens, domestic, hotel and restaurant work. He suggested that many of the women taken on would be receiving army allowances as a result of their husband's war service, and so they were not in great need.[2] In response, James Stark, NUR Branch Secretary, criticised the complainant's use of a nom de plume and his mistaken comments. Stark confirmed that recruitment in Perth was very difficult currently, hence the campaign to encourage women. He pointed out that management and the union had had discussions about pay, to avoid accusations of cheap substitute labour. After three months the women were to be paid the same rate as men, 48s. per week, plus a war wage supplement of 5s. 3d. (as against a male supplement of 7s.). In the workshops women might attract the male rate for a skilled or semi-skilled artisan after thirty-two weeks. The original writer responded, claiming that what he said must be true, 'either because women...are cheaper than men or because there is something wrong with the organisation of labour in Perth'. He felt instinctively that there must be men on Public Assistance who could do the jobs, and went on to assert that because of the war supplement women were cheaper by 1s. 9d. a week, and because they were not getting full pay for three months. He then went on to challenge whether women went through the same rigorous eyesight and medical tests, as he knew men of 50 who had been turned down for that. Stark responded that in fact as more women were needed to carry out these jobs than men, women's labour was not cheap. Also the eyesight test was only required for a permanent position, and that a 50-year-old would not be considered for this.[3]

While it was not unusual for women to work in engineering workshops before the war in the Midlands and North, it was quite novel in the south. At the GWR Swindon Works there had been no women locomotive builders, and so necessary wartime agreements had to be drafted to include women. Most of those recruited were relatives and/or friends of men already working there, demonstrating close family links in the town, and common GWR practices involving widows and daughters. The GWR application form for a woman to complete, to apply for a post replacing servicemen, included a question about the occupation and address of her father.[4]

By July 1941 the LMS was reporting that some of their works union representatives would not agree to the employment of women in 'fully' skilled work such as fitters and turners. They would only agree to using women in 'certain' work, not the whole of a skilled trade, similar to dilution of labour agreements in the engineering industry generally. The companies agreed that they would only employ women where no skilled men were available. It was felt that even after thirty-two weeks women would not have the skills which men had after a long apprenticeship, such as setting up their own machines, and this was used as an argument against equal pay.[5] In fact, equal pay for women working for the railways was only achieved finally in the late 1950s.

The Railway Clerks Association (RCA) in Derby advertised in 1942 for women railway clerks to come to their meeting, keen to attract them to join. Disappointingly the main reason there seemed to be to get female help in the administration of the organisation. Towards the end of the war female membership of the RCA had certainly risen, from 6,350 in 1939 to 21,843 in 1944.[6]

Companies found it difficult to work out what to call these women, for example some went to work as 'lad porters', some were described as 'porteresses'. Clothing was a problem at times, as uniforms for women were sometimes slow to develop. There were complaints from GWR point oilers at West Ealing, taken up by the welfare officer, that they had to use their own overalls, with no mackintoshes.[7] On the other hand GWR porter Violet Ridler was supplied with her smart uniform when she started in 1940.

An image of female LNER goods porters at Edinburgh Waverley in 1941 showed them looking more like cleaners than porters, with wrap-around aprons, although those at Rotherham in September 1941 had a more appropriate uniform.[8] Women sometimes complained that they had to give up vital clothing coupons for their overalls and shoes, which didn't last long, as they might have to walk ten miles or more in the course of each day.[9] Linesman's assistant Mary Woodfield was disappointed that she never got a tin hat. Women talked about the dirty conditions they found in men's rest rooms and took great pleasure in recreating a kind of home for themselves at work, cleaning and decorating areas and enjoying the benefits of ample coal for welcoming fires. Cups of tea and cocoa were important.

There was the underlying debate as to whether women should be allowed to access footplate jobs, as engine drivers and fireman, jobs energetically protected by men. There was much reporting of the Soviet system in the press and at some union meetings, as in the USSR women were employed to carry out all tasks. By June 1942, an NUR representative, following a USSR tour, was saying, 'There are no restrictions on promotion for the many women working on the Soviet railways. They work on all jobs, from signalwomen up to railway manager. Britain could usefully follow this example.' However in July 1942 a *Daily Herald* headline proclaimed, 'Doubtful if Women can Drive Trains', reporting an NUR meeting in Blackpool. Mr E.G. Bowers of Barking was urging that women should be able to go on the footplate or do any other job on the railway. But certain attitudes about female capabilities prevailed and the view of the General Secretary, John Marchbank, was that 'there were limits to what women could do if their health and future prospects in life were to be protected'. The unions stipulated that as far as the 'dilution of labour' was concerned, the substitution of women for men, 'the nature of the works on which women are employed must fall within their physical capabilities and mental outlook'. There were concerns that women might become a 'physical or mental wreck after only a week in a job'.[10]

The railway companies and the press were never able to lose sight of the idea of femininity. Some companies insisted on referring to porteresses, and women signalmen. Women porters from Carlisle protested about an NUR conference delegate who had suggested that women employed on the railway were 'walking around like mannequins'.[11] Surprising claims were made that women were performing jobs that might be classed as 'too intricate' for them, when many intricate jobs have been performed by women in history, for example lace making.[12] Companies were unable to represent women as other than as 'the fair sex' in magazines and newspapers, as Matheson has demonstrated with the GWR.[13] Many railway women were of course married, with children and caring responsibilities for elderly and disabled relatives, but they were still represented as decorative additions to the work place, with curious tendencies. In an *LNER Magazine* article about the running of the goods depot at Bishopsgate, the writer couldn't resist a comment in referring to the women and girls working as van-guards, noting that some of the male drivers worked with their wives as van-guards. 'I was also informed that there is no truth in the rumour that the husband has to do the work of the van-guard when the latter has reached that critical stage in knitting known as 'finishing a row'.[14] A response to sexist attitudes was portrayed in a cartoon in April 1945, drawn by a district inspector, which showed a signalwoman leaning out of her box to say to a passing railwayman, 'Mr Blenkinsop, will you kindly assure me that you have arrived complete with tail lamp attached in accordance with the provisions of Rule 147, and furthermore you are to understand that I am NOT your little popsy-wopsy.'[15]

But these women enjoyed their work, experiencing a kind of freedom not already encountered, with opportunities to work in a team and meet all sorts of people. One of the angles used in publicity campaigns, and seemingly evident from women's own testimony, is that despite the hardship of combining a tough job with large families and shift work, women valued the human contact of railway work, the liveliness and the chance for mobility.[16] Some women, such as LNER passenger guard Mary Buist, talked about the way their male colleagues would often carry out certain of their tasks for them, in support, such as closing carriage doors. Where work was heavy, women learned strategies, for example in pushing barrows and loading and unloading large shipments. The job provided a welcome contrast to piece work in factories, where women were carrying out repetitive tasks in unhealthy and unsafe surroundings. Hard work there was only rewarded by higher targets.

Violet Lee, *passenger guard, GWR*

Violet Lee joined GWR at the age of 17 as a passenger guard during the war.

I was given a uniform which consists of a round hat, with 'Guard' in gold braid across the front. We had the choice of skirts or trousers, because of climbing up and down engines and guard's vans, a brass button tunic top, and a very large pocket watch with Great Western on its face. It was needed to log the times in the log book drivers and guards had to carry whilst on duty. You logged the driver's name, any defect you found, prior to the commencing of... during the journey, the time you left the station, the times you arrived at the stations, and the times you left. If the train was late, you had to explain in writing, 'five or eight minutes late', and you had to explain to Mr Powell, station master, whilst standing on his mat, not a pleasant experience. They gave me a whistle, which had a very loud shrill, a guard's lamp which was lit by wick and paraffin—ooh they were smelly things, we had to clean our own—you flicked the handle round to change the lenses—it had three glasses, green, red and clear. Two flags, one green and one red. I was given a second-hand leather bag. It had two straps stitched on the outside to hold the flags, it also held packets of detonators, road notices (works taking place on the track), speed restrictions. This had to be checked at the office at the start of duty, and you signed to say you were aware of the notices—no excuses! You also checked with the driver. I always wore white cotton blouses, black flat shoes. The latter was necessary for climbing up to footplates, guard's vans, walking on ballast, and platforms, a great number of country platforms were made of a slatted wood. And I always felt very smart. Well, I must have been the youngest passenger guard ever, and I loved it.

Nellie Nelson, *LNER porter, York*

On a night you got a job as a blackout attendant on trains. They used to put us on that. You had to go up to Darlington and back again and you had to go up and down the train to see that it'd got all the curtains down.

We had a uniform yes and a tin hat. It were more or less a replica of the man's uniform. We had trousers and coat and a top coat. We wore trousers, that's when I got to wearing trousers. We got an oil lamp each if we wanted one, but I didn't bother. I used to take me flash lamp, if you were in a van where there wasn't a light you could see what the parcels were.

Well you were more free at the railway, you could go out and do your job, where at Rowntree's you had to do so many, it was all piece work, and if you ever did the number, they put the rate up. They were awkward was Rowntree's, which was awful I think.

We had to get passengers onto different trains. They'd say they want to be on a certain train and it wasn't the right one at all, 'Let's have a look at your ticket where you're going', oh aye, no and they was on the wrong train, they were in the wrong place all't time, you had to take them down subway and across most of t' time.

Nellie was on duty when the King and Queen came

Unbeknown to me I opened the blooming door because I didn't think it was the royal train because it hadn't a lot on it. And I opened the door and I said just, 'All right ma'am?' and she said, 'Yes, love thanks,' that's this Queen says, 'Yes love thanks.' They were passing, they were going down south, they'd been up to Scotland, going down south back again.

We had three shifts, about twelve on each, all women. We had a woman supervisor on each shift. There were some men who were station inspectors and station masters.

With post, one of you used to have a piece of chalk and use to write on 'parcel such and such a train' and nobody else was supposed to take that van. We used to say, 'Oh parcel post have got two, they give us one.' We used to pinch their barrows. Some of the parcels were heavy. But you've such a way of getting hold of parcels, getting round parcels and making it walk itself if it's a big parcel, wobble it and make it walk.

Mary Buist, *passenger guard, LNER Musselburgh*

We had a room for ourselves, we used to go down and make cups of tea in between our train times, because you just had your certain time, then you had to wait to go back. I was in Musselburgh so I just went back and forward, back and forward. That line's all away now. The little side line off the main line.

I lived there and I was based there, it was handy. Edinburgh-London train. The English guards, the London ones used to change over, I think it was, I think Newcastle. The Scottish guards changed over with them and, I remember them being at the Waverley and cooking themselves some potato, they must have been based overnight in Edinburgh. Though the Scottish ones were down at London maybe. I don't know how they did it. You forget. We did interchange, so we did part journey and then part journey because it was a long time, it wasn't a short journey like what it is now, coal-fired engines were slower.

One time the Queen was passing and our train was at Portobello Station and we were held up for over an hour to let her train pass and of course a lot of the surface men were going to their work so they were quite annoyed, it put them off the Queen. They were waiting to get off the train at their work, but she just whizzed by, she'd been on a visit to Edinburgh or up north.

Oh they were all very friendly. I often found during the war that people were much nicer, they sort of shared and they were really nice to each other. I mean we were all in the same boat. There was one women, she was young, not long married and her husband, he was only an ordinary private and a whole lot of the other ones were killed and he was promoted in a stroke right to lieutenant or something like that. A lot of the officers must have been killed too. But the people, they didn't seem to have an idea what was going on because they didn't worry about it, they just sort of accepted that you had rationing and you were glad to get a lot of extra things now and again.

I didn't have really bad hours at all. What I can remember is, about eight o'clock I think I started, that was the first train and it was only for people going up to Edinburgh for work and then at lunchtime you'd have people going back and forward, and in between you had the railwaymen for their shifts, their different shifts and they used the train. And then at night of course you'd everybody going home finishing. But I think I was on two shifts, that's right. It just went to Edinburgh, then it stopped at all the wee intermediate stations instead of just going right through, they had New Craighall, they're all built up now, Joppa, Portobello, and then Abbeyhill and then Edinburgh Waverley.

The drivers used to get the locomotive round to the other side of the train themselves. I think with us being women they sort of did things for you, you know. They were very good the drivers. I mean they had a fireman with them you see. We had hard work right enough. It was tiring work. My husband was away in Egypt. He was away with the Eighth Army, Montgomery. He was away for about five years.

I could walk home and in the blackout, you've no idea what it was like. You had that River Esk at the side and you're coming up from the station and when everything is black like that. I remember one time coming home and that must have been when they were bombing Edinburgh, looking across there and seeing all the explosions you know coming home.

You didn't really see much of each other. I mean most of the time, this room we had you were there and they'd be going away or you'd be on your own. But the trains didn't give you a long time. Anyway, I used to sometimes go for a walk round the station just for a change, just to get away from it. It was a bit monotonous. I'm a good little reader, I was a member of a book place, I used to run up for a book and back again. What energy, up these stairs back from my train.

When we had the pigeon races on, I used to have all these baskets with pigeons and the men came and put them on at Musselburgh and they were taken away at Edinburgh for the races and I suppose they would go back. They were homing pigeons, they'd go back to wherever the men lived.

But the porters did all the work, they were very good that way. Very kind to us women. Aye. They just helped shut the doors at the intermediate stations.

The working day. I think it was eight hours. I didn't get home, I must have eaten something in my room, I must have cooked something. We didn't have any facilities for cooking but I think we just took sandwiches with us and had cups of tea. We must have sat and talked to all the other women.

The men guards had their room and the women guards had their room. But the men were better off than us see, they had a store there. The English guards were always cooking. We were paid eight shillings less than the men, which was a sore point and we thought nothing of it at the time. But I can't remember what I was paid. Would it be three pounds something? Oh it's too long ago. But I know we were eight shillings less than the men. That was a lot of money then. We never bothered at the time but my family always said, 'Women should get the same as men, that's terrible, why did you put up with it?'

I had a rule book, I got it from the station master actually, which told me all the railway rules, but it wasn't issued. I gave it back to him when I left, you had to give everything – your watch and everything like that. My father used to wind that watch up for me, what a size it was. It was trousers all the time. It was just like the men, a coat with buttons, railway buttons and trousers, don't think we had a waistcoat? And a big coat, it was a nice warm coat, and a hat, a cap. It had 'Guard' on it because I remember a woman couldn't spell 'Guard' and I thought to myself, 'That's terrible, it's written on the front of your cap.' We got a wee wireless, was all censored of course, so you didn't really know what was...

Betty Spiller, *porter then lampman, Evercreech Junction, Somerset & Dorset Joint Railway*

I started off as a junior porter, at Evercreech Junction. Same as my brother, who was on the opposite shift.

On working with men. No it didn't worry me, but I think that some of the men were not happy about it, they really weren't. They gave you a hard time. And in one instance the foreman had to step in. We had one guard, and we used to sort what they call 'road boxes' in the morning, that was one of the jobs, to take stuff for various stations and sort of arrange them in order for dropping off. The road boxes contained general goods, such as sides of bacon, and all sorts of grocery items, parcels. It was a kind of parcel train, and Evercreech Junction had a level crossing across the road, so the practice was in the morning, he stopped outside the station, the signal lampman went down, uncoupled the first wagons, which were the road boxes, from the rest of the train, and then that drew into the station, to save fouling the road crossing for too long, for the traffic. And we'd carry on sorting the road boxes, and the guard used to come up with it, the guard of the train. We had one particular guard, he'd say, 'Which ones to sort? Which ones?' 'Well open 'em and see.' He'd give you no help at all, and he got so stroppy one morning the foreman said, 'I'm in charge when you're in this station, and we don't want any of that!'

The 'Pines Express' came down from the north, Manchester and Birmingham, didn't go into Bristol,... it used to come down, and that went straight through to Bournemouth, straight through to the south coast. And then we used to have freight from the Midlands, one of them in particular was always called the 'Burton' and that was the Burton beer train, and that used to come down overnight with the beer. And another one they had, going from Templecombe up was called the perishable, commonly known as the 'Perisher', and that went at nine o'clock at night, up through to the Midlands, with one passenger coach on and perishable freight.

Some of it was heavy. One of the girls, who joined us later, these drop-side wagons, which we called 'dog toe doors' because there was a bar across the top, a pin came out suddenly and that came down and crushed her foot.

We got a jacket and a hat and a skirt, and, that was alright for platform work. And then one morning the signal lampman, Bill Freak, went down to uncouple this particular train that came in in the morning, and next thing we heard was the driver shouting, 'Bill's down, down here.' And they went down and it was a dark winter morning and he'd put his handlamp out first, the driver saw the white light come out and took it as the tip to go, took the handbrake off, the wagons dropped back because they were not vacuum-fitted, they were link couplings, and he was just coming out from underneath, and got his legs, off to hospital he went, and he died.

And they put my brother temporarily on his job, lamping. The inspector came down from Bath, enquired his age, and because he was a year and five months younger than me, he said he was too young and took him off it and put me on it. Well, the station master came down one day, into the station and he said, 'You come with me.' So we went up the line, and he said, 'You go up that signal.' So I went up the ladder, onto the platform at the top. He shook the signal, and he said, 'Are you alright?' and said, 'Yes.' So I came down, and he said, 'Well, do you think you could do the lampman's job?' And I said, 'What about Ted?' And he said, 'Oh.' He said, 'He's too young.' So I said, 'Yeah,' and he said, 'Well, we'd better go and see your father.' So off we went to the marshalling yard and saw father, and he said, 'Well, it's up to her whether she does it or not.' When we went home, mother didn't want me to do it. Any rate I did do it.

Evercreech Junction had a marshalling yard, it used to marshal for Bath in the north and the branch line, and the freight and things to go to Templecombe and go Exeter, Waterloo. There was about a hundred, hundred and fifty signals and signal lights and dummy lights, and I had to take the lamps out, bring them in, clean them, get them back out again. And I had to do all of the brake wagons, they had tail lights and two sidelights on, while they were in the marshalling yard, see that they were filled and useable.

And sometimes if they were short you helped out on the platform for a bit, because they used to have a lot of military traffic. Some of it was very heavy. There was a sausage factory and a clothing factory at Bridgwater, and that came up to Evercreech Junction and was transferred there to go on to Templecombe.

About a hundred and fifty lamps. It was a week's work. You arranged it that each day you did so many in this area, so many in another area. Walked the line. The furthest out would be the distant signal, and the distant signal is three-quarters of a mile from the station, but then you carried on to various crossings out in the country and did the crossing gates and the signals at the crossings.

One thing, when I started, we used to have an early and a late shift. You started at eight o'clock and finished it sometimes at two, and you had shift work, well, I only got that while I was a junior. When I went lamping it was six days a week and it was eight to five. Well, that meant I could never get to a shop, so I said one day, 'Can I have a Saturday off, a Saturday afternoon off?' And he said, 'Haven't got a relief.' So I ask again, 'No, haven't got a relief.' So then I said, 'Well I need some shoes and some clothing.' And he said, 'Well, I can't get a relief.' I said, 'Well, you don't need, cause I can do the work before I go and it won't make any difference.' And I said, 'If I don't get a half day this week I shall take it.' So I did.

Betty was 17 or 18 at the time. So I took it. When I came in Monday morning, he said, 'You took a half day off.' And I said, 'Yes.' I said, 'And look at the state of these shoes that I was wearing.' Cause I knew there'd be trouble. And, any rate he said you'll get a number one, which was a form you had to fill in because you'd done something and you had to say why you did it, and I said, 'Well, that's it.' And I was in the NUR, the union, and I thought, 'Well, the union'll sort it.' I went to the lamp house and started work, and an inspector from Bath came in. So he said, 'How are you managing the job?' and asked various questions. So I said, 'You might just as well know,' I said, 'I took a half day off on Saturday and I got a number one.' He said, 'Why did you do that?' So I told him, and he said, 'Will a half day a month suit you?' and I said, 'Yeah, I'll be very grateful, thank you.' So the number one was withdrawn, but we never did get the half day a month.

For men to get their promotion, they started off as a porter, and then they probably did something like the signal lampman's job, and when there was a vacancy in the yard as a shunter, which was more highly paid, they could put in for that, but they had to come up through the system. So I was given the job, and it was called a 'retention vacancy'. And I got paid what, I don't know what they'd say about it these days, the mean between – part way between a porter's rate and signal lampman's rate, I didn't get the full rate. And I think that was the retention vacancy, so the man, the porter could then still put in for the signal lampman's job, be awarded it, but he never did it. I carried on and he did the next step up.

At 18 I had to register for service. And I still wanted to go into the WAAF, and I thought, well I'm supposed to get a letter because I'm in a reserved occupation, as it was called then, and I didn't go back to the station to put in me keys, I went straight home, next morning I went straight to the labour exchange to register, and I gave my name, and they said, 'Oh, we've had a telephone call from the railway about you, you're in a reserved occupation, you can't register.'

I started at eight o'clock, and cycled three miles from Evercreech New to Evercreech Junction, and further up the road there used to be an old railway coach and it was known as the 'coach café,' and it was a driver's stop off, you know, lorry drivers, and we used to go up the coach café and get a bacon sandwich and that mid-morning. One o'clock I went back to Evercreech, had lunch and then cycled back at two o'clock.

And another time we had a truck of cattle and they were being shunted up in the yard, it was noted one of the cows were down, so they sent down to the station for the cows to be got out into the cattle pen, and the cow got up and put back in again to see if it was injured or not. Well, they got the cows out in the cattlepen, and the one that was down came out of the truck, and because he'd been down, it had cow pats all over it from the other ones. So they went to drive them back in, and we were sort of stood round the cattle pen watching, me and the other girls, the foreman picked up a flat piece of board to bang one of the cows on the back, the one that was down, covered in cow pats, it flew up in the air and it covered one of the girls in her hair and everywhere.

Laura Scott, *sawdust bagger, LNER carriage works, York*

I walked home for me dinner, we lived round there. Facing t' river, round there. Walked home, had me dinner and walked back, every day, and walked home at teatime.

It were dusty. But didn't matter. It was heavy bags, you know. There was only about three of us. Me friend, Nan, and another lady, but the other lady couldn't do it so she had to leave, so there was two of us. We stayed a long time, we've been friends ever since. Well, that's all we did, all day. Empty bags of sawdust. They came, they went into like a big hollow place, sawdust came off the wood that they'd been shaving like. It went off, it went into like a vat thing, and they moved, and then I don't know where they used to take it. And we did that all day. Oh, yeah, it was hard work, really hard work, yeah. They called it 'sawdust hole'. We stood on a plank emptying them. York carriage works. Then after that, we came off that and used to make tea for men, at one time. We got cups of tea and that, but I enjoyed it, you know. I'd worked at Terry's before that, and then when I got married and I was a widow like, me mum and dad brought our Eric and Shirley up. I thoroughly enjoyed it. We had a good laugh. I was fit, I used to be a runner, I used to run round Knavesmire on a morning, before I went to school, walk up there, went running from there, and running about two mile round.

Marjorie Pateman, *lathe operator, LMS Wolverton works*

We had these bands and they were wide, too wide, you see, and then you had to put them on the lathe and then cut off, cut them with the lathe, I can't just remember how it went, and then if they were too wide, you had to put them in a gauge, and then if they were too wide then I think you had to give them to somebody else. Also they didn't rely on you just to do the checking, they had somebody else, and then if they were too wide then you had to take them out, and you weren't very popular, and if they were too narrow, okay, it wasn't any good again. And so that was that. Well, that went on, and we was quite happy, 'cause I worked with a chargehand, a Stony Stratford man, very nice, and I got on, very respectful he was to us, you know, and I got on okay with that.

Very very clean that was, except for the swarf and you know, the stuff that used to come off. I had a very poisoned nose, very bad, and the doctor, the nurse at the works thought it was copper, a piece of copper had got, maybe using a hankie or whatever, you know, in. But that was very bad, but the smell from the lathes wasn't very good, 'cause there was that milky...

Well, then they dropped the bombshell. They called us up the office, we've all gotta go to the frame shop it was, it was called the frame shop. To the rivet carrier.

Marjorie was transferred out of that relatively clean environment. We were all called to the office, and we protested. We didn't do all the banners and all, we just said, 'Oh, no, no,' you know, 'We can't do that.' Girls had never, or women, had never done this before. It was done by boys, before they start their apprentice. Well, it was so hot that you couldn't, I think at some period of the time I tried boiler suits. They didn't supply anything, you had to get all your own. I can't remember whether we had goggles. But you see you were looking at white hot lights, I can't get it out, all the time. The heat was so enormous in the summer it was terrible. The night works were the worst, because the windows were blacked out, for the blackout, and they couldn't obviously have any windows open. Doors had to be shut because of the light, so you just had to cook, sort of thing, you know. I think it was day work, two weeks days and two weeks nights, 12-hour shifts.

I'm trying to think how wide the rivet machines were. It had two foot pedals, and you put, well, you couldn't do them both at once, obviously, but you used to put one, put the rivet in with your fingers, when it was not hot. And then you had to put the other one in, then you had to put the pedals down to put them in, and then up, let the pedals up, and then you had to wait until they got to a certain heat, and they would be glowing white hot, you got to know, more or less. There was no gauges, or anything on the machine.

And then when they got to a certain heat we were supplied with tongs, we had to scrape it up and down the rivets, two at once sort of thing, so keep them even, and then when you thought they was hot enough, you had to take them out, and then walk, perhaps quite a long way to the riveters that were there. So you had to guess that the rivets would be hot enough when you got there, because if they weren't quite right, and then there was, 'Oh, this is no good,' you know. And then you had to take them back and, or get some new ones, and then they wasn't very happy, because you see those wagons was due to go out at a certain time most days, or two days, whatever the time was allowed. And then the noise, it was absolutely terrible. You can imagine being, if you've ever watched the shipyards on the television, you can imagine the noise in a closed area. It was a big shop, but it was still very noisy. You couldn't talk.

Mr Peters, he was the manager, he was very strict, but he was very nice. He used to come round, not at nights, in the day shift, he would come round and he used to stand at the end of the shop, and he would look all over as far as he could see, then he would move along to the next batch and look at the others. Well, after he'd gone, Mr Buck, who was the foreman, he came to me, he said, 'You've been highly recommended by Mr Peters.' I said, 'You what?' He said, 'Highly recommended.' I said, 'Well, I haven't done anything.' He said, 'No you haven't done anything,' he said, 'But he's been in here and he's said every time he's been in this shop he had never seen that girl off her machine,' because he would know, he knows them who went out to have a fag, you know, and he was saying, that's what he said, and I was quite pleased with that, but I didn't smoke, and perhaps I was scared, I don't know, I wasn't any better than the others, but I was lucky probably, I was there when he come in. But we didn't, you couldn't go and skive much, no, no, no.

Florence Brinklow, *parcels delivery, LNER Kings Cross*

At King's Cross They gave me a job with horses at first, you know. Which I liked. I enjoyed it. I used to have to go down and I used to lead the horses from the stables. And I used to go to the city with parcels. Well, it was the goods yard. And you had to go up the stairs and get the horse and bring him down. Well the driver made sure that everything was alright, like. We used to meet the driver. And we'd walk him back down...I do remember going down from number ten platform, which was York Way side.

King's Cross, during the time that Florence Brinklow worked there, had ten main-line platforms, numbered one to ten. Parcels arriving at King's Cross by train were unloaded at platform one, on the east side of the station, with the items transferred into trailers or carts parked in the cabway underneath the east side offices. The access to this cabway was by a slope down from York Way, the adjacent street, at the north end of the station. Parcels coming by road into King's Cross for despatch by train were dealt with either in the triangular area between platform 10 of the mainline station and platform 11 of the suburban station or, particularly in the evenings, in a special parcel loading area west of platform 16 in the suburban station. The horses, while they were used, were stabled in a two-storey building at the north-west corner of King's Cross Goods, and had to be brought down to the station at the beginning of their time of duty. The horse and carts were replaced by Scammell semi-articu-lated lorries. The Scammell tractor had three wheels and was generally known as a 'mechanical horse'. Goods were delivered all over the city and to other mainline stations from King's Cross, and offices in the city used to put out a sign, either saying the name of the station or the name of the railway company, when they had parcels to be collected and taken onto the railway. The carriage of livestock by passenger train was quite normal and continued into the 1960s, even with pedigree calves sometimes travelling in the guard's van of a passenger train.[17]

And we always used to meet up there to take the parcels to the city. You know. Load up your van and take the parcels to the city. And I had a bit of an old so–and–so. He used to make me go up the stairs to the top floor in these differ-ent buildings. But on a Friday, when they used to give the driver a little tip, you know? He used to go up his self. He used to make me go up all the week. And then we'd have to go back in the afternoon and collect different items, you know.

And then I was taken off the horses...and sometimes we used to have to load up a Scammell. You know with the three in the front. And we used to have Lyon's Cakes, down to Addison Road in Kensington. Then the Bedford's, I'd been on the Bedford vans. But I went on night work. We used to collect in the afternoon and take 'em back to the bays at King's Cross. And I remembered when the stables was alight in the goods yard. And my driver, Joe Long, he was really deaf. He should have retired. But they were so short of drivers that they kept him on. And he used to tell me to get up the cobblestone slope and bring down the horses. I was scared to death but I went up and got two horses and they came down to the ... I can remember him cheering, one in each hand, coming down this slope.

They wore trousers. Because, well, we had to do so much climbing too, you know? Especially when we first started with the horse and carts, and jumping up and down. There was such a lot going on down at King's Cross at the time, with, you know, soldiers and sailors and airmen going away. Well, we used to load up. We'd load up the van, or at first the horse and cart. If we was going to Liverpool St, we'd go up Pentonville Road. Going past the Angel and down to Liverpool St. And you'd get down there and then the driver, he used to, a lot of them drivers, some of them was very lazy, you know. They used to take liberties. They used to scramble off while you done all the unloading. And then sometimes you had to take another load back. And you'd take it back to the bays down at King's

Cross. Three or four trips we used to do, I know. But of a night, well the vans used to all line up there of a night to unload. And well, once you got your stuff unloaded, then you could go home.

Down in King's Cross there was a bay for Liverpool St, Paddington, and we took some ferrets to Paddington. And I don't know how it happened. They got out. I couldn't tell you how it happened. And we had people running all over the place to try to, you know, catch these ferrets. Then we used to carry sometimes gold bullion. And you had to have a special convoy for that. You had to have, it was like police protection, more or less. But it was gold, gold bullion.

On night shift. We'd go back to King's Cross. And we'd have, if you was on nights you wouldn't really want a lot, you know. We might have a sandwich in the night, but, it wasn't a bad canteen, it was quite reasonable, I remember. There used to be a lot of Spam about. Awful lot of Spam. There wasn't much food about, no, no.

I remember my driver saying to me once, he said to me, 'Why don't you learn to drive?' So I said, 'I'd be too scared.' He said, 'Come on, sit there.' And he let me drive. And he shouldn't have done it, really. I drove all the way from Paddington right to Euston Road. And he said, 'You'd better change over before I get into trouble.' We changed over. I did want to learn to drive then, you know. But I'd never done it before.

Gladys Garlick, *LNER porter then guard, London*

At Bowes Park. Well it was an island platform there. And coming from Wood Green, all the other stations, the platforms are at either side. So when they get to Bowes Park, people used to get out the wrong side, in the dark. And they had a lot of these enamel hoardings. So we had quite a lot of problems with that, cos we had to call out, 'This side out, Bowes Park, this side out' sort of thing. Because they used to see the reflection with it, I mean the carriages were all dimmed, weren't they. And they used to see the reflection on these hoardings and get out. And then of course we had to rescue them. With a ladder, to get them, cos they'd be on the bank.

It was normal. We never had, when I read about these places being hours late, and that, it was normal. We never used to have a lot of bother. I used to whitewash the edges and trim the lamps, and things like that. The station master was a fat, jolly man. Very nice, fatherly. There was Vic. He was, what, 30-ish I suppose. And then there was Harry. The old chap. He was a nice old boy, he lived at Hatfield. He always reminded me of Grumpy, of the seven, well, he had the biggest nose, like that. But he was a dear old soul. And they were very good then.

Gladys was at Bowes Park from 1940 to 1942, when she was 20. I suppose we were lucky, really. There wasn't a lot [of bombing]. We had the blackout and that. The nearest, they had one up at Wood Green. Cos it was a junction, Wood Green. In a place they called the Khyber Pass, for some reason. And I think that was bombed. And I think they bombed near the tunnel, on the mainline. But there wasn't a lot up our way at all, not really. Until later on.

Ticket collecting. They had another footbridge over the end of the platform that went over. And during the rush hour, you went over there and collected the tickets as the people came off the trains. And of course kept the waiting rooms tidy. We had an early and a late shift. And then a middle shift, where you came home and did a split turn. You did the rush hour both ends. And then when the boys went, they just melted it down to a split shift. So that you helped either side of the rush hour.

In 1942 Gladys went up to Grange Park. And again it was two shifts, early and late. On the early shift at six o'clock, you opened up the booking hall and issued tickets till half past seven, till the booking clerk came on. And then you went up onto the platform, you know, to tend to the trains and that sort of thing. It was a slope, sloped down to the platform. There, a booking clerk. At one time the girl I worked with, she went out to be a signalwoman. And I was going to go as well, but the station master wouldn't let us both go. Said they were poaching his staff, so I couldn't go. So she went into the signal box, I was on the platform, and there was a young lady in the booking office. And, the local paper did a bit about the station run by women. Because there was the three of us in charge, you see.

The station master at Grange Park was actually stationed at Enfield. So we only used to see him once a day sort of thing, he'd just come to see if everything was alright. Cos Enfield naturally was a much bigger station. Cos you'd got the small arms factory and that. You know, they used to have goods come through on the train for the Enfield small arms factory there.

Gladys became a guard. Well, the morning trains. We used to do the busy trains in the morning actually. From King's Cross, that had all the goods on them, you know? They used to be fish, boxes of fish. And things for the Enfield, for the small arms factory. In fact you had things on from nearly every station, all the way down the line. It was quite hard work actually. If you didn't get round to your train in good time, they used to come, the porters on King's Cross used to come round with their trolleys and chuck everything in. Which meant you couldn't get it out very easily. So you had to be round there so that you could position it in the guard's brake how you wanted it to come out. Because it was no good having things for Hertford in the front.

You more or less had to unload everything yourself. They very rarely come up and unload, you had to do it on your own. And you'd just got a knack with the fishboxes. Used to wiggle them forward and then just tip, and over they used to go. Only once did one burst open. And all the fish and ice was all over the platform.

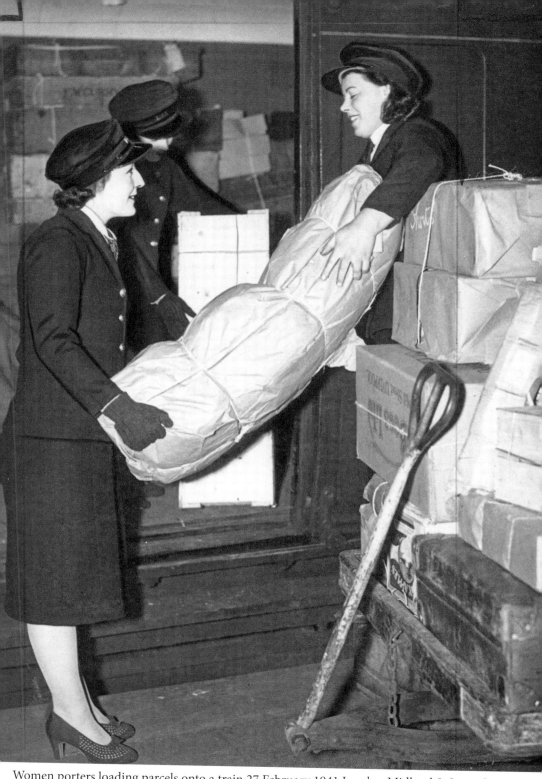

Women porters loading parcels onto a train 27 February 1941 London Midland & Scottish Railway St Pancras. (Daily Herald Archive/Science & Society Picture Library)

First women railway guards
take over duties at London
terminus 19 July 1943
Southern Railway Victoria.
(Planet Pix Ltd – Planet News/
Science & Society Picture Library)

First women take over signal duties on Britain's mainline railways 6 March 1941 London & North
Eastern Railway South Yorkshire line. (Planet Pix Ltd – Planet News/Science & Society Picture Library)

Woman railway worker loading grain sacks 11 March 1945 London & North Eastern
Railway. (Daily Herald Archive /Science & Society Picture Library)

Gang of platelayers at GWR Bristol West Depot, March 1943. (University of Leicester Special Collections)

Finishing rods in the 'AM' machine shop at the GWR Swindon works.
(University of Leicester Special Collections)

A GWR travelling porter. (University of Leicester Special Collections)

Goods porters at GWR Bristol goods station 1941. (University of Leicester Special Collections)

Railway women take over another strenuous job, 30 Dec 1941, Southern Railway.
(Planet Pix Ltd – Planet News /Science & Society Picture Library)

Female porter for
Southern Railway,
Woking, Surrey, 1943.
(National Railway Museum/
Science & Society Picture
Library)

GWR Central Telephone Enquiry Office at Paddington. (University of Leicester Special Collections)

Coping with emergencies at the GWR Central Telephone Enquiry Office at Paddington.
(University of Leicester Special Collections)

Dray horses at the 'Mint Stables', Paddington Station. (Historic England Archive)

GWR goods porters using a battery-powered, flat-bed mechanised horse.
(University of Leicester Special Collections)

Woman cleaning a locomotive in St Pancras Cleaning Yard, 1941, London, Midland &
Scottish Railway (by Cliff Rowe). (NRM Pictorial Collection/Science & Society Picture Library)

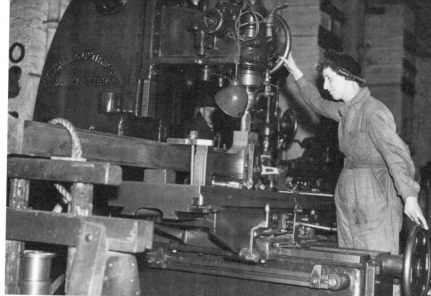

Doncaster Works London & North Eastern Railway. (National Railway Museum/Science & Society Picture Library)

Betty Forrester at Troon in 2002, recreating her wartime role. (Robin Nelson collection)

Betty Forrester with husband George. (Betty Forrester collection)

Betty Forrester in 1944 (then Betty Ross). (Betty Forrester collection)

Evercreech Junction staff at the Bell Inn celebrating wedding of signalwoman Betty Lambert & driver Ron Spiller, inc. George Dyke, W. Newman & wife, J. Reakes, N. Light, E. Phillips, C. Cooper, S. Moore, J. Hill, Joyce Reakes, Betty Simms & A. Fear, with horse & cart, late 1945. (Betty Cox (née Simms) via John Simms, Somerset & Dorset Railway Trust Collection.)

Kit Wheadon, wartime porter, on footplate of 3F class 0-6-0 locomotive, undated, c1939-45. (Somerset & Dorset Railway Trust Collection)

Lady lampsman Betty Spiller (née Lambert) standing on the home signal platform, Evercreech Junction, holding a lamp interior, circa 1945. Photograph by Len Dutton. (Len Dutton via Betty Spiller (née Lambert), Somerset & Dorset Railway Trust Collection)

1, 2 and 3 platforms after raid, York, 29 April 1942. (National Railway Museum/Science & Society Picture Library)

Mrs H.M. Rollason of Nuneaton, London, Midland & Scottish Railway guard.
(Daily Herald Archive /Science & Society Picture Library)

Gladys Garlick and colleagues Rita and Irene at Bowes Park 1942-43 London & North Eastern Railway. (National Railway Museum/Science & Society Picture Library)

Women clerks at the model booking office in the Southern Railway London Central Division Training School at Croydon. (National Railway Museum/Science & Society Picture Library)

Women painters on the Southern Railway. (National Railway Museum/ Science & Society Picture Library)

Women in a Southern Railway workshop.
(National Railway Museum/Science & Society Picture Library)

GWR railway policewoman P. Mitchell at Bristol Temple Meads, February 1942
(University of Leicester Special Collections)

GWR ticket collectors. (University of Leicester Special Collections)

GWR goods porter working on a 'Mercury Mechanical Horse'. (University of Leicester Special Collections)

Southern Railway delivery van. (National Railway Museum/Science & Society Picture Library)

Wartime poster 6 Feb 1943.
(National Railway Museum/Science & Society Picture Library)

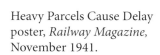

Heavy Parcels Cause Delay poster, *Railway Magazine*, November 1941.

We lived [at Bowes Park] right through the war.

Gladys's mother and the younger children had returned at the end of 1939, but the two boys did evacuate on their own again. But it wasn't very nice where they put them. You know. It was a very poor person. And Mother didn't like it when she went down to see them. She brought them back. But she went to work on the railway then, as a carriage cleaner in Wood Green. Cos my father had gone to hospital. And when I left to go to Grange Park, the station master asked for somebody from the carriage cleaners to come up and take over my job temporarily. And my mother did it. And he kept her there all through the war, which was useful cos it was a split turn. My brothers and sisters knew where she was, and she was able to come home.

When I was on the trains we did 13 days out of 14. We only got one day off. So that was the day I used to go [to see my dad], on Sunday. Because you couldn't work that Sunday, because you were late, late on Saturday night and early on Monday morning. It was all work, really. I mean, if you done one turn on at two o'clock in the morning, and another time it was four o'clock in the morning. So when you came home and you slept, then you got up, then you had to go back to bed again cos you got to get up early.

Our shifts, on one shift, I had to pick up the light engine going to Hertford to make the first train back. That was three or four in the morning, something like that. I used to have to tell the signalman when I was on, so that he could stop the light engine at Bowes Park for me to get on. And the porters, both porters knew. In fact, we had a little arrangement. Because I used to be a very heavy sleeper and I'd tend to switch the alarm clock off. So I used to get up and leave a little crack on the kitchen door. And Charlie or Vic, whoever was on, used to come round, look to see that the light was on and know I was up. And one day it wasn't on and Charlie rung the bell. And the bell press went in and we couldn't get it out again. So there he was at three o'clock in the morning with his penknife, trying to stop it.

The last Hertford used to leave Finsbury Park at eleven something. So we would be at two something, the time we came back. We used to leave the coaches at Hertford North, and come back on the light engine.

They were just the ordinary in-and-out trains. And the guard's brake had a double door. And you pushed the handle down. Eight coaches. There was a shelf along the top with fire buckets and things like that. And there was a handle for a hand-brake, and two little seats either side. Used to be bloomin' cold in there, with a little tiny pipe heater. You never got the heat right through to you, you'd be quite cold.

The engines were always at the front. They were double-four seven numbers, they were. Double-four seven five, or something like that. Different drivers. You knew more or less who they were going to have by the number of the engine, you know, they all more or less had their own engines in those days.

Mary Woodfield, *linesman's assistant, GWR Undy*

Well, this is letting the railways down, but we were not given, you were not measured up for your shoes anyway, to have some stout shoes. Because you were walking in the four-foot, there was plenty of walking to be done. But I always remember going to this shoe shop and they had the loveliest, sturdiest pair. Man's shoes, but they were brogues. And that's what saw me all the way through my four years, anyway.

But how ignorant. Ignorant of the powers above that said, 'Oh, well there'll be a lot of working, walking for the girls. We'd better see what kind of footwear they want.' We weren't geared up with tin hats. Because there was one or two near misses, you know. But I was in my bed, wasn't I. I wouldn't have known about them until you got to work: 'Oh, they had a couple of near misses in the last night.' But no, we were not issued with a tin hat, even. No supervision at all. Oh, I had my own gas mask. But you had that on your one shoulder every day, kind of thing. So yes. And well, you handed them in at some certain stage, I know, it was well and truly after. I only tried it on once. And ooh, claustrophobia set in, but you had to put it on if you'd need it, and that was it.

Dolly Dunning, *oiler and greaser, Somerset & Dorset Joint Railway*

I can remember like shire horses, pulling a truck of coal to the weighbridge. Many times I have seen the driver and foreman cooking breakfast bacon and eggs on the shovel.

I had to oil and grease the trucks and one time there was four engines working. I was the only woman employee with about twenty men. They were gentlemen.

A detective was following a wagon from Glastonbury to Highbridge with shoes. When it arrived all the shoes were gone. Sometimes a wagon came for Bason Bridge. We knew it contained sugar, we didn't go short of a little for our tea.

Joyce Bell, *lengthwoman, Somerset & Dorset Joint Railway*

We used to catch the 10am out from Highbridge Station every morning and travel 'on the cushions' to whichever length of line was allocated to us.[18] When we arrived at a station for the day we all used to go to the gangers' hut, usually made out of sleepers, where we immediately had our lunch. Flasks of cocoa and sandwiches. We then proceeded to walk to the starting point. We all had a pick. The bar had one flat end and one narrow end. We then proceeded to hoe up the weeds and pull up the ballast. We were usually given a set number of lengths to do. A length consisting of the area between the joints of the rails. It was hard work but we enjoyed it and you can imagine the jokes that used to fly backwards and forwards. We would work quite hard to finish our lengths and then walk back to the hut. Here there was always a lovely fire, sleepers and coal being always at hand. We used to boil the old iron kettle and make a lovely cup of tea. By the time we had eaten our lunch and dinner it was time to pack up and start walking back to the station to catch the train back to Highbridge.

We all had knapsacks (army and air force issue). Mine was an old air force pack and I expect we looked quite a sight catching the train with our packs on our backs. Sometimes Dad was 'on the cushions' with his fireman, if they had to pick up their engine at Evercreech.

We were also allowed extra rations, just like the men, and we could have four free passes a year. I can remember one summer, it was very hot and we were working in sleeveless tops, I suffered terrible sunburn on my arms, which blistered. These burst and as we were covered in dirt from the track and soot from the huts, I ended up with poisoned arms and had two weeks off work.

Freda Box, *crossing keeper, Bruton, Somerset & Dorset Joint Railway*

My late husband and I thought the railway would never close, that is Bruton Crossing, the times we opened and closed the gates in all kinds of weather, snow nearly as high as the gates. I hated going on the crossing when it was thundering. People got so angry when they were kept waiting. It was very hard work, my late husband and I worked 24 hours between us and bringing up a family as well. What with no electricity we used paraffin lamps and no drinking water, apart from cans of water from the station most days.

We had a small hut where the signal wheel was kept, it had two arms, one for securing the gates and the other for the signal. I used to count how many times we had to wind, about twenty times each time for signals.

The amazing thing about the railway working, my late husband and I had to work 24 hours between us, but when we had time off the powers that be sent three men to work the gates.

Betty Cox, *porter,* Evercreech Junction, *Somerset and Dorset Joint Railway*

When I joined the S & D I was the first girl to be employed as a 'porteress' at Evercreech Junction. It was a man's world, and I felt that they thought, and no doubt hoped, that I wouldn't last long, but I was there for 'the duration', like it or not. When Betty Lambert and Joyce Reakes joined 'The Firm' things were better, at least I had a bit of female company. After a while things settled down and we were accepted. We knew this when the men stopped being polite to us: at last we were in!

My wages were around £4 per week, uniform supplied, and privilege tickets, which was a bit of a joke, as we never had any time off to use them. One thing stands in my mind, was when the contents of a farm was transported from Sussex to Evercreech Junction. Lock, stock and barrel, including the farmer, his family and the farm hands. Priority was given to unloading the animals from the cattle trucks, Joyce and I fled to the bridge for safety, and to get a good view. It was hilarious with pigs, sheep and cows all going in different directions, but it wasn't so funny when we were told to clear up the mess. The farmer gave us 2s. 6d. between us (we thought it was worth 10 shillings) but he didn't charge for the dung, and the station master's roses got the benefit of it.

We did get 'browned off' when the weather was wet and cold, but there was always a good fire in the porter's room, where we had added a few feminine touches, like a mirror and a vase of flowers, whilst on the notice board we had arranged our current pin-ups.

My uncle, Jack Simms, who was a passenger guard, used to bring us buns from the refreshment room at Bath. I think they were rejects because they were very stale and currantless, but we ate them and thought ourselves lucky to get them.

Vera Jones, *apprentice fitter, LMS Crewe*

Well, when I first walked in Nine Shop, I felt a bit afraid really. Because it was so dark when I walked in. And to see these cranes, fifty ton, two fifty-ton cranes going overhead, carrying a locomotive, you know. It was a bit frightening at first, really. But I soon got used to it.

When I started to work, the work on which I first was engaged was handrails. Off the steam locomotives. These came to us, that is, a fitter and I, from the stripping pits. They were then cleaned and fitted as required with new eye-bolts. Recondition the threads, with a die. And when the appropriate engine was ready, when it had been built up again, to have the handrails fitted on, a fitter and myself would have to take them into Ten Shop. And put them up on the footplates along the side of the engine. And then we would have to climb a ladder. It was about five to six foot high. And then we used to have to fit the eye-bolts in along. And the smoke-box end, they had to get inside the smoke-box to tighten two of those eye-bolts up. But I can leave you to guess who went in the smoke-box.

I eventually went to work with another fitter. Making the fire-box lagging plates for new 2-8-0 locomotives. This was a much cleaner job than handrails and smokeboxes. This started with a large piece of plate, eight by four. By one-sixteenth, that'd be the thickness. This was placed on a steel bench, and a template placed on top of it, used to scribe a line in the appropriate places. On completion of this, weights and templates were removed. The plate was then taken to a man working a drilling machine, and holes were drilled where required. The holes were to accommodate the wash-out doors and brass plugs in the firebox. It was then taken back to the bench, where some cutting with a hammer and chisel was done. And I used to do that, cut these rings out with a hammer and chisel, where the dishes fitted. Then we would have assistance from several other fitters and apprentices. And plate would be cut to shape on what was called a nibbler. It was then taken to a plater who worked on a rolling machine, and the top part would be rolled to make it fit over the top of the firebox. I had to stand at the back of the plates while the fitter riveted the dishes on, and I was holding the dolly.

I started work eight o'clock in the morning. Till half past five. And then some nights we used to work overtime till eight o'clock. Where I worked, there was a chap that used to mix this ... the asbestos in a big drum or something. And the dust, dust was flying everywhere, this asbestos dust, all around where I worked. They used to have a blanket which, I think it was the 0-8-0s, this blanket that they put over, and that was pasted, was covered with this asbestos. Well, quite a few of the men, to be quite honest, they've passed away through illness. Through asbestos. Quite a few men in there. Even in those days, it really wasn't wise to work with asbestos. And yet we were told it was alright.

There was a union. We were in the AEU union. And us ladies, we got a higher rate of pay than what the male apprentices got. But I think the reason was, because when the war ended, they would finish us before finishing the men.

The conditions we worked under, it was very dirty, very dirty. They were block floors. And they were oily and greasy. We worked in artificial light all day, because the roof was blacked out with the war being on. And our clothes smelt oily, really, when we went home, you know. Through working in them conditions. They put some wooden troughs here and there in the shops, where we could just wash our hands. They were more like I call a pig trough. A big wooden trough, so long. With taps coming out where we could wash our hands. That's all that we had. And waste. Waste, to wipe our hands with.

I didn't really want to leave at the time. Because I quite enjoyed working in there. Even though it was dirty and, you know, it was more men's work. But I enjoyed working in there. I didn't feel tied too much, because we were working, I was working in Nine Shop on a bench for a while. Same as doing the handrails. We used to scrape them there, with the fitter. And do the eye-bolts, and that. And then we had to go into Ten Shop after, to put them back on the appropriate engine. Sometimes we had to go to the smithy for different things. So that was another walk to another shop. And it was very interesting really, to see ...

Every time they have an open day I go back, if I can. I go back in there. Because in one way, it brings back happy memories for me. I enjoyed working in there, with all the people. We all got on well together. And that's where I met Harry. And I've always liked to go back and have a look when it's been open day. But there's a big difference now. A very big difference. Some of the shops are empty. And last time I went in it was so clean. And all the floors were painted green and red, and shiny. It was so different last time I went in.

Wartime Memories

Lord Baden-Powell came up once a week. And they ordered ham sandwiches and coffee, or whatever. And so I'd go through to Fred, the chef, and I would order these sandwiches for Baden-Powell. And of course he would cut them beautifully, take the crusts off, cut them in portions and I would take them through. And the first time I took them through, Baden-Powell nearly went berserk. 'What are you doing bringing me sandwiches with the crusts cut off? Aren't you aware there's a war on?' And, I mean, really, wasn't my fault, I hadn't made the sandwiches you know. But he did create. 'You take them back, and you bring me fresh sandwiches with crusts on.' Well, that was the beginning of that. So we were very wary of him in future, because he was a great scene creator.

(Irene Barrett-Locke, refreshments, GWR Paddington)

When looking back at their wartime railway work, women sometimes recalled encounters with famous people or royalty as a special and memorable experience. Others thought about all the different kinds of goods they transported, sometimes these were quite unusual. Somerset & Dorset Railway booking clerk Emily Poole recalls unique documents from the Public Records Office being transported on their trains between London and their wartime storage in a prison. Typist Dulcible Haines worked at the evacuated LMS HQ at the Grove at Watford, and recalls all their efforts to provide overseas prisoners of war with home comforts.

Some expressed their delight at working with horses, sadly replaced by motor vehicles. Most talked of walking or cycling to and from work. The winters at this time were particularly cold. Women remembered special practices they had to learn, for instance feeding information through the system to management, such as the 'nine o'clock position' for goods wagons. There were problems with supervisors and getting time off for essential shopping, fastidious auditors suddenly arriving, and working out how to deal with tricky animals. There were the occasional special delights of bread and dripping with a cup of tea. Clerk Maureen Evans dreamt about complicated piecework calculations and Emily Poole talked of using the 'flimsy ledger' to create copies of documents.

Dorothy Crawford, housekeeper, *LMS Adelphi Hotel, Liverpool*

Dorothy recalls the Grand National in Liverpool, which was still running in the early years of the war. The housekeepers had a very busy time because all the ladies who came had to have flowers in their rooms, they had to have soft coat-hangers and all that they wanted, and the housekeepers had a list from the past and looked it up and saw Mrs So-and-so had so-and-so, Mr So-and-so had something else and they were all produced for them in the room, all around the place. They knew, they took it for granted, that certain people would come and one of the problems was that the people took it for granted too. The hotel wasn't sure whether they were actually coming or not until the very last minute, but they kept certain suites for certain people and they really were very well looked after, for that time. We had extra staff for the floors to give them their breakfast in bed and so on, as well as in the restaurants. And the night of the ball, the day of the race, we had to wait. We couldn't decorate the table, the top table, until we knew which horse's colours had won, so we were all standing by, listening to make sure and the minute they knew whose horse had won, they'd rush out and buy flowers the right colour and get them onto the top table. There was usually 1,500 people. The whole of the lounge, the French restaurant, the grill room and the terrace at the back, it was full of tables and the top table was along that bit, with the winning colours on the tables.

It was a very exciting thing. Once we'd done all our work we were able to go up. Either side of the lounge upstairs, there was a little area where we could all stand and watch everything that was going on down below. It was really fascinating to see all these hundreds of people, all in their wonderful clothes and all the waiters there and producing a wonderful banquet, with everything you could think of. The sides of the lounge were made to look like the fences in the race and of course that made the young men enjoy themselves jumping over that as well. And then you've got plenty of horseplay on the way afterwards. We were always made to walk together and then as soon as they'd gone we had to go round and check up what damage had been done and the thing was, they always paid their bill. They accepted the fact that they had smashed a wardrobe or the bed or done some damage in the rooms. They just accepted the bill and that was it.

You had to surrender your rations and you couldn't get it back unless you were going away for more than a week. Of course the staff found this was very unfortunate, because if they were going home to their families they had to live off what their family produced. And if they got the food, the actual ration, they got it handed to them in the hotels. One of the things that I had to do, when I started going round, was to check with the staff and the housekeepers and the chef and the manager, report and tell them if they were being fairly treated. And I mean I think they did their best, but there were certainly some very poor meals, but they did get the ration of butter and they did get the ration of sugar and that was it.

Marjorie Cawthray, *LNER tearoom Selby*

From one end of the railway where you go in, there's this big building, and at that side it was the restaurant, and there were two bars. And then in between that, there was the dining room. And then after that there was the kitchen, the big kitchen. Very busy during the war. And all the soldiers used to come off the train, and the sailors, and they all used to come in, and we made them cups of tea or whatever they wanted, and then we used to fill these baskets, with all lunches for them and take them back onto the train, for the soldiers and sailors. That was provided by the railway.

We didn't keep open all night, we closed maybe about six o'clock in the evening. But before I got married of course I used to stay in, I was booked to stay in all the time. And then eventually I didn't, I didn't sleep in, I stopped at my own home with my husband. It was not too bad really but of course, there was no really hot water and stuff like that. I had my own room. It was all right, it was quite nice and clean and furniture weren't bad at all. We got our meals, we got our lunch, we hadn't to pay for that.

Irene Barrett-Locke née Davies, *refreshments, GWR Paddington*

I had six wonderful months on the train. And that is when I met quite a few nice people, interesting ones. First one that really impressed me, because I was that sort of girl, was there was a singer, a dark singer called Lesley Hutchinson. And Lord Baden-Powell came up once a week. And they ordered ham sandwiches and coffee, or whatever. And so I'd go through to Fred, the chef, and I would order these sandwiches for Baden-Powell. And of course he would cut them beautifully, take the crusts off, cut them in portions and I would take them through. And the first time I took them through, Baden-Powell nearly went berserk. 'What are you doing bringing me sandwiches with the crusts cut off? Aren't you aware there's a war on?' And, I mean, really, wasn't my fault, I hadn't made the sandwiches you know. But he, he did create. 'You take them back, and you bring me fresh sandwiches with crusts on.' Well, that was the beginning of that. So we were very wary of him in future, because he was a great scene creator.

Joan Cox, *mobile canteen worker, SR Redhill*

I can remember one occasion. It must have been Dunkirk. A train pulled up alongside of the canteen, and all these army men dropped out from the doors and put paper notes in our hands with messages and addresses. 'Please telegraph my wife to say that I'm safe.' And there was money wrapped up in these pieces of paper. God knows how much it was. But I took quite a while trying to get these telegrams sent off for these men. And I really can't recall the troops that they were. But there was injured ones on board as well, cos you could see the stretchers in the compartments. But they were there for several hours, so we was able to do that and we was able to supply them with tea and things like that. But it used to be tight sometimes to do. Very often a troop train passed through, but it only stayed a few minutes and others stayed longer. But that one stands out in my memory, because it was a frightening time of the war.

Betty Forrester née Ross, *clerk/telegraph operator, LNER Thornton Junction*

Well in the morning when they were busy, every line was communal, so of course any message that was going through showed up on every station on that line or signal box that it went through. Every day I got a long, long message, timing a lot of trains and I had to send them to the different signal boxes but usually the men said, 'Don't tell me it all, just tell me the one that's pertinent to myself.'

We had quite varied messages came into Thornton, but most of it was for the station staff. For instance, telling them to attach an extra carriage to a train. This was often 'Attach one third to a special train' et cetera. Well do I remember that, because when I was first trying so hard to understand this Morse, a T and an H is a dash and four dots and I mistook it for a dash and three dots which is B, so I had them attach one bird to this train and I forgot to delete it, so it was kept up on me forever, 'Any birds to go on this train Betty?'

It's difficult to remember all the different types of messages that come. There's quite a lot for the electrician. It's rather unbelievable I suppose, in this day and age of mobile phones et cetera to think that messages had to be relayed from so many different places, but Thornton station was a relay station. And the telephone, the telegraph lines lay at the side of the railway track, so the distance that the messages could be sent was the actual length of the lines, which I think were about 60 to 80 miles. So I remember there was a telegraph office at Burntisland, because I had to work there for a short while. It was also a relay office. Now, they would get messages from Edinburgh, then they would relay it on to Thornton, we were further north. Then I would relay them on to the different signal boxes of small railway stations round about or up the coast. And the strange bit when you were in the office, there was actually six instruments all clacking away together, and amongst all this conglomeration and noise, you could hear your own signal piercing through it all.

They were metallic poles and if you click anything made of metal it has a different sound from another metal. So when you heard your signal, it would be ping – ping – p – ping – ping or maybe [at a lower tone] ping – ping – p – ping – ping. You went to the instrument and you sent the letter K, and the message was sent to you, then you sent R for received, and sometimes you sent K for thank you and you'd written down the message and it either went through to the stationmaster's office or to one of the outside staff. If it was outside staff you'd put it on his hook and he would eventually come to look at it. Sometimes it was marked 'urgent', you couldn't really leave the office, so you found somebody to deliver it for you. The inspector was just within calling distance and he would maybe deliver it for you.

Another thing we did at ten o'clock. At ten o'clock there was a time signal and it supposedly went right through Scotland, and all the instruments, the little hammers waggled back and forwards and you grabbed as many handles of the different hand instruments that you can and you waggled them as hard as you can, and also the telephones, to let everybody know that it was ten o'clock. And I used to often wonder by the end of everybody letting other folk know what the time was, if it was still ten o'clock by the end of the line. But I think the signalmen all waited for it and they knew that it was just gone ten o'clock. Ten am in the morning.

Unfortunately there was nobody else who could read Morse in our actual Thornton station. On two or three occasions when the stationmaster was on holiday we had a relief stationmaster who could read Morse and if we were lucky enough to be back shift, when he was on duty, he would relieve you later in the evening and say, 'Off you go home,' because very few messages came through after about six o'clock. I think we must have worked on a Saturday, because Saturday I often used to get away if he was there. But Sunday of course there was no telegraph. It was difficult, annual holidays. I remember I had to get an emergency holiday and they weren't going to let me off and it was imperative that I get away and I think the person on the other shift did an extra shift for me, because they were short of people. Of course it was wartime and a lot of the men had been called up. I suppose this is why I got the job quite easily, because I read the Morse and so.

Thornton station wasn't a big station. There was an up line and a down line, but running into the middle of the platforms, not quite touching, were two lines with buffers at the end and they stood extra carriages there. I would say the platform was shaped like a letter H if you can understand that, and unfortunately if there wasn't any carriages standing in those dock platforms, people didn't realise in half dusk that the platform didn't continue straight across and often people fell into the platforms. And in our office we had a sink, and the first aid man was rather apt to bring bleeding people into our office to get attention. I remember one lady she had hopped off her train going up to Inverness and thought she'd plenty of time to run across to the bookstall and get a book, hadn't seen the rails and fallen off the platform into the dock. Of course, there was no lighting, there was nothing to show that, unless you saw the buffers, but of course the buffers were down within the dock platform.

Annie Lageu, *shorthand typist, LMS Leeds*

The Passenger Manager's office was in temporary accommodation above a tailor's and there we did have a little typing pool. There were just the four, five of us in it. And then when they had almost finished the offices in Aire Street, the new offices, adjoining the Queen's Hotel, the lease ran out of the offices that we're in, so we had to go in before they'd completely finished refurbishing the top floors in the Aire Street offices. We hadn't a little typing pool there, we went in a big room that was eventually a typing pool for both the District Goods and the District Passenger Manager's office. We had a supervisor, all the supervisors were spinsters because when a young woman got married she had to leave, they didn't employ any married women, the only ones were widows from the First World War.

We were more or less supervised. You couldn't go out of the office unless the supervisor knew where you were going, except of course to the toilet, which was something that annoyed me, because I was a person of very regular habits. And every morning about half past nine I would go to the toilet, two mornings she followed me and I said if she did it again I would report her to the welfare officer. Anyway she didn't do it anymore, I don't know whether she overheard me or not. But these women were all spinsters, over us, and some of them not very good as typists, because this one particularly wasn't. One of the men once asked me whose initials these were, because we had to put our initials on the top of the letters. And they said, Who was FG? 'Cos I don't want her typing my letters.' So I said, 'Well you'd better tell her because she's the supervisor.' And one time I was doing some very confidential typing and all the typing we did, she collected it and put it in a basket and then we had a messenger came and distributed it to the different departments and she wanted me to leave this in the basket, and I had to ring the man concerned, because it would have caused a riot in the office, because the men weren't very happy. They'd come from Manchester with such wonderful promises which hadn't materialised.

Our windows overlooked City Square and we saw all the children be brought to be evacuated, that was something that really was upsetting.

Until Easter 1942 I was not very happy working in the typing pool with this supervisor and I applied for a clerical job, and I went down into the offices after I came back from Easter break, and I was only there a week when I was called in and told that as a shorthand typist I'd been in a reserved occupation, but as a clerk I wasn't. So I could be called up, into the forces, or into nursing, or armaments, you know munitions or something like that. Well, I was much happier. Having been in from the beginning I knew a lot about the work of the department and typed for different people in the different sections, and I was much happier there. But they got me a six months deferment, so instead of being called up straight away it was November before I went into the ATS.

Christina Pettigrew, *shorthand typist, LMS Glasgow*

Now all the deliveries on this goods station were done by, as they called them, 'carters'. They were all horse-drawn carts and the horses were stabled at the foot of the Goods Station, beautiful great big Clydesdale horses. Absolutely lovely, used to be down regularly to see them and they were beautiful. Most of the carters kept their horses perfect, brushed, and their great hooves were brushed and white. And I think it was once a year they used to have a parade or a walk through Glasgow, or a part of another parade. The horses were all dressed over with ribbons, blue red white, and all their brasses were polished to the hilt, beautiful. If the weather was very very bad, and at that time it was all cobbled streets in Glasgow, and up Hill Street was very very high and they used a second horse, he was brought up by a young, probably a junior or a learning carter and he was attached to the front of the horse to help draw these great heavy loads up cobbled streets. And sometimes if they were slippy or icy it was terrible, they would fall.

And I loved to go down to the stables. I went down as often as I could to see these lovely horses. One carter was not a good carter, he didn't keep them very nice, but nobody liked him. But the horses I used to know all their names, and the man who looked after the stables. He was extremely nice, and took me round and spoke to all the horses.

But they were all finished, I think before I actually left college, they were just beginning to be motorised. Now I went from College Goods station, into the army, the ATS.

Mary Hodgson, *LMS clerk Chesterfield*

As well as looking after the switchboard I did what was called the nine o'clock position, the state of the work. So that at nine o'clock every morning, I had to have in my possession the number of goods wagons that were in the shed, waiting to be unloaded, and the number that had already been unloaded from five o'clock in the morning. The goods yard was full of wagons in those days, and especially during wartime. There'd be hundreds of wagons in the goods yard, and the number-taker would've been round, and taken the numbers of every wagon, and where they'd come from. I had to have all that information given to me, and then sort it all out for this nine o'clock position. Which at nine o'clock I had to phone through to the Farm Buildings at Sheffield, to a certain office.

I was there at eight o'clock in a morning. We also had spare capacity in what was called the Hollis Lane Sidings, which were over the other side of the main line, for wagons waiting to come across over the main line into the goods yard, when there was room for them. The goods wagons would be emptied in a certain order, so that there was a whole string of empty wagons, hopefully by a certain time when the engine came into the yard, pulled all those empty wagons out. And then some of them from the Hollis Lane Sidings would be brought across the main line, when there was time on the main line to bring them over, because in those days the main line was busy. Not like it is now. But at a certain time, the full wagons would be brought, and put onto the road that the empty wagons had been taken out of. The goods agent could be told exactly how many wagons had been unloaded, how many were waiting to be unloaded, and all this information could be given through to the headquarters in Sheffield. So that there was a very good system, of knowing really exactly how the railway stood at any particular time of the day. And I had to do the same thing at four o'clock in the afternoon. I had to phone through to Sheffield, and tell them how many wagons had been unloaded during the day and how many were waiting to be unloaded. So that there was a full picture, of what was waiting to be done, the following morning. I also did another return called 'sheets, ropes and chains', because in those days there were a lot of open wagons, but if they were loaded with any goods that needed protection from the weather, then we used to have huge, dark red sheets.

The staff who worked an afternoon shift were called the shippers, and they had to write out all the invoices from the consignment notes, from the goods which had been put into wagons ready for transport during the night. Now those shippers had made out hundreds of invoices, which all had to be put into strict alphabetical order. Because there were so many invoices to go through, if for any reason you had to trace through them, if you were looking for a consignment that had got lost or something like that, everything had to be done in the very strictest of alphabetical order. And it was amazing, the number of people who didn't know their alphabet, in order to work out this strict alphabetical business.

I also eventually dealt with the staff uniforms, measuring the porters, which they thought was lovely you know? Putting your arms round them with a tape measure. The Chief Clerk had done it for many years, and then he decided, well he'd let me do it instead. And also another job that I did quite a number of times was to accompany the lorry driver, who was taking cash to the bank, 'cos in those days we used to have cash transported by rail, and if any bullion boxes that came in needed to be delivered to various banks up in town, I was asked if I would accompany the driver, and be security for him in case he got attacked.

Then after I'd done the four years, in the Chief Clerk's Office, I worked in the Delivery Office. I started at eight o'clock in the morning and alternated with the shipping shift the following week. We did a week on delivery and a week on shipping and it kept alternating. The strict laws that were enforced for the female staff, we were not supposed to work as just one female, amongst the male staff. So actually on this shipping turn, there ought to have been two females, with the male staff. But there wasn't, there was only me. But in those days we were not so conversant with trade unions and people like that were we? Or else somebody might have reported that, but we didn't, we never ever thought about it, so many a time there was just me.

Sometimes when you got to work, if the caretaker wasn't there, many a time I've gone out on the shed, on the inward shed, and asked if they'd got some firewood, and you'd have to set to and light the fire before you could start work. Cos there was no central heating or anything like that. You really did have to look after yourself. And when the auditors arrived, they never announced that they were coming, the first you knew was somebody, up in the accounts office window happen to look out, and you'd see the auditors walking up the goods yard. The first thing they wanted was the money and the stamps, you'd no time to put anything right if you'd done anything wrong.

Doris Maley, *shorthand typist, LMS Broad St, London*

It was always difficult to get food in London; there was so many restaurants going up in smoke. We didn't have a canteen, but there was a canteen down below us, which occasionally, if they had a lot of dripping they would let us have slices of bread and dripping with our cup of tea, which we thought an absolute wonderful thing! There were the British restaurants, but we had to go quite a long way for those. It was near St Pancras Station, and of course in forty minutes it was very difficult. I think we managed it once or twice, but not very often. It was a difficult time, and so was the fog in London. That was very difficult getting from Broad Street to Fenchurch Street. It was always amusing to see the lamplighters with their bicycles, lighting the lamps as they went along. London was so different from now, and it's hard to imagine that there were really very few buses and very few cars. And even less lorries. No traffic coming in and upstairs we were dealing with traffic going out, and there it was, mostly horse and cart, and I always remember, the last horse and cart there, because the poor carter loved his horse so much he hung himself in the stable. And the men who looked after the horses, they were so devoted to them.

No uniform. Lavatories weren't very good in those days, we had to traipse over to the station and had our own key, but had to go to the station. Even at Liverpool Street, in some of the offices, they still had to go on the station.

Joan Richards, *parcels clerk, GWR Hartlebury*

At the time there was a big maintenance unit there, they carried all the spares for the Royal Air Force and other forces. But the main thing was Air Force supplies, and every day, four or five lorry loads would come down, and my job was to stick a little docket on everything that went away. If there was a place to stick it, you had to put a docket on it. And all these dockets, you know the little stamp piece you had, for putting the numbers on, they all had to be stamped with a number. And there was of course an invoice with every one, the number had to be put on the invoice and that was my job, walking around with a tin of paste and a brush and then stick the docket on, put the number down, and I did that up until the war finished, 1945.

Lunch, you could take it with you, but the RAF had a special dispensation. They allowed you to go through to their canteen, and you could either have a hot meal or you could go in the snack bar part of it and just have a sandwich. As long as you were in uniform you were allowed in.

We only saw the passenger stuff. Two trains a day that you mustn't put anything on, and that was the London trains. They must not be loaded up. They mustn't be held up, taking parcels and that off. The other trains could run late, but not the London trains. And if they were late, the station master had to send a letter of explanation as to why the train was held up. They've got to go on time, but the others, sometimes, it'd take half hour to load the stuff that was on. If it was too much to load on, it'd got to be loaded in a truck and the truck was hooked on the back of the train.

There was a diesel that ran. The diesels came out, and there was a little diesel that ran, what they call 'the triangle' of Stourport, Bewdley and Kidderminster, and that ran three or four times a day. And once on a Sunday, in the morning, and once in the afternoon, and it was mostly fishermen from the Black Country coming down, men going down to do fishing and stuff, and you got a bit fed up with them asking you when the next train was coming. And I know that one Sunday the one chap got a bit annoyed about it, and some boy went up to him and said, 'How long's the next train, mister?' and he said, 'It'll be an engine and four coaches when it comes.' And the poor lad, he just looked open mouthed, he couldn't make anything out of that.

There were some funny situations. One chap that worked in the RAF, he worked for the railway, but he worked in the RAF loading and checking off the goods wagons. He came down one night and he fell asleep on the platform, and apparently he'd done it once or twice before, and they'd gone and woke him up when the train came, but this particular night, I suppose they got the devil in them or something, they decided to let him stop, and he usually caught one about twenty five to six, and that night he slept right through the train. I said to them, 'Aren't you going to wake him up?' 'No,' they said, 'Let him stop.' And he was still there when I caught the quarter to seven train on that night, and apparently he caught the next one, about eight o'clock at night when he got home. He wasn't very happy.

Well, the war had finished by then, when I came to Kidderminster. And that was funny. I had some funny experiences in the Parcel Office there, because a gentleman came up one day and he'd got to send a calf away, and he wanted of course to go by passenger train. So the lad which worked in the Parcel Office with me, he was a nice lad, but he could be a bit dim sometimes, he'd never sent a calf away before, so he had a look in the book and it said it'd got to be weighed. So of course the question arose how do you weigh a calf? And it'd got to have a napkin on, which the chap had put a napkin on it, and he'd done that part of it. So he decided he was going to weigh it on the scales that they weighed the parcels on. Well, when he got the two front feet on, he couldn't get the back two on. Well, he tried about three times to get this calf on these scales. 'Course myself and the parcel porter, we were killing ourselves laughing, and the man that the calf belonged to was getting very agitated, and so was the poor calf, and this lad, he just didn't know what to do. Anyway, the man it belonged to, he was getting really annoyed, you know, and he said, 'I can't get the damn thing on there!' He says, 'The platform's not wide enough for him to put all four feet on at once,' he says, 'This is damn ridiculous!' So the parcels porter, he whispered to me, he said, 'He'd be better on the big scales, out on the platform.' Because on the platform there was some scales sunk into the platform themselves, and they were for weighing the trolleys, you know, that you put the parcels on, and of course, he could have stood on that perfectly. So I went in, and I said, 'Wouldn't it be better to put them on the scales in the platform?' 'I was just gonna suggest that,' he said, this young chap, and I said, 'Were you?' And he said, 'Yes, that's what I've been thinking.' He'd forgot all about these flipping scales. Anyway, of course, the man they belonged to turned to me, said, 'You seem to be more sensible,' he says, 'Could you please see to this poor animal for me?' I said, 'I'll bring him out here.' So I brought him out, of course, stood him on the platform, by the scales, we'd done it in two minutes. And he turns round to this young chap, and he says, 'Thank god,' he says, 'they've got employees with brain,' and off he went.

Oh, there was a poor goat that ate his label. They came in the one day and said did we want a goat? Just said, 'No, we don't want a goat.' And he says, 'Oh, the poor guard, he doesn't know what to do.' I said, 'Why?' He got a goat in the guard's van and it'd ate its label, and he didn't know where he'd got to leave it! I think in the end he took it through to Birmingham, and they took charge of it there.

When I went to work down in the goods office the farmers were only allowed to grow so much, so seed potatoes would come in. You'd have the truckloads with seed potatoes come in, and there'd be so many bags for each farmer, and they'd have to be checked in and the farmers would have to come and get the bags that they were allowed, and it was the same with the grain. There was a big grain shed down there, where they kept all the bags of grain, and they could only have so many, because only so much grain could be grown at a time, and it was all stuff like that when you were moved over to the goods office. And then they wanted somebody in the correspondence office, and I'd been messing about with a typewriter, and the one in charge of where I was, he said, 'You can type.' And I said, 'I can with one finger,' and he says, 'You can do more than that.' He's, 'Why don't you go and have a go?' So I said I'd try it. So when I finally left I finished up doing all the typing for the correspondence people.

So I had a variety of jobs, because when they knew I'd been on the switchboard at the Fire Station, that was the job they wanted somebody for in the goods office. They'd got a miniature switchboard, and they wanted somebody to work the switchboard, and be at the counter and get the farmers and that to sign for their potatoes and all that sort of thing, and also enter up the weights of the different coal wagons. It was quite interesting, there. You've got people coming in all the time with different... I quite enjoyed that.

Working at Hartlebury the main problem was you couldn't do any shopping, because I used to have to catch the two minutes past eight train in the morning, and I wasn't supposed to finish till half past five, but if the five o'clock train was late, I could sometimes catch that. But if somebody came up with a parcel, you've got to stop and deal with it. It meant I didn't get home till perhaps there was one about six o'clock something like that. So of course the shops were always shut when I got home, and there was no Sunday opening then, everything closed down on Sundays. So the Sundays I had off, I started going up to the YMCA, and doing teas and that for the soldiers. They came in on Sundays, and of course there was nothing open for them, not till the cinemas opened at lunch time, so they used to go in there in the morning and have a game, ping-pong or something like that, and a cup of tea and perhaps beans on toast. Until the cinema opened, or the pub. 'Cause the pubs didn't open then, twelve o'clock till two was the pub opening time. So they could only wander around the streets. So we used to get quite a few coming in, pass the time away till the pictures opened sort of thing. So I had to work every other Sunday, but at least I got one Sunday a fortnight off. But when the invasion was on, they were short-staffed, so I had to work every Sunday.

Maureen Evans, *messenger then clerk, LMS Crewe*

We took sandwiches. And of course the men had their own little sort of cubby-hole where they used to go and have their 'snap', as it was called. And Mrs G and I were very privileged. We had a railway carriage to ourselves. This was in a sidings, a disused sidings. And again the pot-bellied stove was there. We had to stoke the pot-bellied stove in order to get some hot water to make our drink and eat our sandwiches. It was all very cosy. I was there from eight o'clock in the morning until half-past-five at night. And then I would dash home for tea. And I had to go to night school till nine o'clock at night.

It was doing the wages for the railway works. Well, not just the railways works, it was a lot of little sort of outside places as well that we did wages for. But I actually did the wages for the signal shop. There was piecework prices to be worked out. And you'd get great piles of tickets on a Monday morning coming up from the railway works. You'd spend the entire day, Monday, possibly into the middle of Tuesday, working out all these piece-rate work prices. And it was quite intricate really to work out, doing fourteen of something, at fourpence three farthing for 27, ridiculous amounts of money, the way the piecework had been worked out for each particular job. And then you had to work out the War Wage, so you worked out the piecework prices and the War Wage and then you did the income tax. And then about Wednesday all these bills would go in, to be put into the machine room to be put on a big sheet to work out.

It was all done by hand, and brain work, really. Well, we had the Burroughs adding machine. There was one on each desk. It was like an old chipmaker. And comptometers. We used to use the comptometers for certain things. A comptometer on the end of each desk and there were two comptometer operators on each desk. But they worked entirely separately from us. But occasionally we'd ask, could we, if it was a particularly difficult calculation to work out, we'd say, could we borrow the comptometer to work out a difficult calculation? Or sometimes they would do it for us. If they were feeling kindly towards us, they would do it for us. But mainly it was the Burroughs adding machine, for lengthy additions.

I got six pounds a week. Yes. Big money indeed, yes. My father was getting less money than me, for doing his job in the machine shop. And also I could have as many quarter-fares as I liked. And I think it was three free passes. I think it was a fortnight [holiday]. You had to put your name down, and of course the longer you'd been there...it was based on your length of service, really.

We weren't allowed to wear trousers at work. And of course one winter, I think it was 1947 winter, it was a very bad winter. We asked if we could wear trousers. They allowed us to wear trousers *to* work, but you had to change into a skirt *at* work. So you had to go into the changing room.

The heating. Well, it was a long pipe running along. But of course, when there was a fuel shortage, the offices were very cold. They couldn't heat the offices.

So, my husband will remember this, there was a period one winter when the girls took to wearing, you couldn't get stockings or nylons as they were called in those days, unless you knew somebody really. And everything of course was still on coupons. So we took to wearing boys' three-quarter length socks, really to keep our legs and feet warm in the winter. Because they lasted a long time, you know, you bought one pair of socks with your coupons and they would last you then throughout the winter. I used to walk to work. Occasionally I would cycle. If we had to work overtime, we would cycle. Because there was no buses. In the office we had to work overtime most Mondays and most Tuesdays. And everybody used to moan about this working overtime.

And then moving up into the General Offices, I suppose there'd be about 150 people in my estimation, working in this office. It was divided into two sections. One was the section where the wages were actually being done. And the other section was the procedure after that, where accounting was done on the cost, it was the costing section, the costings of all the transactions and things. So the two sections didn't really mingle. It was more or less equally divided. We didn't know what they did and they didn't know what we did, really. But, there was a lot of girls there, so there was a lot of companionship and friendship and what have you. And yes, I did enjoy it. I didn't enjoy the actual work. The work was very tedious. And on a Monday and Tuesday, when I was asleep at night, I'd be dreaming piecework prices all night long. I mean, this happened really every week. I'd be doing piecework prices throughout all Monday and Tuesday night when I was asleep, you know. But I didn't enjoy the work because basically I'm an outdoor person and I felt cooped up in this office.

There was no pressure really to join the union, but I did join the union. Yes, my father was, being an engineer, he was in the union, and having gone through periods of, threats of unemployment, and periods of working one week on and one week off and being short of money in his married life. The union was the only one, the only people that seemed to help the situation. And he always said to me, 'Join the union, Maureen, because they're the only ones who's going to stick up for you if there's any problems.' So I did join the union, this was wartime, you see, so things were quite different in those days, and the only thing you had really was you could get discounts on various things. But somebody would come round and collect the money from us about once a fortnight. And we used to get paid once a fortnight. And then they would come round and collect our union subscriptions from us. It was the [Railway Clerks Association, later the] TSSA.

Irene Adgie, *typist, SR Woking and Waterloo*

We worked from, officially it was 8:45 to 4:30. Because they had adjusted the hours from 9 to 5 in order to fit in with the trains, as most of the other members in the pool worked in London. And we worked on Saturdays from 8:45 to midday. But we had to do a lot of overtime. We were paid for it. But the government in its wisdom insisted that everybody had to do a minimum number of hours. So that meant we all had to work two hours overtime twice a week. But also, because we typed all the notices of special trains, somebody was needed in the office until 8:30 at night. So, there, every four weeks we did a week of late turn. And although we started two hours later, we were still doing two hours overtime every night that week. And we also had to work weekends. And the Sunday was a long day. That was I think from 8:45 to six o'clock, something like that. We had to work weekends and that came about once every four weeks.

It was a hut, beside the railway at Woking. They had no linings really to the walls of the hut, not anything that was insulating. The roof was the ceiling, with no lining to it. And in the summer they were unbearably hot. In the winter they were unbearably cold. The only heating was a coke stove in the centre. And because of fuel shortage it had to go out during the night. So when we arrived in the morning it had only just been lit. And often the oil in our typewriters was frozen. During the day of course it heated up and people sitting near it got over-heated. But those on the edges remained cold. So a few minutes to spare and we'd be standing round the stove. The other thing about the hours, they needed someone on duty from 8:15 in the morning because there were two reports to be typed. One, the control log book to be copied for the previous day, and the other dictated straight onto the typewriter by one of the rules department, of the various incidents that had happened. When the bomb dropped. That sort of thing. And engine short of steam.

Because I lived locally, I came in for quite a lot of those early turns. Walking or cycling. I was a mile and a half from the station and I usually cycled, because I used to go home at lunchtime. There was a canteen. But it was very grim. It was run by Gordon's Hotel, who at that time did the catering for Southern Railway on the trains. And I don't know what the catering on the trains was like. I could never afford a meal. But the catering in the canteen was abysmal. It wasn't just a shortage of food. We knew there was a shortage of food. It was the cooking. It was dreadful. Later on, when I started having lunch at the canteen because I'd gone into lodgings, my friends and I used to go sometimes to the British Restaurant in Woking. Sometimes to the Yorkshire Café for a treat, where we had cauliflower cheese and chips and it was lovely. But we couldn't afford that very often.

My father moved down to South Wales in 1944. And I went down with them but I couldn't get work that I liked. To my surprise, the LMS and GWR didn't want to know. They had plenty of staff. And after three months typing invoices at an oil refinery, I phoned the supervisor at Woking and said, 'Please can I come back?' And she said, 'Delighted.'

Doreen Dickenson, *goods clerk, LMS Liverpool*

The train, the carriages were blitzed. They got incendiary bombs on them. And so for that period I was sent to Aintree station. Well, you want to see Aintree station now. They've made it a bit upmarket for the racecourse. But before, it was just like a little bridge over the railway, the ticket office was like a wooden platform extension. And you went down the steps and you used the waiting room of the passenger trains. And there was a bit of a shed down the garden at the back. And that's where we were housed as a goods station. At least, part of a goods station. I was in the accounts department by then. And so the ledgers and things were brought up. And we had to do the account current and the monthly balance and things like that. There was a bit of a joke about, we were a penny out of balance and somebody put a stamp, stuck a stamp on the other side. And the auditors wouldn't have it. Put a penny stamp on the side you were short of, you know? But anyway, I think that was a bit of a joke.

But those days the toilets we had to use were the passengers' toilets, where you had to put a penny in the slot. And of course what they did, we couldn't put pennies in the slot. We were staff. So you had a six-inch nail which you put on the track so that the engine flattened it. And we bent it slightly into a sort of a hockey stick sort of shape. And you shoved it down where the penny was, and twisted it, and it opened the door. So all the female staff were given a nail to go to the toilet. It's primitive, isn't it.

And we were there for a month, or something like that, until we came back and the Canada Dock was ready for us to come back. And do you know, they'd built us offices underneath Derby Road in the old stables. Of course it was just an arched brickwork tunnel, about 40 feet long I suppose. We were in there, and they'd whitewashed all the bricks over the top like that. And we had stable doors… And two foot outside were a track where the engine went up and the wagons were loaded and shunted about, right outside the door. That again is more fun, because then we had the Americans over and the Movement Control.

We had to have special permission later on, to wear trousers. But because we couldn't get any coupons and things for nylon stockings, we coloured our legs with gravy browning, or something like that. But we couldn't wear trousers without asking permission. And men couldn't turn up in a sports coat or anything. Only on a Saturday morning. You could turn up in sports coat and trousers if you were going off to your cricket match. But you always had to wear a suit and a tie.

Most people at my age started at 15 shillings or 17 shillings. I got 19 and sixpence a week. I started on a Monday morning. And payday was once a fortnight, every other Thursday. So I was paid on the first Thursday because I started the pay week. And I didn't expect any money, but on the railway they didn't work a week in hand. So on Thursday morning I was given the grand sum of eleven and sixpence, which was four days' pay. And I was paid up to five o'clock, and I got it at eleven o'clock in the morning. A ten-shilling note, and one-and-six-pence in me hand. That was me first four days' wages.

Half past eight till half past five. Nine o'clock till six. We always did a Saturday morning... Half past eight till half past twelve. Or nine till one. We did four hours on a Saturday morning. 42-hour week, I think, the outside men did 44 I think, that's right. After a while we did every other Saturday. But to do every other Saturday, we had to put our two hours in, in the week.

Normally men came in at twelve o'clock, and went home midnight, two o'clock in the morning, whenever they'd finished. They were invoicing goods which were going on the wagons to be distributed all over the country. And on the side of the wagon, in those little squares you see on the side, they put the invoices. The invoices were, you know, 'Canada Dock Liverpool to Birmingham', or wherever you were going. And I think we used to know nearly every, almost, village places all over the country. Places you've never heard of. Well, I was on the railway, I've heard of it. And it used to go to a different mainline station, to be delivered by road or cart. And underneath we would write, so many packages, or so many tons or whatever it was. And the weight, in hundredweights, tens and units. And a copy of it would be passed over to a charger. We were rating and charging. So they'd put a rate on it, and somebody would work out the cost of that transport, at so many tons, hundredweights, quarters and pounds, at so much a ton. And you had calculators to do it. So that was done in the office. But the girls were asked to work shift-work with them, to do the typing part of it. And we came on at half past twelve till nine, I think it was. So we'd come in half past twelve in the day and work till nine o'clock at night.

And there was still a war on. Okay, so we weren't so terribly blitzed round here then, because the Blitz had subsided a bit. But it was blackout. Dark nights, and I had to travel to Southport from Canada Dock. We were working those days underneath the arches, as we called it. And there were no windows. In fact, the hay boxes' brackets were still on the wall, where the horses had been. So we were in there. Brick floors, concrete floors. I think they did try to put some kind of lino down on it, after a bit. And we were there from half past twelve till nine o'clock. You had a half hour break for your tea, or something like that. And we typed these invoices.

I was happy at my work. I mean, it was fine. We typed the invoices and we used to make a score. You had to have a score of how many you'd done in the night, you know, and all that kind of thing. The lists used to come in on printed invoices, which had the columns for tons, hundredweights, and pounds, shillings and pence, you see. We had big firms to deal with, shipping firms and all that. We went out all over the place. It was the sheets that came in from the checkers outside. Cos they would check off what came in on the wagon from the docks. And then they would put them into other wagons to sort them to which, north, south, east and west, all over the country they would go, you see. And we had to invoice them. The invoices to go on the side of the wagon. And the ones they brought in to us, they'd have a weight flashed across the page. It was wagon numbers, you see. And many a time, the wagon numbers happened to go slightly lopsided. But in the weight, many a time we charged out tons and hundredweight and quarters, and they were wagon numbers. You get a wagon number, 71463 or something. And it'd be seven tons, 16 hundredweight, three quarters and some. And you charge those out, and think, 'Well, where the hell's the wagon number?' That was the wagon number. Those sort of things. But only on odd occasions. And there were hilarious jokes if you charged out a wagon number. You must have been thick, you know. But it was the way they used to never write things in the right place, you know, and you had to find what they were, cos they scribbled it outside in the dark in some cases, you know. If you charged out wagon numbers, you were crackers.

In the Delivery Office, and then when we started on the shipping, we had to come in and do the late turn. You're supposed to be a week of earlies and a week of lates. But you'd find out that somebody would go sick on their late week, and they'd ask you, would you do their late week for them. And you'd do two weeks of lates and one of earlies. Nobody ever complained, they just did as they were told. Didn't say 'It's not my turn', or 'I'm not doing all that'. You got 19 and sixpence a week, or 25 shillings a week, and that was your lot. Anyway, we did this until they decided that all this rating and charging was to be done in a centralised accounts office. And it was the centralised rating shed. And they opened that in Great Howard Street office, opposite the Waterloo Dock. They selected people from each of the districts like Edgehill, Canada, Huskisson, and all that. And we were all in the same office, doing the rating and charging. And that started in, well, I was seventeen years there, and I was 21 years old, and so I must have been about four years on the dock. And so after four years, 1944 or 1945, towards the end of the war, when they decided to centralise the accounts, the men weren't coming back then. Cos Netty got married once we got into the accounts office. It must have been before the fellows were discharged, because she got dismissed as soon as he came home.

We were members of a trade union. And it was one and elevenpence a week, I think. A fellow came round and collected our one and elevenpence, or two shillings a week, two shillings a week. I don't know, probably less than that in the earlier stages. But we were members of a train union. It was the Railway Clerks Association. Which became the Transport Salaried Staff, the TSSA. And of course a chappie used to come over. And he had the book, and he ticked you off, and he took your two bob off you, whatever it was, you see. Now I had a friend over there, he said, 'Do you realise that a couple of coppers a week go to the Labour Party?' So I said, 'No.' He said, 'Well, I'm a Conservative. And I don't think they've got any right to take my, misappropriate my money. I want me money back.' You see. So he said, 'If I want to give me money to the

Labour Party or Conservative Party or any other ruddy party,' he said, 'I'll do it. They're not doing it. I want to know what they're doing with it.' So he asked, and they gave him a form to fill in to withdraw his support for political dues or whatever it was. And they gave him a pink one and a white one. And the first one was to fill in to say he didn't want to pay the money to the Labour Party. And the second one to say that his Labour Party money was to go to the Railway Benevolent Fund. So he didn't fill the second one in. And I did the same. I didn't fill the second one in. And the fellow said to me, 'Well, where's your other pink form?' I said, 'You're not getting it.' He said, 'That's to go to the Railway B ...' I said, 'And what's to stop you tearing both of them up when you get outside the door, and I still haven't got me penny back? So if I'm having the penny, I'm having it in my pocket and I'll put my money to the Railways Benevolent...' I don't trust anybody. My father was a customs officer. You never put your name to anything that wouldn't stand up in a court of law. That was his doctrine. And I'm still the same today. Can't help it. How do I know somebody's not going to tear those papers up as while me back's turned? I mean, we didn't know Labour Party from political party. But it was just the principle of the thing, that they took your money and presumed that you wanted it to go to the Labour Party. So everybody on the railway contributed to the Labour Party's funds, whether they liked it or not. So we put threepence a week or something in the Railway Benevolent Fund, on principle, you see.

Gladys Garlick, *guard, LNER London*

I can remember one bank holiday. It was a lovely bank holiday. The weather was gorgeous. And of course people used to go down to Cuffley and Bayford. The Boy Scouts used to go down camping and things like that. We got to Bowes Park and the train was full. They couldn't get any more people on this train. So they stopped booking tickets at Bowes Park. And we had about three lots of Boy Scouts. Of course in those days they used to have a truck, a cart. And the wheels used to come off and a long handle used to come off. Well, they used to cart all their stuff to the campsite... they used to walk there with all their stuff. I had about three lots of those all got in. Well of course you couldn't organise it because they were just pulling, you know, tipping in, sort of thing, all up the front brake. And of course the ones that wanted to get out at Cuffley were behind the ones that wanted to go further on. So we had a right old muddle to get them off the trains, as it were. We were an hour late by the time we got to Hertford. And in my brake I had a load of bicycles. And then people was trying to get in as well. It was really, you know, it was laughable really. But it was a gorgeous weekend, that was. But it was really funny. And as I say the people at Palmer's Green and every other station couldn't get on, because it was so full. The old train was chugging along. I think it felt the weight, actually.

Mary Woodfield, *linesman's assistant, GWR Undy*

The same work all the time. Summer or winter. I enjoyed every minute. And I cycled from Undy, which was about three miles, I expect. There and back, every day. Cos I loved my bike, anyway, and I still do. I liked the work. I don't care how mucky and all it is. There's always water in the tap. And knowing that when you were done all around one of the boxes, and got a lot of the gunge off, you just look back and say, same as any cleaning job that I've had. And I've done a few cleaning jobs, mind. You look back and you say to yourself, 'Now that looks nice, that does.'

At the tunnel, I had one narrow squeak on the railway. My tummy turned to pieces after. Because we'd had our cup of tea up in the box. It was the middle box, and the London trains come from Newport, pheeeewww, right up against the box. To turn down to go to the tunnel like that. But of course I'd forgotten that, hadn't I? And of course got out to lower deck...and was just going to step out, on the railway rails. And oh, here comes the London out of nowhere. Oh, almost in front of it. That was one time when it actually crept up on you. I thought nothing of it then, but it was only when you thought after: 'Good God, that was a narrow squeak.' But you got to know the times of the regulars. I always knew when it was three o'clock. Because there was a certain train every day went through at three o'clock. And on time, too. Always. But I've never known anything but the railway.

Freda Box, *crossing keeper, Bruton, Somerset & Dorset Joint Railway*

Around 1940 or 1941, my husband was waiting for the bell to ring to open the gates for a train, and we could hear a plane about, it seemed to go around the crossing a few times, getting lower and all of a sudden, a loud bang, the wing of the plane must have caught in the telephone wire and suddenly we heard a very great bang. It being the war had started in '39 we thought it was a German plane, well my husband found someone with a car, got in touch with the station master at Evercreech and he got through to Templecombe. And it is so funny and so unreal, the train came as far as the crossing and the pilot of the plane got off the train, wanted to know where the crashed plane was, he said the three or four of the crew had all got out safely. During the night there were about ten or twelve RAF personnel guarding the bits of the plane, being war time no-one could photograph any of the plane.

Norah Cook, *passenger clerk, Highbridge, Somerset & Dorset Joint Railway*

As I worked on the S & D during wartime, many of the employees at that time were over 65, having been kept on, so that younger men could join the forces. Despite the fact that it was wartime, I always had a huge coal fire in my office during the winter months, the footplate staff were very generous! The waiting room on the down platform was quite large and there was usually a good fire in there too.

There used to be a train on the GWR from Paddington, arriving at Highbridge at 3.10pm, which was supposed to connect with our 4pm passenger train to Evercreech Junction. However, it was not unusual for the Paddington train to be late, and although our staff hung on to the 4 o'clock train for a while, they sometimes had to let it go. Then the passengers, if any, from the GWR train had to wait until 6.50pm for the next!

When the clerk, whose place I had taken during the war, returned I was sent to Shapwick, further down the line. That was in 1946 I believe, and that was quite a bad winter. There weren't many passengers, but large consignments of peat to be waybilled. The booking office was quite large, and the only light was from an oil lamp, but it was quite comfortable, as once again there was a roaring coal fire. I remember that during that winter I caught the usual 10am train to Shapwick, but the snow was getting deeper, so I'm afraid I caught the next train back to Highbridge, as I didn't fancy spending the night at Shapwick.

Shortly after this a vacancy occurred at Highbridge Goods Office and I was transferred there, which was much more convenient, as by this time I had married Driver Maurice Cook and the goods office was quite near our home. Most of the goods traffic consisted of cattle cake, which the lorry drivers distributed to the many farms in the area. Of course there were also consignments of coal and timber from the wharf. Unfortunately for me, the cattle cake was my undoing. I developed asthma, and my doctor thought that the cattle cake dust was probably the cause of it, so I tendered my resignation.

Emily Poole, *booking clerk, Shepton Mallet, Somerset & Dorset Joint Railway*

I transferred from Evercreech New to the Goods Department, Shepton Mallet in 1942. My duties were accounts, invoicing all goods outwards, raising charges for them, including anything sent from Masbury. Stone was sent from local quarries, special goods trains from Masbury, with USA gasoline jerry cans for southern destinations. Food and stores were received for the Air Ministry and also for the small British naval base here, the military prison and US troops. I worked with the chief goods clerk, who was also captain in the Railway Home Guard.

Interesting to note, all stationery was buff colour. We did not have carbon paper, the accounts were handwritten, using purple copying ink, then at the end of the week, each statement was transferred to the 'flimsy ledger', a very heavy bound book which looked as if it was filled with tissue paper, by today's standards. The statement was placed on the left-hand side page, a flimsy page placed on top, then quickly a 2" wide brush dipped in water was liberally brushed over the flimsy (the statement was facing upwards underneath). The ledger was then closed, put into an iron and screwed down with a crossbar attached to the top, taken out later in the day, it would be dry, leave a perfect copy on the flimsy, the statement then forwarded to the customer. This ledger lasted many many years, very economical.

A vacancy then arose for a clerk in the passenger and parcels depts, and I was transferred, where I worked with Cecil Tulk, and then he retired soon after. Bob Gilham came and he was my colleague, we worked shifts and had twelve passenger trains per day. Passenger tickets were issued, enquiries, bookkeeping for all monies transacted. Parcels department, consisted of inwards and outwards parcel traffic, charged up same, racing pigeons to be released, forwarded Old English sheepdogs to America, handled young calves which had to be bound in sacking for travelling in the guard's van, despatched horses, which were put into a horse box and then attached to a passenger train. Also delivery sheets to be made out for the Scammell driver, Bill Cummins, for delivery of cheese and local parcels. We had cloakroom tickets, to be issued mostly for cycle storage, but we had to keep our eye on the school boys, as they used to try to dodge paying, and one mischievous boy, because I told him he had not paid, jumped in a large puddle of water which splattered over me and he ran off. And yet I met him twenty years later, and he apologised and said the incident worried him after and he was ashamed. The clerk also had to collect tickets from passengers alighting from the trains, so there were also plenty more enquiries, especially as we were situated a mile from town. Many girls from northern cities came to be land girls in Somerset. They would arrive at awkward times, sometimes they had to walk several miles to their farms, as there was no transport, or wait till the farmer came with a horse and cart.

The old red teapot and cups were always on the mantelpiece, no formalities here, the water had to be collected by crossing over the line to the water column, fill the kettle and put it on the open fire. The coal ration used to run short and we had to beg a little from the engine drivers. Derby coals were OK for heat but if it was Welsh coal no heat at all, it would hiss like the gas lighting we had, and that was turned down to half power by the gas company for economies. Our seating was high stools, which we sat on whilst doing our work, which was at a very large high lidded desk.

Mr G. Coles was the station master, till he retired and then Mr Hanger took his place. The station master collected the wages, but that was one of our duties, to dispense the wages for about forty men. The wages were placed in very small lidded tins, set on a tray, very handy for issuing out, when they all trooped into the office on Fridays. It included platform staff, signalmen, permanent way, and signal and telegraph departments.

We had the Public Records Office from London evacuated to the prison, all important documents were stored there, such as the Domesday Book, and when the war was over, they used our passenger parcels service to send neat discreet parcels to London from time to time. The custodian would come, book it in, wait for the train, to see that it was safe in the hands of the guard, who would take it to Templecombe, and then it would be transferred to the Waterloo train and met at the destination.

With our twelve passenger trains per day then, there were cheap day tickets issued to Bath, Burnham-on-Sea, Poole and Bournemouth. Business was good, and even a Sunday service to Bournemouth was introduced, helped to cheer people up after the long war years.

During all those years the books were regularly and meticulously checked. Everything had to balance, even if a halfpenny difference, it was taken forward to the next month, whether a debit or a credit. We had no adding machines, so it was mentally calculate, everything was handwritten. The different staffs were all hard working, happy, and pulled their weight whatever the weather, as we were situated quite high on the Mendip hills and it could be very very cold in the winter.

Men were called up for war service, got on a train probably for the first time, to some unknown destination, and the train ride was something they always remembered, whatever part of the world they were in, emotional partings from loved ones and happy homecomings. Country railways were a lifeline to villages and small towns, it brought work and prosperity, but that has all gone now. During the war, railways were noted as our first line of defence, people may not agree with this, but there was nothing else, except for bicycles, horses, and there was no petrol.

Theresa Roberts, *booking clerk, Midsomer Norton and Welton, Somerset & Dorset Joint Railway*

As a booking clerk I worked early and late shifts on alternate weeks, to cover all passenger trains. The early shift started at 7am and the late shift at 10am. On the early shift the first train was 7.38am, and on it went, without fail, the previous day's takings in a cash bag. We also did parcels and goods. The coal that went out from Norton Hill colliery kept me busy between trains, logging on blue invoices. The trucks to various firms ran on for a month, and at month's end they were totted up and transferred to other bills for payment. There were train time queries on the phone and at the ticket hatches, and tickets to collect off each train, and at month end, a little man round Midsomer Norton collecting from local small business people their monthly dues, I used to like that bit.

Edna Simms, *booking office clerk, Evercreech New Station, Somerset & Dorset Joint Railway*

In those days there were many searchlight battery soldiers stationed around Evercreech, on the high slopes and hills, at Batcombe, Westcombe and Alham. Sometimes our telephone would ring and a soldier would say he was going on leave and hoped to catch the next train. He had borrowed a bicycle and hoped to make it, and asked us to do what you can to hold the train, I'm just leaving. Well! you can imagine can't you, what to do for the best when the train arrived and no soldier! I would watch the goods yard entrance road and somebody would watch the little path that ran into the passenger entrance. The bicycle would be quickly abandoned and the gate held open and usually the soldier was lucky. Obviously there were times when we could not help these soldiers.

   In those days of food rationing we all seemed to be 'black marketeers' if you know what I mean. I had one or two friends who helped the food situation. I remember one morning (very dark and frosty) I left my home at Castle Cary (which was approximately five miles from Evercreech) on my bicycle, and hanging on the handlebars were four rabbits, and how I managed to cycle that distance with my 'cargo' I don't know. We used to exchange food items with one another when we could.

Mary Purell, *clerk, LNER Murrow*

The staff consisted of myself and another older clerk, Mr Bateman, and the stationmaster. It was a very busy office. The railway line ran from Peterborough to Great Yarmouth. The passenger trains called at all stations along the line. At the end of the day we had to balance the books down to the last ha'penny. Fortunately everyone would pull together to see that we did so. Every three months or so the auditors would arrive, without warning, to examine the books.

   When I started working in the office, it was impressed on me that the policy of the railway was that you accept any goods, from an elephant to a pin. Traffic, passenger traffic, we had lots of other goods. Potatoes, sugar beet in season. There were a lot of strawberries grown around the area. Merchants would hire a wagon and send them to London and the Midlands markets et cetera. There was also a lot of grain loaded. Farmers would hire the railway sacks for their corn. Each railway company had their own sacks. Ours were all stamped M&GN. That was the railway that I worked for. There was another station at Murrow, on the LNER line. We also always had to be careful that we did not accept their sacks when they were returned. Demurrage was charged on the hire of sacks.

   There was always a great excitement when the royal train went through on its way to Sandringham. The station was always spruced up. In those days, everyone took pride in their station. We always had a competition for the best-kept station. Flowers, et cetera, were set. I remember that every week the edge of the platform had to be whitened, as we still had a blackout. This was so that people could see when they were alighting from the trains.

A lot of troops travelling on the trains when I first started at Murrow. There was a great shortage of wagons for loading goods, as well as everything else. All tickets were written by hand, then pushed into a cylindrical date machine. The price had to be entered on every ticket.

There were three porters, as well as the lamp boy. The signal box was operated by three signalmen on a rota basis. There was a waiting room on both platforms. I remember the toilets were on the far side platform. The station itself was always busy with passengers, this was the only means of people travelling. There was only one bus that went to Wisbech on a Saturday. The people in the village were mainly employed on the land. Some caught the train to either Wisbech or Peterborough to work daily. There was a wonderful camaraderie amongst the staff from the stationmaster down. It was a lovely atmosphere to work in.

I used to cycle to work every day. Some days I had to be there to book passengers on the first train at seven o'clock. We took it in turns to do this. The M&GN was a single track in places, so the driver of the train could not proceed until he had the purse from the signalman [the purse was a kind of token used in railway signalling to secure single line working]. This was then passed on to the next signalman down the line. We inserted it into a special machine to clear the way for any trains coming in the opposite direction.

When we sent any freight wagons, they had to be clearly labelled with a destination, plus the route that they were to go. So you wrote 'via such-and-such'. This way we had to know our geography of the British Isles. Every year in February, we received a wagon loaded with sugar beet seed from the local beet factory in Peterborough. Some sacks only weighed a few pounds, depending on what acreage that had to be set. Each farmer had to be notified that the seed was in and ready for collection. The office was always busy with people sending parcels, et cetera. I didn't like it very much when they brought birds, fowl et cetera, tied by their legs with a label on, with their destination. In the summer people would send their friends strawberries. Again, with just a label tied to the handle. I often wondered what condition they would be in on their arrival, and how many would be left. Some people sent cartons of eggs to their relations on a weekly basis during the war.

There was a coal yard at the station. The coal merchants must have rented these facilities from the railway. There was also a big goods shed, that housed the railway sacks et cetera. Twice a year there was a special train that ran from Aberdeen to Great Yarmouth, with the fisher girls, who had come for the herring season. You could always hear them singing as they went through the station.

Murrow was unique in that it had a diamond crossing. That is, when two railways cross each other. I believe there were only two such in the country. The LNER from Spalding to March and the M&GN, called 'Muddled And Good For Nothing', that went from Peterborough to Great Yarmouth.

Dulcible Haines, *typist, LMS Watford*

And then I finished up in 1939 just before the war, in the Labour Establishment Office, this dealt with all the staff work over the railway. The war came in September 1939, and we were working in Euston, but we were then transferred to the Grove at Watford, during the war. Which was very nice, down there. I liked it. Being Watford, it was quite convenient for me. Because lots of the staff came from the other side of London, it wasn't so good. Particularly when they'd been up all night with air raids.

And I think the Grove had belonged to the Earl of Clarendon, or somebody like that. And it had been used after that I think as a school. But we took it over. And it was a big area, it's a lovely area. The railways had erected big huts for the staff, and it was lovely, because we got fresh vegetables. It had a nursery garden with several big greenhouses, and they'd been growing all sorts of lovely fresh vegetables and salads. And the railway kept it going. We were able to buy the stuff from it. So during the war those things were a bit scarce. We were quite lucky, it was so lovely to have the things all freshly picked. And they were so much nicer than anything you bought.

Oh, they had a canteen. They'd thought of everything. There was a canteen for us. They also ran buses from Watford Junction to Hempstead Road. The Grove in Hempstead Road. To take us to work. They thought of everything. They provided for us very, very well. The people over the other side of London, you know, it was a long journey for them. They used to grumble like mad. But for me in Watford it was nice. I could even walk there in those days, which was quite a long walk. But I could walk back as well, and I liked walking.

Well, soon after the war started, well, I suppose it must have been 1940 when they had Dunkirk, lots of men were taken prisoner. And the railway started the LMS prisoner of war fund. They appealed to the staff to give a penny a week to contribute to it. And of course I should imagine practically everybody did. There were a lot of staff. They had a lot of money. And we were able to write to the relatives and ask their permission to send a three-monthly parcel to these relatives at no cost to them. Cos we had plenty of money. And most of the people did agree to it. But of course some of them wanted to do it themselves. They loved them, and wanted to do it. So we understood. But we sent them a three-monthly parcel of warm clothing. Cos they needed it. There was long pants, long fleecy pants and vests and shirts and socks and everything. I think we were allowed a ten-pound parcel for them. And it used to be sent to London to the Red Cross, to make sure that nothing... they used to inspect it. Make sure everything was as it should be. It was sent over to the men. I mean, I think quite a few of the parcels were stolen obviously. But the men did write back and thank us. Because they were very grateful for the warm clothing and that, that we were able to send them. Anything they asked for, we tried to get for them. For instance, they often wanted military badges, cos they were very proud of their regiments. Small musical instruments like the Jew's harp. And anything small that could go through. They were also allowed cigarettes and tobacco. Goodly amounts of that, which was sent, we paid for and sent. Sent them when they wanted it. But I think they were quite grateful. Because they did get everything they wanted that was allowed.

Surviving Air Raids

I saw York bombed. That were the night I saw York bombed. We just went on our break, our suppers. We come on at ten and we said, 'We'll go and have a drink,' and we went and had a drink and there was an aeroplane going round we said, 'Oh, that's a Jerry.' So we went to what was number four platform, I could see York Minster was all lit up because he were dropping incendiary bombs and he managed to drop some bombs – some incendiaries on a train that was coming into York. He hit it at Colton Lane first. Smashed all the glass on it, and they were dropping them on the station. They were putting them out as they were dropping them, you know. We had the fire thing we kept and squirted 'em when they dropped them.

(Nellie Nelson, LNER porter, York)

A woman's decision to apply for railway work meant that she was frequently putting herself in danger. Railway stations were a prime target for German air-raids, vulnerable to serious damage which affected vital services. But the railway companies responded rapidly to meet the needs of the service. In their 1943 publication *Facts about British Railways in Wartime*, the British Railway Press Office proudly reported that they could very quickly restore damage to engines and trains from high explosives and incendiaries. They boasted that their rapid repair organisations could renew main line tracks within a few hours and, amazingly, restore bridges and signal boxes in a day, using standard bridge spans and extra steam breakdown cranes at the ready. In some cases shuttle bus services were arranged within minutes, to divert perishable goods traffic such as foodstuffs and newspapers.[1]

Women had a tough time working under these circumstances, often having moved from other towns and cities such as Birmingham or London, where their houses had been destroyed by bombing. Sometimes they were able to move to areas where their husbands were stationed. At Chaddesden Sidings, 41-year-old Christina Axworthy, the first LMS woman wagon examiner, was working with her goods checker husband at Derby LMS after being bombed out of their London home.[2]

Other women had to take strategic action to carry out their jobs in these conditions. During air-raids on Paddington, the telephone girls at the GWR Central Enquiry Bureau reverted to an 'under the counter' service, when they had to curl up under desks to answer phones.[3] A press report in 1943 described how women railway workers avoided machine gun fire when enemy aircraft attacked a 'south east of England inland town' in daylight.[4]

Heroic acts were celebrated: railwaywoman Mrs Kelly walked several miles in the middle of the night to open up her station during a bomb attack, and worked with others to ensure safe opening the next day.[5] A carriage cleaner, Mrs Ethel Lee, had been a stewardess on a cross channel ferry which travelled across to Dunkirk to rescue survivors. When the ferry was bombed, Ethel refused to get into the lifeboat until all the other women on board had been saved, at which point a bomb blast capsized the boat. She was in the water for an hour and a half before being rescued, but luckily she was a strong swimmer.[6] A Lloyds War Medal for bravery was presented to Miss E.M. Owen, GWR Stewardess, following the bombing of SS *St Patrick* in June 1941, possibly the first woman on the staff of GWR to get such a medal.[7]

Women seemed to accept the difficulties and dangers of bomb damage. LNER porter Nellie Nelson's bike was destroyed in the bomb raid on York Station. Booking office clerk Edna Simms had a near miss under machine gun fire on the platform at Evercreech. Dorothy Crawford tells of the housekeeper at the Adelphi Hotel in Liverpool, playing whist during air raids and returning to play her hand after checking for casualties. Betty Chalmers and female colleagues operated their replacement York switchboard in a shelter under the bar walls, in abnormally hot, unventilated conditions. Even getting to work was a problem for LMS shorthand typist Doris Maley, travelling between Broad Street and Southend during raids. The Liverpool blitz hit the railway offices where goods clerk Doreen Dickenson worked and, as in the case of many railway workers, they were temporarily housed in railway carriages. Irene Barrett-Locke left Paddington Station because of the dangers of air-raids, but decided to return because she was bored.

Dorothy Crawford, housekeeper, *LMS Adelphi Hotel, Liverpool*

In September 1939 I was on holiday. I enjoyed my holiday in Cornwall, except that I stood all the way from London to Glasgow, full of troops, and then got home all right and they announced the beginning of the war on the following day. I stayed home and had my week there and went back and found that the rest of the staff had been absolutely run ragged. They were making blackout curtains or painting the windows that didn't have curtains, so that every room was black from the outside. I think they boarded up a good many of them.

There were 16 successive bombing raids on Liverpool in 1941. The hotel had terrible damage in the coffee shop. The whole side of the hotel really had, was a mess after that. There were several people killed. I think Liverpool people were the nicest I've ever had to work with. I can tell you the names of most of the staff that were there in 1939, '40, '41, partly because of course we gathered together very much more because we were bombed, and spending nights in shelters. We were lucky, we got the Turkish baths' couches. Somebody was supposed to walk round all afterwards, to make sure that everything was all right. Eventually we got so blasé when the bombs were going off that the manager and the head housekeeper and two other housekeepers used to play solo whist and she went round the rooms and made sure that everybody was all right and came back and took her hand the next time.

It was a landmine. They were aiming for Lime Street Station and they hit in between, so that we got most of the windows blown out and quite a bit of damage due to the broken glass and so on. Half the hotel had its doors smashed. All one side of the hotel nearest the station. I was lucky my bedroom was on the other side. And we'd just walked out of the housekeeper's office, otherwise we would have had the window smashed in on us. We had to tour round and knock all the lights out that were on, in case another bomber came and wanted to bomb us again.

When we had the landmine the grill room and everything was ... the troops came in the following morning to help to clean up. The morning after it actually, the manager arranged for us all to have our breakfast in the French restaurant. All staff, just as if nothing had happened, well except we were in the best room and when the soldiers came they got out a roast of beef and all the soldiers had a jolly good lunch of roast beef, sitting in the corridors all along with their plates handed into them.

Florence Brinklow, *parcels delivery, LNER London Kings Cross*

An unexploded bomb near the picture house in King's Cross. And Joe's van actually went into the hole. Joe's Scammell actually touched the hole where the unexploded bomb was down the hole. Frightened the life out of us, me and my old mate Ivy, we'd just finished work. I waited a couple of minutes for her. And we was walking up the slope that's at the side of number one, that leads onto York Way. And over on the right hand side was the Legion Poppy Factory. We was going past there and they dropped a bomb, it couldn't have been far from there, because we were smothered in debris. As we were walking up that slope, there was a wall, to get out onto York Way. And I think if we'd been at the top we might have been really hurt. But I think it was the wall that covered us, more or less.

Irene Barrett-Locke née Davies, *refreshment rooms, GWR Paddington, London*

Those lovely shops, selling gorgeous fruit and artificial flowers, it was wonderful. I loved it. And it was more exciting when the war came and there was a blackout of course. Because you were doing something very exciting, even to be on the station, which was jolly dangerous then, when they started to bomb. All round Edgware Road, Suffolk Gardens, Sussex Gardens and all round there, absolutely wiped out some of the places. It all revolved around the station then. I lived in the girls' dormitory, Westbourne Grove.

I left for a few months. I came home because the bombing was terrible really, and I had met my RAF husband who was then at St Athan, and he insisted that, with the bombings so intense, when the docks were hit or ablaze. And I remember from Paddington, seeing the sky blood red, where the West Indian docks had been bombed and were flaming up. It was really quite dreadful. One side of Sussex Gardens had a landmine and been completely taken away. So that Paddington Station was in a very, very dangerous position then. Everything total blackout, everything changing then. You know, it was war, so it was different and all the men in uniform, it was pretty terrible then. So this boy I had met who was at St Athan wrote and said, 'I want you to leave London, because you know, Paddington Station will be hit, there's no doubt about it.' So I went back for a couple of weeks and I got so bored and so fed up I thought I'd rather face the bombs any day. So I went back, but I didn't go back to the station. I got a job with Lyons, the Corner House.

Maureen Evans, *messenger then clerk, LMS Crewe*

It was 1944 and we'd had plenty of air raids, but I remember either an air raid warning or the sound of a buzz-bomber coming over. I was cycling to work one morning, or cycling from the station, and I can remember pedalling like mad because there was a bridge just by the Carriage and Wagon Department. I can remember jumping off my bike and sheltering under this railway bridge. So whether there was a buzz-bomber or whether it was an air raid warning or whether it was my imagination, I'm not quite sure at this stage in the game. But there was something that happened on this one particular occasion. Of course everywhere had got blackout blinds, going up to the station, of course the station would have been all blacked out during the war.

Betty Chalmers, *telegraph office, LNER York*

1942. Well, the bombing – we were on the station [at York]. Fortunately I wasn't on duty, but there was one girl on duty and three men, and apparently the bomb hit the station. They'd already put a thick concrete thing on our glass roof, which was stupid of course, but they thought it was to save us, keep the light out as well. Two o'clock in the morning of course, they hit the station, because that was an important thing to do, and to my knowledge it's the only time that York station was closed for two days while they cleared the rubbish because it was terrible. So I cycled into work next morning, dodging broken glass and, carrying my bicycle, got to work, no office, completely destroyed. But they had taken the precaution, two or three years earlier, of putting a duplicate switchboard in the shelter under the bar walls.

They'd put a duplicate switchboard there, which they switched over to every night and that's partly why we had to work nights, because we needed an extra one, on the switchboard. So that was a godsend because the other one was completely destroyed. And when I got to the office, amid the rubble, the boss was there and the girls were sorting out wet railway tickets. The water had come in over the booking office, and of course, there was nothing for us to do, nothing, and my mother was ill so he said, 'Well, I think you'd better go home for a day or two,' which I did, very good.

The board was kept going, they hastily got teleprinters from such places as West Hartlepool and Middlesbrough, places that weren't as busy as us, and they managed to put them in the shelter. We were in a corridor [under the wall]. It was awful, and they were there for nearly two years, until they cleared some of the muniment rooms in the new offices. That was the bombing, April 1942. The board was all right, the switchboard was all right. It was terribly hot in there, the air conditioning was rough, so in the middle of winter when you got there, you got down to your bikini nearly, not quite in those days, but nevertheless it was happy. The control were in there, they made a lot of fuss of us girls. There was a central control and a district control, the central control was obviously the main one, the district would be this area, the north-eastern area. Yes and the District Intelligence they were down there, so we just had to be in the corridor. They were very good because we were on our own. They'd say, 'Do you want something to eat?' And we had a little kitchen and they would give us something or make us something, or the messenger would go over to the canteen if we wanted it and brought it over. It was terrible, no windows, and it was hot it was, when you went in on a winter's morning about six o'clock, oh. You were so cold cycling down, but you know you got used to it.

There was no toilet. Ah, well now this was tricky, because we had to go, we had to go through the central control, and as you went through they held their hand out for a penny! And we were only quite young but we just had to put up with it, that was all, and in those days, of course, things were, you weren't so free with people. And then I, during my time on the switchboard, I was working in the office normally, but it was my turn on the switchboard and there was a group of Royal Engineers stationed in York. They had come back from France and they were a railway construction company, and some of them started ringing up the girls, realising there were girls on the switchboard, and I know a few of my friends did, and I used to say, 'No, I'm not doing a thing like that.' However, one night this Scotsman came on and he said, 'I'm a Scotsman from Wales.' I married that man three years later!

Doris Maley, *shorthand typist, LMS Broad St, London*

The journey to work was always difficult. We didn't really know how far we were going by the train. It was all right the Southend part going, but when we got to Barking or further afield, well when we got to Upminster you began to see the results of bombing. Sometimes we were turned out at Dagenham or Barking and we had to find our own way to Broad Street. But often there was a lorry waiting, and we were lucky, sometimes got a lift, I think I was nearly always pretty lucky to get a lift, but otherwise it was extremely difficult to get to work. But I don't remember any time when we failed to turn up at some hour. Often we might not turn up till dinnertime, but we would leave home at the proper time. Going back was just as bad except it was dark and we had to put our suit-cases up against the window to protect ourselves, but the carriage was in total darkness, and not once did I come across anybody who abused it. It was really quite good fun, it was friendly. I suppose it was mostly women, and young girls, and towards the end we had two or three 17-year-olds we used to travel with and they were very good. Sometimes we'd play cards on the train.

You know it wasn't wonderful, there was a lot of stops and starting and you did wonder if you were going to get home, but of course when you got to the station to get home, having shown your pass to get out of the station and be allowed to be in Southend … if the siren went when you were walking down the road, bad luck! And mostly I found my mother and the cat and dog in the air-raid shelter, and I'd have to have a meal or whatever we had down there, but invariably it was straight down to the air-raid shelter. Later on, when I worked in Southend, twice a week I would have to, I was in the Red Cross and St John's in the war, and I used to do nursing at the hospital two nights a week and then go straight back to work after I'd finished night duty, so we worked quite hard.

It was very difficult during the war. There were a lot of women employed in the goods yard rather than men. And being a first aider I was always on duty and the women always seemed to be pushing barrows and hurting themselves, so I was often called away from work to deal with them. If there was an air raid, as we were vulnerable, we had to go down flights of stairs into the bowels of the earth where there were vaults, warehouses for wool and tea. And we were down there for quite a time. We had to take our typewriters down with us so that they would always have a typewriter.

We had bombs in the high street but they never actually bombed Southend, but we did have a plane come over spraying us with, with shells and bullets and, what d'you call them. But we had nowhere to go, at all, we just had to sit in the office.

Irene Adgie, *SR typist at Waterloo and Woking*

Woking wasn't that far from London. It was on the edge of the raid area. But of course the line went up into London. And there was still night-time bombing at that time, when I started. So there would be bombs dropped on the line during the night. One incident I remember very vividly was when there had been a fog. Thick fog. And a train was delayed because the guard had had to climb the signal pole to see the signal. It was one of the old semaphore signals.

About reports. ...anything that delayed trains in any way. It had to be available for the District Superintendent's telephone conference with the Superintendent of Operations, who was based at Dorking for, I think it was 10 o'clock in the morning. There were nine copies of each report, all with carbon paper in between. And we had to be accurate, because we didn't have time to stop and rub out.

Before the end of the war, we'd had a lull in the bombing. And then the doodlebugs started. And that of course did a lot of damage on the railways because quite a number did land there [near Woking]. But they were mainly ones that had cut short, before they reached London, which was their target. But I do remember the first night that they came over. I was in bed and I think I was sharing the room with the evacuee then. And we heard a lot of small arms fire. And I said, 'What's that?' And the evacuee said, 'They're playing soldiers.' Because we were very near Pirbright and various other army camps. And the next day we found that it was the first doodlebugs coming over and the army didn't really know what was happening, and they were letting off small arms at these things. But we knew very well after that just what doodlebugs were. It was the only time, that time, was when I had to go down the shelter at work. I think about twice we had to, because there was one so close. But we were very lucky. We didn't get hit ourselves. And the Woking area generally, things fell in the fields and the woods and the commons around. There was very little damage.

Doreen Dickenson, *goods clerk, LMS Liverpool*

We were blitzed, in the early... before the May blitz, there were incendiaries on that warehouse. And the young lads, and some of the older men, who were in the Home Guard, used to have their Home Guard uniform. They used to call them the LDV, Local Defence Volunteers they were at first. Then they became the Home Guard. And they learned rifle shooting and that. And they used to go and shoot the rats in the warehouse, you see. Well many a time they'd got on the roof and put the incendiaries out, and things like that, otherwise the warehouse must have gone up.

Anyway, it got a direct hit in the May blitz. And by that time my father had met this friend who had the boarding house in Southport. And she said, 'Look,' she said, 'I've got a couple of rooms. Would you and Nelly like to come out, if it's only for a weekend, and have a couple of nights' sleep? We don't bother about the bombing up there.' And it's only a fraction, in an aeroplane, a split second, to drop a bomb in the wrong place. So we went out there. We left our house here. And the local Home Guard here put a few incendiaries out on our roof. But it was never really damaged other than that. And of course we travelled to work on the train of a morning.

So the night of the May blitz, we stood on the promenade at Southport, outside our house by the Floral Hall, and watched that place being bombed. We watched Liverpool being bombed. It was absolutely a nightmare. And all of a sudden there was one huge explosion that didn't [get] put out or die down. My father said, 'That's the match factory.' And he was right, it was the match factory. That was Bryant & May's, where he worked. And so that was a Saturday night. So we were devastated. We thought, 'What are we going to go back to, if that was the match factory?' I was working at Canada Dock. We'd no idea what had happened. So we went out early. On the Sunday, Netty, the girl I'd started work with from Birkdale, her father came round to our house on a bicycle. We didn't have cars in those days. And he said, 'Netty doesn't know her way around.' He said, 'She's got to go and try to go to... can we meet you somewhere and can we travel with you on Monday morning?' So my father and Netty and I, we all met under the clock at Southport station at about half past seven in the morning. Because we had to try and get some kind of a train.

We were due in half past eight, those days. It was only half an hour on the train. Well, we stood on that station with crowds and crowds of people. And there weren't any trains, I think we were there until about nine o'clock, I should think. And eventually a train came through and we got on it. And it went as far as Waterloo South Road, which is a station up the line, nearer Southport than Seaforth. And we all got out there, like refugees. There were people in bowler hats and pinstriped trousers with their briefcases. There were scruffy old dockers and kids and oh, there was everybody. And youngsters like us, just starting work. And we walked then along the road towards Seaforth station. And when we got near Seaforth Station, then we saw the dereliction. There were bricks all over the place. Part of the warehouses had come down. We walked past Gladstone Dock, Langton Dock, Alexander Dock, and then Canada. And we walked along the road just, just crocodiles, straggling like, the pair of us were crying our eyes out. We just didn't know what kind of a world we'd come to, that we'd got into.

And when we got to Canada Dock, part of the overhead was down, just broken in the middle, on the floor. The water mains were burst. And you couldn't get across the road because about three foot of running water had... the road had caved in and it was one puddle, and cobblestones they were, in those days. Well the fellows from Canada Dock, the checkers and the Home Guard that had been on duty that night, and all that, they carried us over the water. They carried a lot of the women over the water. Some of the fellows took their shoes off and rolled their trousers up and waded through. It was a world we'd never known before. We were only kids, at 16, we were only kids. And there wasn't really an office to report to. But when we got there, some of the staff were there and Mr Umpleby. And the chief foreman. The chief foreman was a fellow called Andy Campbell. Oh, he was a great big hefty brass. But he was a lovely man really. But there was no nonsense out of him. And every other word was a swear word. It was a 'bloody this' and a 'bloody that' and whatever.

We carried on and walked a bit further and we walked past Huskisson Dock and Sandon Dock and we walked right into town, to Waterloo Dock. And really and truly it was just patches and patches of brickwork and broken roads. They'd had a good go at the docks that day. We got to Waterloo Dock warehouse, which was still standing, and Great Howard Street Warehouse on the other, cos they'd seemed to do from that end towards Seaforth. They didn't do much, the Liverpool side. And fortunately they never did get the Liver buildings or the India buildings. I don't know what preserved them, but they were very good about that. So we got to Waterloo Dock warehouse, and we reported there to the staff office there. Well, by this time it's one o'clock. And we had our butties. They gave us a cup of tea. We sat there for half an hour, told them what had happened. And I'm afraid we were weepy. Feel a bit of a fool now, you know, but I mean, you can't help it. And then they said, 'Right, well, you'd better get on going home again.'

I think we went in the next day. But because Canada Dock had been hit, and half the warehouse had gone or something, they got us railway trains in the yard at Canada Dock passenger station. And we worked in the carriages. But apart from that, we got home that day from Waterloo Dock on the back of a coal wagon. You see, the local traders and the local lorries and everything, they were very good. They came round to pick people up and try and get them to their destinations. Well, you know the coal wagons, the back tail dropped down, that sort of thing. They covered them with newspapers, and old sacks, or whatever it was. And we sat on the side, we sat on sacks of coal, covered with things, and were driven to Waterloo Station, where we went home again, Netty and I. It was a Monday morning, I know, because the Saturday night was the blitz and we went on the Monday. And we got home. I think we were a few days, I think they said to us, 'You'd better stay off for a few days and we'll let you know.' Whether we got a letter or whether we rang. We weren't on the phone. I think we must have rung somebody or something. Because we came in and there were railway coaches for us to sit in. And they put the switchboard in the railway coaches.

The switchboard was fine, you can get the wireless on the switchboard. You got the local radio. Well, we were there for a couple of months and they went on fire. We got incendiaries there. When the railway wagons, the coaches went on fire, we had to go to Edge Hill. Now the trains weren't very good, because they only went as far as Waterloo for ages. They never repaired the line for donkey's ages. Waterloo LMS on the Southport line. So we went on the old Cheshire Lines railway, which was the old steam railway, we used to call it, from Cheshire Lines station which is the south end of Lord Street, near the Garrick Theatre.

But we got the train from there. And it took an hour and a half to get to Edge Hill. So we were only in Edge Hill office for a month or so, and then we came back to the coaches. We came to Canada Dock when we'd got the office set up. We had about three railway coaches. And we were in this shipping office there, doing invoices and all that kind of thing.

Nellie Nelson, *porter, LNER York*

I saw York bombed. That were the night I saw York bombed. We just went on our break, our suppers. We come on at ten and we said, 'We'll go and have a drink,' and we went and had a drink and there was an aeroplane going round we said, 'Oh, that's a Jerry.' So we went to what was number four platform. I could see York Minster was all lit up because he were dropping incendiary bombs and he managed to drop some bombs – some incendiaries on a train that was coming into York. He hit it at Colton Lane first. Smashed all the glass on it, and they were dropping them on the station. They were putting them out as they were dropping them, you know. We had the fire thing we kept and squirted 'em when they dropped them.

They said, 'Shall we bring the train in?' And then they decided to bring the train into the station, because you've got to look at the passengers first, you've got to get them to safety. So we got the passengers, most of them off the train. There was one was all cut in bits where there was flying glass, and I was wiping it off. I had a bag full of wet cotton wool in one pocket and dry cotton wool in the other pocket to wipe them off with. And we had a foreman called Billie Milne and he was with the accident and ambulance service and he said, 'I'm going back for some more sticky tape to 'em'. I said, 'Oh I'll come with you.' He said, 'No you stick with them lot,' so of course I stuck with them lot. I'm here now, because he was taken when that bomb dropped on York Station you see.

The passengers that were injured got off. There was a few killed on the train but they were got off and away. The bomb dropped about four o'clock and we stopped [till] about seven o'clock and I had a pal my mate with me, she was a little lass and she lived on Leeman Road and she said, 'Let's go see what they've done up Leeman Road,' and they'd dropped bombs on Leeman Road as well you see. They'd taken the coal thing at Leeman Road and they let the horses, they used to have horses then to take parcels down, and the horses were running wild, they'd let the horses out.

I biked to work and I lost me bike that night. It was in the left luggage office and the whole lot went up, the left luggage office went up. Well we didn't go the next night for two or three nights, because we were frightened to death. Because you know he said he were going to take all the cathedral towns in England and he took Canterbury and he took Liverpool didn't he? He bombed them. One at Coventry as well, he bombed all that lot and saw... oh well York was left, and so he bombed York that night.

We had a telegraph office, the telegraphers were under the City board, you had to go round the old station to get to it, the old station to get into it you know. And we could hear them up above click, click, clicking. They were machine gunning round the following night or two. Machine guns were going round and they said on Bootham you could see where all the machine guns had hit all the house, hit all the houses.

Gladys Garlick, *guard, LNER London*

About a V2 incident in 1944. Well, it happened around teatime. I'd been up to C&A's in London with my mother. And I came back to go on duty. We were a bit late getting to Palmer's Green, and as we draw into Palmer's Green station, the train went... So I put on the handbrake. And I don't suppose that made any difference. But I automatically put the handbrake on. Anyway, we came to a stop. And I got out of the train and the first thing I saw was the two porters, there was two sisters that were porters at Palmer's Green station. And their porter's room was under a bridge across the platforms. So it was where the guard's brake was. And they came up covered in soot, because the soot from the chimneys had come down and they were absolutely black. So we didn't really know what had happened.

And as I walked along, there was paving stones on the roof of the train. And glass, and all sorts of things all over the place, you know. And cos it was dark, darkish, so you know, it was bit of a muddle, as it were. And I'm gradually walking along. It took me about an hour, I think, to get from my train brake down to the engine. And the only person that I can remember was badly injured was a girl. And she had a nasty cut on her head. And there was nobody about. So I went up onto the road and there was an ambulance. I said, 'Oh, well I've got a badly injured person, can you come and pick her up?' And they said, 'Oh, we can't come onto the railway, it's private property.' So they gave me a stretcher.

One of those with two poles and material in between. They gave me that to take down to the station. They wouldn't come. So I took that down. We got her onto the platform, onto the stretcher, and I got two passengers to take her up to the ambulance. So I never really saw the going of her, cos I stayed downstairs. But I never know why they refused to come really, because you know, it seemed a bit strange. Whether they didn't want to see a bad sight or what, I don't know. But they said they couldn't come down, it was private property.

I made my way along, helping people out, and various things. Got down to the driver and fireman. He looked very shocked. He was very white. And the hole was huge at the bottom, front of the train. You could have got a bus in it quite easily, a double-decker bus quite easily in it. It was huge. And I don't remember going home. I must, they must have put buses on. But I can't remember that. I suppose I was in a bit of a shock myself. Can't remember that at all. But the next thing I remember, we were the first train over the hole. They'd filled it up in a day, and we were the first train over the next day.

In front of the engine. If we'd have been on time, we would have been leaving and I probably wouldn't be here today. Because it would have hit the train completely.

Norah Cook, *passenger clerk, Highbridge, Somerset & Dorset Joint Railway*

One day the war came a bit too close. There was a search light battery at Highbridge and a German plane machine-gunned down the beam. When I got to the station the next morning for work, I noticed there were bits chipped out of the stone footbridge. One of the carriage doors was also smashed. At that time there were loads of American troops around. They more or less took over the loco. They had sidings there, where I think they kept all the stores and ammunition. I often wondered if that was what the Germans were after that particular evening.

Edna Simms, *booking office clerk, Evercreech New Station, Somerset & Dorset Joint Railway*

One morning will always remain in my memory of railway experiences. I had opened the waiting room door to go onto the platform from my office, and imagine my surprise when the porter on duty gave me a backward push and I landed on the waiting room floor with him falling on top of me. The reason being, a German bomber was machine-gunning the line right through the station and we were so lucky to be inside.

Tricky Situations

During the war the trains were bumper to bumper, there was no space at all. And at that time in a morning the wagon tappers were out. I would stand and I would call, hoping that there was somebody in that cabin, but very very often there wasn't. So how did I get all that information? I used to stand down, between the wagons and listen very very carefully because of course, as soon as a train started to move its chains started clanking. And if everything was deathly quiet, I'm under the wagon, to get that information. To this day I feel apprehensive at the thought of it all.

(Mary Hodgson, LMS clerk Chesterfield)

Young women found themselves in new jobs, responding to entirely new scenarios, without any experience to guide them. After just a few weeks young porter Betty Spiller, at Evercreech, had to cycle four miles to a local branch line station and look after it in the absence of a sick man. Clerk Mary Hodgson had to stand down between the wagons to collect information about goods wagons, hoping the train wouldn't move off. Clerk Maureen Evans found herself challenging an overtime instruction, a decision which came back to haunt her years later. Sadly LMS clerk Georgina Huber was sacked on the spot one day because of her Austrian father.

In 1944 three LNER women workers at Ecclesfield near Sheffield managed to save a dangerous situation in their lunch hour by hitching a runaway barrage balloon to some stationary railway wagons, to stop it hitting a local foundry works. The trailing wire ropes had also been in danger of hitting a nearby passenger train.[1] In July 1945 booking clerk Ida Luff, wife of the St Helier stationmaster, was applauded for her bravery in rescuing a boy from the live line at Carshalton. She made sure the current was cut off and then grabbed some rubber gloves to rescue him, but unfortunately he did not survive.[2]

Passenger guard Phyllis Parsons, who worked from Templecombe on the Somerset & Dorset Joint Railway, had an extremely fraught experience just after the war. The Bath Road Viaduct, north of Shepton Mallet, had been widened when the line was doubled, and during a gale in February 1946 one half of the viaduct collapsed, reducing the line to single line working until the viaduct was rebuilt in August 1946. After the collapse Phyllis remembered, 'we were the next train after the goods safely got over, returned to Templecombe safely on a goods. We were soon going over again on the single line... the other rail was hanging.'[3]

Betty Spiller, *porter then lampman, Evercreech Junction, Somerset & Dorset Joint Railway*

I'd been on the railway a few weeks, so they said to me, 'There's nobody out at Pylle station,' which was the branch line from Evercreech Junction to Burnham-on-Sea, 'You go out there and see to it.' I said, 'I don't know really anything about it.' And they said, 'Oh, you'll be alright, go on.' So I cycled from Evercreech New to Evercreech Junction every day, and cycled off about four miles to Pylle station.

And the person there was off sick apparently. Blackouts were up, I mean I didn't know how to get the blackouts down but I managed it eventually. Only person there, and I only been on the railway six weeks! 16. And I was out there for the day. It's a very tiny station in a hamlet, not very busy, I suppose they thought, 'Well, she'll manage.'

Two passenger trains in the morning, a couple of freight, two more in the afternoon and a late train at night. And I got out there, I didn't see anybody for half the morning. Went up the signal box and there were tomatoes and chrysanthemums growing up there. It was a one-man station, the man always ran it, but of course he was sick, so later on when the morning train came in I had one passenger get off from Glastonbury, didn't see anybody else very much. During the afternoon the phone rang and somebody said, 'I want to go up to Manchester, how do I get there?' So I directed them that you went into Evercreech Junction, time of the train and what train you got, you got the 'Pines Express', and they said, 'Now I want to come back, and how much is first class?' And I thought, 'Well, this is a bit beyond me, I haven't got any timetables.' So I said, 'Well, I think you ought to ring Evercreech Junction and get the full details.' And there was a lot of giggling at the other end. That was only the other ones at Evercreech Junction having a game.

So the afternoon train came in, it went at four o'clock. About five o'clock a farmer came in, with about fifty rabbits he wanted to send to Crystal Palace, so

I had to weigh them, stamp them up. I got that done, and I rang the station at Evercreech Junction. And I was started at eight and I should've gone home at five, so they said, 'Oh, well you'll have to wait for the milk train,' which came through at half past seven, 'and put them on.' So I waited, I put the blackouts up, and I waited. Didn't see anything, didn't hear anything. About eight o'clock I rang the north box at Evercreech Junction and I said, 'Where's the milk train?' And they said, 'About Wincanton by now, I should think,' that was way down the line. And I said, 'Well how did it go through and I didn't know, I've got fifty rabbits here for Crystal Palace?' So they said, 'Well you'll have to stay there and wait for the last up.' Nobody, you know, thought in those days to enquire if I was alright, or anything else!

I remember, I think it was about 1944, it rained and froze. As the rain came down it froze, at that time, and I remember seeing icicles on the telegraph wires and sometimes it was so heavy the wires came down, and the ladders were iron and they were wet and I remember climbing one of the ladders and holding on to the rails while I did the lamps. When I went to lift me hands off they were frozen on. I had gloves on mind. And it was so cold that everything froze in the lamp house, and they moved me into the weigh room for a bit because there was a fireplace in there. That winter was so cold. And very often if I'd gone out and got really wet, if there was an engine in on the turntable in the marshalling yard, I used to get up on the engine and stand in front of the firehole doors to dry out. The steam used to come off my clothes, and I remember one of the drivers saying, he said, 'Carry on like that and you'll be out with rheumatism by the time you're thirty.' And one day I stood in front of the firehole doors, with me back to them, and the driver went to move and he shoved the regulator over and we got a back draft, and the fire shot out of the firebox and singed the back of me hair.

Edith Stretch, *booking office clerk, LMS Hanley*

The Grand Hotel's opposite the railway station. And we had a theatre in Hanley. Well, some of the Shakespearean actors used to stay at the Grand Hotel. The page boys used to come across with money, and they wanted a ticket to so-and-so, and I'd get them all ready, put them in an envelope. No cheques. I'd never seen a cheque. But this time the ticket collector was coming in, he was bringing a chappie in. Big tall man. A cloak on. A trilby hat, turned up at the sides, you know. He only wanted a feather and he'd have been with *Gone With The Wind*. Anyhow the ticket collector, Alf, he says, 'He says he wants for you to find about tickets.' And I thought, 'Well, they usually come to the grille, the front.' So he must have been somebody important. I've forgotten who he was, but anyhow I asked him where he wanted to go and I told him how much it'd be. And he gave me a fifty pound note. Well, I nearly, I'd got no money. The station master had been to the bank and taken all the money. Cos they never left you much in. But I'd never seen a fifty pound note. It was white and beautiful. And I said, 'Well, I'm sorry, I can't give you the change.' I said, 'But you're at the Grand, aren't you?' He said, 'Yes.' I said, 'Well, I'll get you the change, and I'll get your ticket, and I'll bring it across.' This was all in overtime, cos I'd finished my shift by then. So we had a big store in Hanley. And I rang the cashier up. I said, 'I've got a bit of a dilemma.' I said, 'I've got a fifty pound note I want changing. None of the banks are open.' Cos it was Saturday afternoon. And she said, 'Well, I can change it for you.' She says, 'Are you coming up now?' And I said, 'Yes.' And I told her what it was all about. I said, 'Some daft bloke's given me this and I've got no change.' So I went up. And course they took me right up to the top of the store, where the cashiers was. She says, 'Have you got any identity?' I said, 'I've just ran up here, you know.' I said, 'Well, ring the station up.' I said, 'And the other booking clerk'll tell you what I'm like.' So she gave me the change and I went back.

Marjorie Pateman, *lathe operator, LMS Wolverton works*

Well, my brother-in-law, we were all courting in those days you see, and my brother-in-law and my sister, we went up to Blackpool. Course I'd just come off night work you see, and I wasn't very sort of with it, well, it was dark and there wasn't many lights or anything about, cause it was still the war. But anyway, they got me on the big dipper, which they would never have got me on if I hadn't been half asleep and not knowing, and it was the most dreadful experience I've ever had. And when we came back from the weekend, my sister and I slept together, and the two brothers slept together, 'cause there wasn't any of the other sort of sleeping together in those days. And then when we came back my husband was always very insistent on getting the times of the trains, but my brother-in-law wasn't, so we got to the station when we thought my brother-in-law said that we'd be all right. When we get there we can't get on the trains, there's no trains all night, and there's no food, because the soldiers are on the station, and they must have the food, so you can't buy sandwiches from the buffet or drinks, nothing. My sister-in-law had a fur coat, and looked very posh, we don't know where to go, so we go into the gods, because we haven't got much money, at the cinema, and my sister-in-law sits up in the gods in her fur coat, in the cheap seats ... all we could eat was peanuts, and we arrived back next morning on the train at six o'clock in the morning, so that was a very eventful weekend in the wartime.

Florence Brinklow, *parcels delivery, LNER Kings Cross*

One night I was sitting on the tailboard of a van. Inside was a coffin draped with the Union Jack. A young airman with his cap and his bag on the top. And Ivy was late and her driver was waiting for her. She sat on the tailboard of the van.

And as she got up, we used to have coats that had buckles, and the buckle got caught on the tailboard. Her screams were so loud it made her bad. It made me bad as well. I had to take her home. Now my driver, he said to me, 'When you come back, after you've took her home, meet me at Euston Station.' Well, I had to take her to Edward Square. That was up Caledonian Road. And I took her home and I thought, 'I've got to get back to Euston now'. See, he'd already gone from King's Cross on his own to Euston. And I had to go back there myself. Walk. And as I was walking up Euston Road, a sailor asked me the way to Euston Station. As we walked past, there was a hospital on the right-hand side. I think it was called Elizabeth Garrett Anderson. And he turned round for no reason at all and smashed me straight in the mouth. And he knocked two of my front teeth out. There was two paratroopers coming, and they picked me up and one of them ran after the sailor. I don't think he got him. Anyway he took me home, I remember that. And my grandma... they was very strict on having men near the house, you know. Never no fellas near the house at all. And of course when he rang the bell, he took me home, this soldier, paratrooper. When my uncle, who also lived with us, opened the door he said, 'What's going on?', he said. So he said, 'This young lady's just been attacked. I've brought her home.' Well of course they asked the fella in, you know. And he left my grandma with a rosary and he said, 'When I come back,' he said, 'I'm coming to collect this.' But he didn't ever come back. No, he never came back. And I had the following week off with that. It was all over taking Ivy home, walking back, you know. And getting a smash in the mouth.

You had to have a torch. But after time you was even afraid to use that, you know? You had to put blackout curtains up at windows. I remember, I was attacked once, as well. Again. In York Way. He was asking for cigarettes and I said, 'I don't smoke'. I didn't then. He said, 'Yes, you've got cigarettes,' he said. And went to rifle my pockets. I put me hand up like that, you know, to stop him. And I can remember he hit me in the mouth as well. That was twice.

Betty Forrester née Ross, *clerk/telegraph operator, LNER Thornton Junction*

There was such a lot of difficulties in wartime which aren't really documented at all. At this particular point it had just been the beginning of our forces going to Normandy and my boyfriend had a sudden leave and I got a telegram to say he would be arriving in Kirkcaldy the next morning. And I naturally I wanted leave and I was refused it. When he arrived at Kirkcaldy station in the morning, he had gone to his own home town in Peebles and then come the next morning to Kirkcaldy and expected to stay in my home in Kirkcaldy for about a week. Unfortunately, as he usually did, he'd taken off his army uniform and he was in civvies and he had no identification to show that he was a soldier and he was a sergeant on reconnaissance. The railway stations in Fife, of course it was a restricted area, they had soldiers on duty to stop anyone without their identification staying at the station and he had just to get back on the train and go all the way back to Edinburgh. So, they couldn't replace me unfortunately and it's a wonder I didn't get the sack, I just didn't turn up for my work. So I didn't know who took over my duties for that week. [Betty went on to marry George, a railwayman in a reserved occupation.]

Mary Hodgson, *goods clerk, LMS Chesterfield*

I moved onto what was called the FRS, that was the Freight Rolling Stock. And for that I dealt with wagons other than the ordinary ones. Any of the private sidings that had got any out-of-gauge loads. And they wanted bogie bolsters or covered vans, or special flat wagons. The type of wagons that were used in those days were slightly different. But they were the more unusual type of wagons, and firms would get in touch with me, or the man who we used to deal with out-of-gauge loads, from headquarters, he would perhaps go out to a firm and examine the load and measure it up and tell them that they needed a certain type of wagon, and he would get in touch with me. And I would order these wagons from control, because, they would know exactly where they were, and where they could get them from, and they would make arrangements for them to be brought perhaps from another station, and up to Chesterfield, and put in at these private sidings.

And also part of that job, I did wagons that were needing repair. They were stopped for repairs at Chesterfield, and we used to have what they call wagon tappers in those days. They went round passenger trains, they went round goods trains tapping wheels, and they could tell by the sound that the tap gave them as to whether or not the wheel was okay or whether they'd got a flat wheel. If they were on goods wagons, then it was up to the goods staff to notify, both the forwarding and receiving station, that that particular wagon had been stopped at Chesterfield for repairs. And a clerk had to do that and that clerk was me. So I had to get this information from what we called 'The Wagon Tapper's Cabin' which was on the up platform – it's still got a siding in it for slow trains going south. Beyond that there was double goods lines. Beyond those goods lines was this wooden cabin which these wagon tappers used. And I'm here at the station having got off the train at eight o'clock in the morning, and I'd got to get to that cabin. During the war the trains were bumper to bumper, there was no space at all. And at that time in a morning the wagon tappers were out. I would stand and I would call hoping that there was somebody in that cabin, but very very often there wasn't. So how did I get all that information? I used to stand down between the wagons and listen very very carefully, because of course, as soon as a train started to move its chains started clanking. And if everything was deathly quiet, I'm under the wagon, to get that information. To this day I feel apprehensive at the thought of it all.

Thinking about it by rights, I should have reported it to the goods agent and said I'm not going any more. Very often you see the goods agent was not on the premises. He would come in the morning, read all the correspondence, and he would go out to the firms during the day. He would come back about four o'clock, just before four o'clock in the afternoon, because it was the four o'clock position that I had to phone to the Farm. I had to go and tell him the state of the wagons in the yard and Hollis Lane and wherever, and sometimes he would say: 'Well you can't show all those. Knock so many off.' So that some days it was not a true position. So he was away say from ten o'clock in the morning, until about half past three in the afternoon. He didn't know what anybody was doing.

Joan Richards, *parcels clerk, GWR Hartlebury*

My hours were from eight till five on early, and of course I had to travel by train from Kidderminster, and the late shift was eleven till seven at night. Supposed to be every other Sunday, from ten till six, but when the invasion started it was a month of working Sundays as well, so it was a month before I had a Sunday off. And then, because they didn't think I was doing enough, I had a letter telling me I've got to report to the Fire Station in Kidderminster once a month, and I had to go down there and spend all night there, relieve the firemen, and then go to work the next morning. And I remember one night I went there, the siren went just as I got through the fire station doors, and it was a hayrick, right on the top of a bank. They didn't know whether it had been set alight or whether it had been, you know, internal combustion, or what it was. Anyway, of course we could hear the planes going over, and it'd got to be put out as soon as possible, and oh I forget how many fire engines were there, they were there all night anyway, had to pull it all apart, to finally put it out. So that night, normally you went down and you were on duty till about half past ten, and then a fireman took over, you were allowed to go and rest in their dormitory. If there was no callout that was all right, but if there was a callout, of course he had to come off the switchboards, you had to come down and take over. On that particular night there was nobody to take over, so I worked on the switchboard all night, then I went home, I had some breakfast, caught the train and went to work, fell asleep when I was having my lunch. Somebody woke me up, got home, I don't remember having me tea, mother says I fell asleep while I was having me tea. I don't remember climbing the stairs or going to bed, all I remember is half past seven the next morning my father waking me up. So that was one experience, but we got through it all.

Maureen Evans, *messenger then clerk, LMS Crewe*

On one occasion, by this time I'd met my future husband. He wanted to go somewhere on a particular Monday, and I said, 'well I'll be working overtime.'

And he said, 'tell them you're not working?' So brave Maureen decided to tell them that I would not be joining them on this particular occasion. So I walked out at five o'clock and left everybody behind doing the overtime. And at a later date this was to come back and haunt me.

Well, in those days of course it was traditional that if a female married that they had to leave the railway. So I think during the war years, and with the coming of British Rail instead of the old railway companies, of course things had changed. And so we were allowed to stay on, but we had to request to stay on [in the early 1950s]. You had to write a written request to stay on. And so I wrote out my request to stay on after I was married. And of course this was when I was taken into the Chief Accountant's office. The Chief Accountant's office was up about half a dozen steps and he had a window there so he could look down upon the minions doing all the work, you know. And I had to come before this Chief Accountant, only to be reminded of the fact that I was the young lady who'd refused to work overtime on one occasion. He knew this, yes. And reminded me of the seriousness of the situation. And here I was, asking to be allowed to stay on. But he accepted it, yes, that I could stay on.

Gladys Garlick, *LNER guard, London*

We used to take the trains down into the sidings at Finsbury Park. And one day I'd left the train at Weston sidings. I was coming back up the lines. You were actually supposed to walk right across and walk along the edge. But you never did that. And I'm walking towards Finsbury Park station, and of course as you're walking the lines are verging, aren't they. They're getting narrower and narrower. And I'm walking and sort of not thinking. And the signalman's waving madly. And cos I'm just getting nearer and nearer, and there's a train coming along behind me, you know. So that was a moment of carelessness, or youth, on my part. And I wasn't worried, but he was having a heart attack, because he thought I was going to get knocked down, you see.

Georgina Huber, *clerk, LMS Crewe Arms Hotel, Crewe*

Georgina started at the Crewe Arms Hotel from 1926, and worked right up to the outbreak of the Second World War. Her father was Austrian.

I was sacked. I had a letter. Then one morning, two huge men came into the office and demanded to see me and give me an interview. I was sent into the manageress's office and seated at the table, while they sat opposite me and asked me questions.

Well, I was an enemy alien. The company would not have been happy employing people with foreign, enemy connection. Cos it wasn't just a foreign connection, it was an enemy connection.

It doesn't really concern the railway company, but I was secretary of the local Peace Society, you know. From before, from long before the war. And we just went on. And we were rather accused of getting hold of young men and trying to stop them from serving their country. But it wasn't like that. But we did try to help those few young men who were clearly honest conscientious objectors. Who actually believed. We had one or two very knowledgeable people on our committee. One was a local magistrate. And what they were doing was just giving the boys an idea of how they should behave before the tribunals. Cos they all had to go up to a tribunal to be assessed, to see whether they were... And some of course were put in prison. But some were put in non-military jobs in the army. And some accepted that. But those that didn't accept it, of course they just went to prison. And that was that.

They sent for the manageress to come in. And she was in tears. She said, 'And I have to give you this, Miss Huber. I'm sorry.' So I opened this envelope which had come from London, informing me that my time with the railway company was now at an end. And I was to leave immediately. Not to stay another night, you know. So I had to go and collect everything up. But one of the police officers that belonged to the railway company was most kind and most helpful. He did say to the other policeman, 'I think that you've been rather precipitate. And Miss Huber, if you've got nowhere to go tonight I'm sure my wife will put you up for a couple of days until you can get yourself settled.' Which was really extremely kind of him, and thoughtful. And I was very happy about that.

Yanks, Canadians and Italians

Main railway. All goods coming through. American soldiers by the thousands and all, let's face it, I mean if you didn't get a wolf-whistle once or twice. It made you wonder, what had I done to you boys? There was plenty that went through, not on the passenger trains. But still, you know, a troop train coming through. And all right, we'd stand back. It was lovely, to wave to all them hundreds.

(Mary Woodfield, linesman's assistant, GWR Undy)

As military service had removed many of the young fit and 'eligible' men from the railways, the attractions of waves of American soldiers arriving were understandable. Many of the women workers were thrilled to see them, as heroes, in the place of the British men away for long periods. Booking clerk Theresa Roberts even suggested that being able to say hello to an American GI might be the height of her railway ambition.

Some overseas soldiers spent extended time locally, and some women, such as LMS clerk Maureen Evans at Crewe, were able to develop long term correspondence with the Canadian soldiers when they moved on to Europe. She also enjoyed seeing American soldiers passing through, thrilled by the wondrous gifts – coffee, gum, soups and magazines – which were tossed out from the trains. LMS goods clerk Doreen Dickenson was intrigued by the American soldiers based in Liverpool and delighted by some amusing repartee, at the same time commenting on racial differences and attitudes. This was at a time when women's magazines were advising their readers to be careful about 'coloured soldiers', choosing their words carefully: 'These men are not only fighting for us, they are, like all other Allied servicemen, strangers in a strange land. It would not be fair though, either to them or to you, to form such a close friendship as might lead to romance. It is by no means a question of them being 'inferior', but *different*, and, certainly today, only in the very rarest cases do such marriages succeed.'[1]

There were language issues. Miss J. Everett, writing in 1945 in the *LNER Magazine* about her time as a booking clerk at Lincoln, acknowledged the stereotype of a booking clerk as 'a species which asks unnecessary questions, pries into private affairs, and takes an unusually long time to issue tickets.' Conversations with American soldiers could be tricky – an American soldier, when asked if 'Single?', thinks he is being propositioned, and she suggests that you should say 'One Way?' or 'Round Trip?'[2]

Another group of overseas men that some of the railway women came into contact with was the Italian prisoners of war, sometimes employed on railway construction work locally. Stories about Italian prisoners often included tales of cooking, but women frequently recalled resentment at what they saw as greater quantities of preferential rations being awarded to the Italians, such as butter and bacon. The Italians however made good use of the odd vegetable abandoned in a truck, and were able to cook delicious meals as a result, although clerk Mary Hodgson failed to appreciate her offering and discarded it.

Maureen Evans, *messenger then clerk, LMS Crewe*

There were troop movements. And in the Carriage and Wagon Department itself there was a platoon of Canadian soldiers actually working in the department. I suppose there would be about 20 or 25 of them. Well, of course, being a young girl, and being brought up in the war, you don't question the things that were happening round you, because it was just part and parcel of the growing up process. But of course afterwards I realised that they'd been there actually getting ready for going over to Europe to help to restore... they were sappers, you see. And they were keeping a hand in at what they would normally be doing, in order to help in Europe when they got over there. And they were there for several months while I was there. And then just one morning they were gone. I went into work one morning and they'd gone, departed.

There was three or four of them used to write to me. And they used to send snaps. Pictures, you know, from Europe, what they were doing in France. There was pictures of big engines with lots of little scruffy children, badly clothed children. And they were showing where they were working, what they were doing, mending railway carriages and wagons and trying to get the rolling stock moving, I suppose. Over in Europe, in war-torn Europe. And yes, it was obvious that these children had gone through a very bad time, you know.

We were actually based on the Crewe to Shrewsbury line. And the trains to Shrewsbury had a lot of troops going backwards and forwards, including Americans. Sometimes the signals would stop the train just outside the office, and you'd look up and see this train outside the office and all these American soldiers would spot a female in the office. So there was a lot of whistling and calling and waving and 'come on out, come on out'. I would call, and we'd go out and stand on the edge of the Crewe to Shrewsbury line. And these American soldiers would throw out all sorts of things. Magazines and gum and chocolates and biscuits. Powdered coffee, which we'd never seen. Cos we only knew Camp Coffee, you see, in those days. Packets of soup. We'd go back into the office armed with all this stuff, you see, and divide the spoils between us, yes, yes. I'm sure we weren't allowed on the Crewe to Shrewsbury line but nonetheless we used to go and... they couldn't get out of the train. The signals would change and they'd be gone. Until the next time another lot would come along.

I enjoyed being in the general offices. I enjoyed the first part as the messenger, because I had quite a lot of freedom, I suppose, in those days. And nobody seemed to mind as I used to go trotting off. When I got bored with doing the filing I would trot off into the workshop and the Canadian soldiers would tease me and get me to say 'apple pie'. And I would say it in my Cheshire accent, you see. And they used fall about laughing at this 'apple pie'. And there was one or two of the younger men used to tease me a bit, you know, and I'd have a little bit of fun out there, and then I'd go back and sort of pretend I'd been doing something, you know, collecting a few clock cards or something.

Doreen Dickenson, *goods clerk, LMS Liverpool*

When we came out, some of us went to Sandhills station, which was a bit of a lonely walk. I walked up to Sandhills and I could get the train from there on my line. So one of the staff used to walk with us from Sandhills. And we were walking along Derby Road – it was occupied then by the US forces. Because there was this Lease-Lend business then, and they had their own Movement Control. And we had our Movement Control over here. And some of them... the railed-off places that you walked past, along Great Howard Street, to go to Sandhills station, were picketed by black men. And all of a sudden the voice would say, 'Who goes there!' Or they'd talk to you through the railings and you think, 'Oh, run like mad!' American soldiers, well, black people, were very very low in American ratings. They wouldn't go on the same bus with them, walk the same side of the street with them. But it didn't bother us, because well, we didn't care what colour they were, and it doesn't matter now what colour they are, as long as they're decent upright citizens.

While we were underneath the arches I had a spell on the switchboard again. Well of course I was on the switchboard one lunchtime and some American had been told by his major to get the Canada goods station on the line. They wanted to speak to Andy Campbell, the chief foreman, you see. So you got the chief foreman on the line before you put your major on. But I couldn't find Andy Campbell. So he came back, he said, 'Mr Campbell?' And I said, 'No.' He said,

'Who are you?' I said, 'I'm the Goods.' 'Oh,' he said, 'are you the goods?' I said, 'I sure am!' That was it, you see. Well, we had a little laugh. I said, 'This is the switchboard. I'm very sorry, I can't find Mr Campbell, but I'll take a message for you and get it to him.' Cos I had a little lad who was a runner – he'd go up the tunnel, you know. So he said, 'Oh,' he said, 'My name's Major – ' So I said, 'Yes.' So he said, 'Right,' he said. 'You tell your Mr Campbell I'll be over there to see him.' He wasn't a coloured man but he was a Southerner. Well, about half an hour later, before I could get hold of Andy Campbell, up the yard comes an open Jeep with a black driver and this fellow sitting in the back. He was Major – . He came up and he wanted to know 'Where's this girl who "sure am the goods"?' Well, I came out with me headphones on, because it was those plug-in switchboard things with the cords, you know. And of course the agent was walking down the yard. He wanted to know who this fellow was who was coming to speak to his girls, and 'Oh dear, I shouldn't encourage people like that to come in here. If he'd come to see the chief foreman then he should see the chief foreman.' Well, you know, I was the talk of the wash-house, wasn't I? So we had fun like that with the Major, he was quite nice really, but he did want to see what was going on.

Mary Woodfield, *linesman's assistant, GWR Undy*

Main railway. All goods coming through. American soldiers by the thousands and all, let's face it, I mean if you didn't get a wolf-whistle once or twice. It made you wonder, what had I done to you boys? There was plenty that went through, not on the passenger trains. But still, you know, a troop train coming through. And all right, we'd stand back. It was lovely, to wave to all them hundreds.

Emily Poole, *booking clerk, Shepton Mallet, Somerset & Dorset Joint Railway*

Something happened when the prison was occupied by the US troops. One very dark and wet night, in the winter, there arrived an escort of eight US soldiers, complete with batons, and one prisoner, who had murdered a taxi driver in the North of England. One of the escort came in and said, 'Say Red, bring your scissors to the waiting room' (I have auburn hair). I went and was asked to cut off the stripes and insignias of the prisoner before they proceeded to the 'stockade', which was their name for the prison.

Theresa Roberts, *booking clerk, Midsomer Norton and Welton, Somerset & Dorset Joint Railway*

During my time at Midsomer Norton Station, American troops were stationed on the Mendips a few miles away, prior to D-Day, and occasionally we would have them call in at the station in their American trucks, to pick up the odd wooden crate, the contents of which we never knew! They were very chatty lads, but any fraternisation was very frowned upon by the station master, but at least I got to say 'Hello' to an American GI. What a record!

Edith Stretch, *booking office clerk, LMS Hanley*

When the Americans came, they used to come into Hanley, cos there was a lot of ladies of the night in Hanley. They used to come and they used to catch the last train. It was ten past eleven to Stoke, and ten to eleven up the loop line. And they wanted to go to so-and-so. I said, 'Well, I can only book you to Stoke.' I said, 'Then when you get to Stoke,' I said, 'find ...' Cos really they probably only wanted to go round the corner. So they'd put all their money down like that. I could have diddled them right, left, and centre. And I'd say, 'Well, it's so-and-so.' I said, 'There's your change.' And they'd say, 'All that? (American accent) Yes ma'am. Thank you ma'am.'

Mary Hodgson, *LMS clerk Chesterfield*

We also had two Italian prisoners of war, who worked at Chesterfield for quite a time. And because they were Italians they had a ration of butter. Now our ration of butter, I can't remember exactly what it was, but it wasn't very much per week, but these Italians used to come to work with a lump of butter each. They worked out on the wagons that were being loaded and such as full wagon loads, which were dealt with out in the yard. And we had a firm called Ernest Shuntall's in those days, who were wholesale greengrocers, so of course they had full wagon loads of potatoes, and onions, and carrots and all sorts of things like that, fruits when they were in season. After these wagons had been emptied, there would be an odd potato, or an odd onion or something like that in the corner of the wagon which their men weren't going to bother jumping out of the lorry and going and picking up one odd piece of vegetable. And these Italians went round these vans, they would gather enough in the way of vegetables and bring them back into the men's cabin, and they would set to and cook them in butter. They used to make beautiful [potato] scallops in butter, but you'd got our English men working on the railway, bringing a packet of sandwiches to work, spread with margarine or dripping or something like that, and there's our butter feeding these Italians.

  And one Italian in particular when I was working in the Chief Clerk's office, in a piece of newspaper he'd bring me a dozen scallops that he'd cooked in butter. But they were in a piece of newspaper. I used to thank him very much, wait until he'd gone, and the Chief Clerk used to say to me, 'You mustn't eat those.' And I would throw them on the fire. But those two Italians in particular, they had a very good time while they worked on the railway. We had two more, who didn't come anywhere near the offices. They weren't with us for very long. We understood that they were fascists, and they were eventually moved to a camp up in Scotland, where these fascists were all kept out of harm's way. But the two who'd been in the Italian Navy, they worked along with our men quite OK. They were brought to work in a morning, they were taken back home at night, and I think they were quids in when you think what happened to some of our prisoners in Germany. But they were a couple of nice fellas.

Dorothy Crawford, *railway hotels, LMS Liverpool*

The Admiral of the Port of Liverpool had a suite [at the hotel] and we had people coming in back and forwards all the time. Navy. At one point we had a manager who'd come down from Gleneagles before that, in 1939, and he was Italian and eventually the night that Italy went into the war, he and half the staff of the restaurant and the kitchen and so on were taken away by the police. Most of them were released afterwards but he didn't come back.

Joan Cox, *mobile canteen worker, SR Redhill*

We opened up. And it turned out to be a caravan. It was presented by the Buenos Aires Railway to the railwaymen of Southern Railways and it was a well-equipped canteen. It had a flap that came down, that you used as a counter. It was rather exposed because it was put on the siding of Redhill Loco Yard. It was quite near to the turntable but there was no shelter for it. So at that time Italian prisoners of war were working there. And Mr Pipe and Ernie somebody-or-other got these Italian prisoners of war to come and build a shelter. It was made out of old railway sleepers and it was really like a wooden-sided thing, with just a door in the front and they put in a couple of sleepers to act as seats. The men used to be able to come round there and shelter from the weather, because it really was exposed. And they used to have their cans filled up and get cheese rolls, things that their wives couldn't always supply at home because cheese and all that sort of thing was rationed so hard at home, that to be able to buy a cheese roll and have it in their tucker bags was ideal. We used to have all sorts of pork pies and sausage rolls and bits and pieces like that. Nothing hot, no hot meals as such. Coffee and tea was hot, obviously. And Mrs Flint that I worked with, Elsie, she used to make apple pies. Because her garden had trees and she used to pick up these apples. And with the help of the rations we could scrape up from the canteen, she used to make these pastry apple pies and things. The men loved them because it was a treat you couldn't get at home.

We were rationed at that time. We had to account for every spoonful of sugar, tea, milk, butter, marge, everything was rationed. But we also had an allowance.

Because we were a canteen serving railwaymen we used to get extra pies. Pork pies and all that sort of thing was all rationed but not to the canteens, there was an allowance. Only a certain amount. Once it was gone for the day it was gone. But we did seem to manage to eke it out. Most men could find a meal of some sort when they came round to us.

It was only railwaymen, because as I say we were on a siding. I think it was the Tonbridge line through. It really was on a siding away from everything and the public never ever came that way. You had to come across railway lines to get to it. The Italian prisoners of war used to use it. How they got the money to use it I don't know. But they did. They used to come round and they were quite a friendly bunch. But they were in the charge of army chaps and the railwaymen used to tell them where they had to go and what they had to do and what work they were doing. But of course they were enjoying life, weren't they? They were out of the war. Enjoying themselves.

Joyce Bell née Pearce, *lengthwoman, Somerset & Dorset Joint Railway*

There was a PoW camp at Penleigh, I think that was the name of the place, and the prisoners used to be allowed out to work on the farms, and when they saw us 'girls' go back into the hut they would come to the door in their brown overalls with a big yellow patch on the back. As you can imagine, being Italians they would try to flirt with us. We used to give them cups of tea, as we felt sorry for them. It was hilarious trying to make conversations with them.

Betty Cox, *porter, Evercreech Junction, Somerset & Dorset Joint Railway*

As time went on we saw the arrival of Italian prisoners – they were brought daily by coach to work in the sidings, and I remember looking on in envy as they cooked their breakfast of bacon, while we ate our bread and marge – we thought it was a funny old war.

The Railway Family

Even then, to a young girl, there was a feeling that if you belonged to the railway, you belonged to a family. It was a wonder. Does it exist today, do you think? No?

(*Irene Barrett-Locke, refreshments, GWR Paddington*)

The railway family, the idea that the workforce was part of one 'family', with strong ties and loyalties, was an important concept, deliberately constructed by railway companies and trade unions, and especially the Railway Women's Guilds. Hannah Reeves has been studying the railway family in Gloucester, looking at how it was able to support the political objectives of railwaymen, while based on traditional ideas about roles within the family.[1] Part of this was the idea of working on the railway as a job for life, with the railway family looking after you, and bolstered by the promise of travel benefits. But during wartime these women were being appointed on a temporary basis, so they didn't fit the mould. However the railway family also related to the way that people gained jobs on the railway because of other family members, and this certainly applied in the case of many women, who were often influenced by their own fathers and brothers and uncles. Their fathers often worked within the 'railway family', able to find out about opportunities easily and recommend daughters. Somerset & Dorset Railway Porter Betty Spiller recalled, 'Well, I wanted to join the WAAF, and family were not in favour of that, and my brother was already a junior porter at Evercreech Junction and father with being a shunter, and a vacancy arose, station master spoke to my father, said would I be interested and they kind of made me interested and shoved me in that direction.' Family ties were strong in other ways, for example Phyllis Knapp worked as a messenger at the LMS Chief Mechanical Engineer's Office at Derby, doing her husband's job while he was in the army.[2]

The women interviewed here recount the ways in which their fathers often guided their entry into railway jobs and how they progressed, with a mixture of authority and support. The role of their mothers in guidance was much more opaque, as they were much less involved in the work of the railways.

Maureen Evans talked of the way in which her father took command of the situation, in deciding which of three job options she should take. Ironically she was eventually earning more money as a railway clerk than he was in the machine shop. But he supported her, in paying for special lessons to help with her railway examinations. He was keen that she should join the union, as he had suffered periods of unemployment himself. Irene Adgie's father wanted her to take a railway job, as he felt it had 'prospects'. Although she first pretended she was happy in other work, she took his advice and became a railway typist. Doreen Dickenson's father wanted her to follow him (he was a customs officer) and take the Civil Service examination, but when these were cancelled and she ended up on the railways, he told her they would pay buttons. However while she was working as a goods clerk she was able to draw on family ties by discovering a relative of her father's who was able to shield her from difficult situations. Mary Woodfield, a lineman's assistant and a married woman at the time, tells how her father was proud of 'a daughter of mine going on the railway'. He too insisted that his daughter join the union. Mary felt the need to make the workmen's hut more of a 'home'.

LNER guard Gladys Garlick had originally wanted to join the army. When she had no response to her requests for information, her father told her they were looking for railway booking clerks. She flustered her interview and so her father suggested that they were looking for lad porters at his station, and that was how she started her railway work. When she eventually became a guard, one of the first two on LNER, it was because one of the inspectors knew her father – 'a lot of people knew my father'. At the same time Gladys's mother moved from being a carriage cleaner to take over Gladys's portering job for the duration of the war.

Porter Betty Spiller was given the chance of being a lampman, but the station master insisted on seeing her father in the marshalling yard for approval. Although her mother was unwilling, Betty did take on this new job. One of the prevailing concerns of fathers was that their daughters might be subject to bad language in this new type of work. Parcels clerk Joan Richards was warned by her father that she would have to get used to it. But the men felt the need to apologise to him after swearing slipped out, and seemed to feel guilty. Joan took this in her stride.

Fathers could be supportive in other ways. Booking clerk Theresa Roberts's father bought her a second hand Francis-Barnett two-stroke motor cycle to get to work (most workers had to cycle in the absence of other transport). Mary Buist's father used to wind up her guard's watch for her.

In the early years of the war, the female worker featured rarely in railway company staff magazines, save for the occasional photograph of a female clerk or secretary leaving on marriage and being presented with the obligatory inscribed clock or canteen of cutlery. The idea of the railway family was however highlighted by the celebration of the 'Railway Queen', with applications open to railway employees' daughters from 14–16 years old. Edinburgh girl Helen Forrest was the Railway Queen in 1939, and toured Switzerland on a goodwill visit as part of her duties.[3] In 1941, it was Dorothy Norwood of GWR, and in 1945 it was the 16th Queen, 14-year-old Greta Richards, from Feltham in Middlesex, whose father worked for SR.[4] In 1946 a 'Princess' was introduced, as a 'lady-in-waiting'. Surprisingly 'it was the duty of each Railway Queen to stimulate a spirit of goodwill amongst railwaymen of another country, with a view to combining for the abolition of war.'[5]

At the end of the war GWR decided to pay tribute to 'Great Western families', actively encouraging readers to send in photos of groups of four or more 'on duty', for example the Warrington family, including Phyllis who was a porter-guard at Aberystwyth, with brothers and father.[6] The Loveridge family of seven celebrated Mrs Loveridge and daughter Miss D, both porters at Oxford alongside her husband and four sons.[7]

Betty Spiller, *porter, Evercreech Junction, Somerset & Dorset Joint Railway*

There was a pride in the job. And anybody would help somebody else. You didn't say, 'Because you're the signal lampman and I'm something else, you can do your own thing,' or anything like that. When you first came they were very conscious that it was women, but after a bit they forgot you were a woman, you were just another workmate. I mean it's the same now, I'm working in a garage now, doing cars, and the men in the workshop, they don't take any notice of me at all, well, when I make the tea.

Irene Adgie, *typist, SR Woking and Waterloo*

I enjoyed it. I still get that feeling when I come in contact with railwaymen. Like going into the office at Salisbury to reserve seats for a train journey. I still get that feeling that railways are special, and railwaymen are special.

Doreen Dickenson, *goods clerk, LMS Liverpool*

The railway life was a wonderful, it was an experience all its own. It was a world of its own, really. Because it had its own telephone system and its own communication system and that sort of thing. The people you worked with were characters. They had life, and experience. And when we were young during the war, there was only the older men that were left behind. Or some of the older spinsters. We did have one or two older spinsters which were quite an example to all of us. We weren't going to look like that. But they talked to you. I mean we had time to go for a cup of tea and get to know people's life experiences. And I learnt a lot from them. The friend I had who was interested in operas. And he'd learnt Latin and German and because I did a bit of Latin, the good old days, he'd write to me. Notes. He used to work on lates and he worked in the Time Office. He was a time clerk, you know. They clocked on the outside staff at various hours. And at one time when we worked under the arches in the stables, the switchboard was in the same office as the time clerk. It's lovely, the switchboard duty, you learn an awful lot. You sit on the switchboard and there were all plugs and you plugged in and waited for the operator to answer. And he was coming on duty at half past twelve. And he had a habit of saying 'Merry Christmas' when he [the time clerk] came in and hung his coat up. And I used to say 'And a happy New Year to you.' Well, I was on the switchboard and I'd just plugged into the operator. And she didn't answer in a hurry and she said, 'Don't be so rude. We have thousands of people to deal with here,' she said. 'We've got...' I said, 'Listen, love, I'm very sorry. I wasn't talking to you.' It was he ... as he came in, I said, 'He always says a merry Christmas cos he comes in at one o'clock in the day.'

I picked everybody's brains. You learned from people, their experiences. And it was a wealth of knowledge really. I really enjoyed my time on the railway. Because with all due respect, apart from a silly boss who wouldn't let me go on a holiday, the rest of them were nice people. And they were all, I don't know, cuddly sort of fellows. Daddy kind of fellows. They didn't mean any harm. They'd come and put their arm round you. And you'd get a bit of angora fluff on their suit, sort of thing, if you wore one of these jumpers. I mean, Barbara did. She'd been to somebody one time and I said, 'Ooh, where have you been?' Cos Alan had all this angora fluff on his suit, you know. I said, 'Don't you go home to your wife with it like that.'

Gladys Garlick, *guard, LNER London*

I liked the job. I enjoyed myself. And I knew everybody. A lot of people knew my father, and that. And I had a good time really. It was a good war for me, really. I enjoyed myself in the war. It used to be cold in the winters, perhaps there'd be snow, but one of the porters would come along and say, 'Here you are, Gladys, I've bought you a cup of tea.' And then I'd go along a couple of stations. 'Oh, I've bought you a cup of cocoa, Gladys.' You know, used to bring me drinks and things like that.

Irene Barrett-Locke, *refreshments, GWR Paddington*

Even then, to a young girl, there was a feeling that if you belonged to the railway, you belonged to a family. It was a wonder. Does it exist today, do you think? No?

Mary Woodfield, *linesman's assistant, GWR Undy*

Part of a big family. The men, signalmen in their boxes. Honestly, they must have spotted us from miles away. We didn't always walk from one box to another because our length was from Tunnel Mouth down to Magor. Now that was quite a span. But it was convenient to wait for the train from Severn Tunnel. So we just had a ride down on the train from there to Magor. And then do our jobs. And if there was time to kill, well I'm sorry, you had to kill it. Until there was a train stopped to come back from Caldicot, from Magor, back up to the Severn Tunnel. Well, to finish your day off really. Get back to the yard. Get back to this filthy dirty hut. Well, I mean two men had been living in it as well. They appreciated everything we done. It got that we'd almost wallpapered the place before we left. Honestly. And it was a case of 'Now you girls stay here. We'll go and do this.'

No shifts. That wouldn't have been allowed. If the men were called out, you'd get to know the next morning. Well, you know, 'where's Harry?' or 'where's Ben?' 'Oh, he was called out for the night.' So once he'd had his hours maybe come in and show his face then, kind of thing. Because we were not taught any of the wiring or anything to do with the wirings. I think we saved manpower by us doing the jobs all round the boxes, which the powers above, kind of thing, must have thought that was a safe job for girls. And if they had somebody that they called, somebody out from Newport as well, they were more geared for the wiring.

No technical training. If you were nosy enough you asked, and it was a case of 'Oh yes, but you girls don't want to be bothered with that.' So if you'd wanted to learn you couldn't.

Most of the time, doing around the gubbins, underneath the boxes. We went up in the boxes where the levers were. Because the love from the signalman and the boys would be a case of, they would spot us coming along the line. And I was told this, here's the words they'd say. 'Here's the girls coming. Put the kettle on.' We always had a cup of tea there with them. And I pulled the lever over once, with the duster, and all the rest of it. And everybody in the world didn't get to do that, did they? And watched how the ding–dings all went, all along, the bells, you know? We were thrown in the deep end. And I'm sure the ones that took us on were thrown in at the deep end. Because nobody in officialdom come up to the tunnel ever to see us. They might have had reports given through. But they never have come to see us.

Edna Simms, *booking office clerk, Evercreech New Station, Somerset & Dorset Joint Railway*

The period of my employment on the S & D Railway was a very happy and interesting time. Everyone was prepared to help one another and we seem to still keep in touch with many of the inhabitants of Evercreech and the business people who are still alive at this time.

Edith Stretch, *booking office clerk, LMS Hanley*

I liked it. The station master asked me, we'd been there about a month, 'How do you like it?' You know. I said, 'Well, I don't know whether I like work. I'd rather be at school.' And he looked at me, you know. 'Got to buckle down.' I said, 'All right, all right.' He was a nice man. He'd got a daughter himself. So I think that was what happened. He was great.

Vera Jones, *apprentice fitter, LMS Crewe*

Well, wartime didn't really seem to affect my relationships with other people, in a way. Sometimes we had to work till eight o'clock at night. We had to work Sundays some weeks. If we worked a Sunday we'd have a day off in the week. But we was all friends together in there really. And if we went out, some of the girls, we would go out together. You know, like when we weren't working. But of course I met Harry.

Harry worked on the same job that I started on. He was moved off a few days before I started, and went on to B-belts in the erection shop. He has always said that I took his job, so he got his own back by marrying me, and says that I have been paying for it ever since. We started courting at the age of 16 and were married in 1946. I was 21, he was 20. Well, when Harry was on nights, I used to see Harry for a few minutes in the morning when I went in work. Next morning, when I went in to work, I used to see Harry for a few minutes then. Each morning, when he was on nights.

And then the Men came Back

The railway sent a letter to the station master at Gordon Hill to thank me for what I'd done. They didn't send it to me. They just gave it to him to show to me. Which I thought was... I think I should have had that letter really. On top of which, I was on early turn and I'd had to get off at Gordon Hill to go and see him when I'd been up at two o'clock in the morning, to look at this letter and wait an hour for the next train back. So you can imagine I wasn't very happy about that. Even today. I think I should have had a letter myself for that. Not given it to him to show me. Somebody up head office, I suppose. Somewhere. I don't know. But I do think that was wrong really.

(Gladys Garlick, LNER guard)

What were the aspirations of these women at the end of the war? Some, such as clerk Mary Hodgson, were able to catch of glimpse of what might have been. She was proud to discover that her abilities matched those of fellow male night class students, but then had to make a difficult choice between marriage and studying for the Institute of Transport exams and getting letters after her name. She chose marriage, and frustratingly had to see her husband achieving this much later.

As the men started coming back from the war, most of these women seemed to accept the inevitable loss of their jobs, although they did have some not very enticing options, such as trying for a cleaning job. Because of the staging of demobilisation, some women were able to transfer to other jobs for a few years, but many were made redundant. Joyce Bell, née Pearce, lengthwoman on the Somerset & Dorset Railway, recalled, 'We were all very sorry to leave, as we really enjoyed our time "labouring"'. Despite the demobilisation of men from the services, GWR were still employing 16,000 women at the beginning of 1946, and a film celebrating their work was made by the company: *Women at War*.[1] They also set up a training school for girls at Paddington after the war ended, to train girls as shorthand typists for railway service.[2] At the end of 1946 LMS were still advertising for women clerks for telegraph work at Gloucester Station.[3] In May 1946 at the RCA conference at Hastings, there was a debate about the retention of women clerks after marriage.[4] It was agreed that this should only be allowed 'in exceptional circumstances'.

In many cases there appeared to be no positive recognition of the contribution of these women. LNER guard Gladys Garlick was refused a written reference, told that this was not done, presumably on the basis that the railways usually employed men, for life. She had to negotiate a verbal recommendation on the telephone. Furthermore, a letter commending her service was sent to the station master, to be shown to her at some inconvenience.

Women workers did take part in the victory parades, such as the Victory procession in London in 1946, when three representative women LMS railway workers took part.[5] The role of his women workers was honoured by C.J. Vidal, district LMS manager at Motherwell, when he paid tribute to them, including 69 signalwomen in his area, but he was pleased to be welcoming back 60 men.[6] A number of other women leaving featured in press publicity in 1946.[7]

There were problems with protocol. A court case in February 1945 heard that three women goods porters at Hastings had left their jobs without the permission of a National Service Officer.[8] After working there for three and a half years, following the bombing of their house in London, they had made an application for release in September 1944. Their work had been very heavy and they did not realise that they had to wait for approval of their request, a rule that was only removed in 1946.[9] It was decided that although they had committed an offence, there would be no penalty.

Many of these women accepted that the jobs they were doing belonged to men who were gradually returning to take them up again, and that there was 'no room for us', as porter Nellie Nelson at York said.

Betty Spiller, *porter then lampman, Evercreech Junction, Somerset & Dorset Joint Railway*

'45, '46. And then the men came back.

Nellie Nelson, *porter, LNER York*

Well, there were no getting back, because you see the men had gone back, all the men, we were doing a man's job like, the men came back to work so there were no room for us then.

Mary Buist, *passenger guard, LNER Musselburgh*

That's right, [the railwaymen] came back for their jobs. Well you got the chance of going in for cleaning or something like that, but my husband was back so...

Laura Scott, *sawdust bagger, LNER carriage works, York*

After children grew up a bit, me mum and dad looked after them and I got a job at British Rail with me friend Nan, cleaning carriage seats, they'd never ever been cleaned before.

Mary Hodgson née Wainwright, *LMS clerk Chesterfield*

At the end of the war, the railway started its night school classes again. I decided to join, in September 1946, and the classes were held at Wicker. I worked at Chesterfield. I used to leave home at 7.15, walk down to Dronfield station and get to work at eight o'clock. And then I would work until five o'clock. Then I would come out and catch the express, which was about 5.10, that had come up from St Pancras. And get off at Sheffield, and then walk from the Midland station down to Wicker. Which is about a mile and a half walk, and do the night school class, which finished at nine o'clock. Then I would have to run from Wicker to Midland station, because the last stopping train to Dronfield was the postal train. That left Sheffield at nine o'clock, and I got here about twenty past nine, on a slow train. Then I had to walk all the way home, uphill, all the way home, which is about a mile and a quarter from Dronfield station and I got home perhaps about quarter past ten. And every time I went to night school I worked those hours, because there was no day release in those days, you did a full day's work. And then you went to night school.

But the first year's exams, I got a first class distinction. And there was one male, he got a point of a mark more than I did. And for that he got a London Midland & Scottish prize. I wish he hadn't been there and I might have got the prize. Not that you wanted the prize, but you wanted the honour of it, looks of disgust from the other males who were down below me. I don't think they thought females could do anything in those days you see. I took the second year exams as well, which were harder of course. I got a first class pass in those.

And then eventually I was asked to work in the Accounts Office, I only worked in it for about three months, because by this time, late 1949, Albert and I had managed to get a house to rent, which was almost impossible in those days after the war. You could not get housing. And we took the bull by the horns and decided to get married.

But then the Chief Clerk came to me with a letter that had been sent, offering Miss Wainwright a four year study for the Institute of Transport, and I don't think it had ever been heard of before, not for a female. But this four year course was then going to come into us having this house, and getting married. They wouldn't employ a married woman, so I had to refuse. But many a time I've wished that I'd been able to take it, because then I could have, and don't think I'm doing it from a swanking point of view, but wouldn't it have been marvellous to have been able to say, 'Mary Wainwright MINST', Member of the Institute of Transport? Years later my husband studied for it, and he got one of the magazines, and I used to look purposely for a female's name, down all the list of passes. And it wasn't until a long time afterwards that a female came up on those passes. I would have loved to have the opportunity, to have tried it. But because of the railway ruling, that they would not employ married women, I had to leave on the day I got married. And yet I could have knocked some of the young lads into a cocked hat.

Joan Richards, *parcels clerk, GWR Hartlebury*

Well, they were, you know, demobbing them, and they were coming back, and things were getting to the state where everything was carrying on as before, sort of thing. All the rush had gone out of it. The last few months I was at Hartlebury, things had slowed down, you know, the invasion had started – well, it was well underway then – and they were starting to wind down then. I'd left because the chap was coming back out of the forces, so they started demobbing then. The man was coming back whose job I'd taken, but there was a vacancy in the parcel office at Kidderminster, so I moved to Kidderminster, and I was there for about twelve months, and of course the chap came back. That job was that. But there was a vacancy in the goods office, so I moved down to the goods office and I was working down in the goods office when we got married. I left in 1948, that's when my daughter was born.

Irene Adgie, *SR typist, Waterloo and Woking*

Marriage. It was the rule. Well, no, not really. They did allow people to stay on once they were married, because they'd had to during the war. And I could have stayed on, but with Jim doing shift work, if I'd been working, we'd hardly have seen each other. He was getting plenty of overtime, so we could afford to live without me working.

Doreen Dickenson, *goods clerk, LMS Liverpool*

We were taken on as temporary staff. The idea was, we would replace men who went during the war. And when they came back, well, they didn't want us any-more. That was the idea. But war was only going to last six months, like. That was the idea in those days. So by that time I think we'd become well established. Nobody gave you a letter and notified you. They just notified you that when you were married you'd have to leave, when the people come back from the forces. But after that, paying superann, we were fully employed, you couldn't sack us or anything like that. So when I got married I didn't pay a full stamp. Because I was not likely to be on the dole. Guaranteed employment or something like that. Like being in the civil service, you'd got a job for life unless you murdered your grandmother, that was the idea. They couldn't really sack us. There was no point in me paying a full stamp because the only benefit I got out of it was if I got sick pay. You didn't get the same rate as the men. If you got the dole, they got something like 27 shillings a week and we got 17 and sixpence. So I thought, why pay the same rate of stamp as the men, if you were not going to get the benefit? The only benefit you got was maternity allowance. If you left to have a baby, you'd get a maternity grant and maternity pay for so many weeks. Well, that wasn't going to affect me, I wasn't going to leave and have a baby. I wasn't even married. When I was married, I wasn't going to have any either.

Gladys Garlick, *guard, LNER London*

After the war. I could have stayed on even then, but I was really getting tired, you know? And I'd met my husband then on the railway in 1945. So that making it a bit difficult cos we were both on shift work, and didn't always gel, like.

Well, I had seen him on the train, on the fire end, you know, up the other end of the train. But I hadn't had a lot to do with him, really. I knew all the young men there, naturally. But funnily enough, we actually were introduced at another fireman's house. He had Arthur and another chap round. And he invited myself and another girl round to his house. And Arthur took me home, and that was it, wasn't it.

Well, I was getting tired with the shift work and that. So I decided to turn it in. And that was funny, really, because I went into the shop at Southgate, you know, where the underground is at Southgate. It's a big draper's shop there. And I was got a job as under-buyer. And they wanted a reference, didn't they? Of course. Naturally. So they said, on the railway, at King's Cross, 'Oh, we don't give references.' So I said, 'Well, they asked for two when I went on the railway.' And they weren't going to give me a reference. So of course I marched up to the big chief top hat, you know, at King's Cross, and said, 'Well look, I've been handling money.' Cos you used to get money on the train. Go from station to station, things like that. I said, 'And I'm going to a job where I shall be handling money, and you say you can't give me a reference.' I said, 'Well, give me back the two that I gave you when I came on the railway.' Naturally they couldn't do that, but he said, 'Oh well,' he said, 'Tell them to phone this number and I will verbally give them a reference.' And that was that.

They said they don't give references. Well, cos I suppose normally people lived on the railway for life, didn't they? You didn't have to give a reference, did you, in those days? I mean people didn't leave, did they? So I was a bit annoyed about that.

The railway sent a letter to the station master at Gordon Hill to thank me for what I'd done. They didn't send it to me. They just gave it to him to show to me. Which I thought was... I think I should have had that letter really. On top of which, I was on early turn and I'd had to get off at Gordon Hill to go and see him when I'd been up at two o'clock in the morning, to look at this letter and wait an hour for the next train back. So you can imagine I wasn't very happy about that. Even today. I think I should have had a letter myself for that. Not given it to him to show me. Somebody up head office, I suppose. Somewhere. I don't know. But I do think that was wrong really.

Joyce Bell, *lengthwoman, Somerset and Dorset Joint Railway*

As the men started coming back from the war we were made redundant, we were all very sorry to leave, as we really enjoyed our time 'labouring'. When I left I went as a cashier in the old International Stores in Burnham-on-Sea. After a few years I went as cashier in the canteen at the Royal Ordnance Factory at Puriton, where I met my fate and married in 1955. But I shall never forget my time 'on the railway'.

Betty Cox, *porter, Evercreech Junction, Somerset & Dorset Joint Railway*

When the war ended we stayed on, but as the lads came home to reclaim their jobs, we knew then that our days were numbered. Joyce and I left the S & D on the same day – we were sorry to say goodbye to Bill Cornell our foreman, who had been a good friend, and a shoulder to cry on when things went wrong. I wonder did he miss us, or was he glad to get back to normal?

Theresa Roberts, *booking clerk, Midsomer Norton and Welton, Somerset & Dorset Joint Railway*

I was with the S & DR for six years and enjoyed it very much, particularly the work, but the late shift started to clash with my social life so I left to take a job with regular office hours and longer evenings. But it was a happy time even though there was a war on, but I suppose that's why I came to work there anyway!

Dulcible Haines, *typist, LMS Watford*

And then at the end of the war, of course, it was disbanded. And I went into the Estate Department. And after the war, some of the men came back to thank us and say hello, you know. And that was quite nice.

We was still at the Grove. But not long after, about nine months perhaps after that, we went back to Euston. And I was then supervisor of a small typing bureau.

Violet Lee, *GWR passenger guard*

Still in my thoughts are the Great Western Railway – I can still see the huge rocking monsters, blasting out steam and smoke, the fireboxes roaring, straining round uphill bends, disappearing into tunnels and cuttings then emerging triumphantly out of the other side with an echoing blast on the engine whistle. I still think back to those years, deriving a sense of pride for the years of my girlhood on that wonderful engineering structure, the railways, which we have lost.

Epilogue

At the time of writing, sadly it appears that only one of the women whose voices were recorded so carefully about their wartime work is still alive, 96-year-old Betty Forrester, the LNER telegraph operator at Thornton Station in Scotland. But even now Betty remembers working the instruments, listening to the sound of the 'pings', over seventy years ago.

It has proved difficult to be precise about exactly how many women were working for the wartime railways. Reports of totals at the time varied, depending on which organisations and which types of work were included. Before the war, in 1939, the railway companies and the railway undertakings of London Transport appear to have employed around 590,000 workers, of whom 25,000 were women (4.3%). Three-quarters of these women were clerical and technical workers or hotel, refreshment and laundry staff. As the war developed however, by 1942, when 100,000 male employees had gone off to serve with the forces, there were around 74,000 female railway workers working for the 'big four' and LT railway undertakings (12.3%). By the peak of 1944, there were 93,000 (15.1%), falling to 91,300 in 1945 (14.7%) and then 58,000 by September 1946.[1]

Although Bevin announced his big labour recruitment drive in 1941, in fact as soon as the war started railway companies were considering recruiting women to fill gaps. The Railway Executive Committee and British Railways were also taking steps to coordinate recruitment campaigns for women to meet wartime conditions. By early 1941 the GWR was already employing over 2,000 women, the vast majority as porters, and the LNER was employing 2,500 women at this time. But there was resistance in places, for example in the GWR locomotive running sheds, where the attitudes of their shed foremen restricted female recruitment.[2]

In the early part of the war there was some local union resistance to the idea of female labour, with concerns about local men being available for these jobs as a result of redundancy, and worries about the effects on the railway employment hierarchy. In engineering work there were concerns about 'dilution of labour' agreements, but women were eventually allowed to work in railway workshops to meet wartime emergencies, encouraged by the Restoration of Pre-War Practices Act 1942, which laid down in law that after the war women would have to give up 'men's jobs' to accommodate returning servicemen.[3] Generally the unions were cooperative however, recognising the problems in keeping the railways running, although they never allowed women to work on the footplate, and they were also rather suspicious of the capabilities of women at times.

The women's stories in this book have shed light on the nature of wartime female railway labour. While there are many accounts elsewhere of women working in industry, in the services and in the Land Army for example, there has been little to date drawing on the major role which women played in railway work in wartime. These women were able to counteract myths about such work being too heavy for the 'delicate' female physical and mental constitution, and about some jobs being too 'intricate' for their potential skill set. This study has demonstrated how they experienced working with men, often for the first time, and the kind of strategies they adopted for coping with potential problems.

It has enabled us to recapture a feel for the kind of world they encountered on the railways, with a testimony of their vicissitudes which brings this world to life in a way that is hidden from other sources. Many of these women were young, in their teens and twenties, and many went on to marry one of the railwaymen and servicemen that they met in the course of their work, binding them to the railway life, even if they had to leave at the war's end. It does seem that there is a noticeable flow in the lives of these women, coming in and out of railway work and the services. It appears that these both had the appeal of a highly organised operation, with lively company and varied activities. As we don't have evidence in the NAROH collection from women who were older during the war, we cannot unfortunately look at how women coped with large families and responsibilities for elderly and disabled relatives, but we know from newspaper reports that thousands did.

These women took on their new roles conscientiously, working in difficult and at times dangerous conditions. To many of them it was a hugely enjoyable experience, meeting a variety of people, proving themselves, appreciating fresh air and good company and discovering surprising capabilities. It is hoped that this book has paid tribute to their sterling contribution to wartime work.

List of Contributors

(Names of the railway women at the time of interview have been used in the text, usually a married name. Maiden names are included here where known.)

National Archive of Railway Oral History

Irene Adgie 37, 50, 61, 103, 123, 147, 154

Born 1926. Railway work 1942-48. Joined SR as a typist, at Woking, evacuated from Waterloo. Worked there in Traffic until she was married, at 21, when she decided not to seek permission to stay on.

Irene Barrett-Locke née Davies 34, 92, 120, 148

Born 1920. Railway work 1937-41. Started as a kennel maid at a greyhound track in Gloucestershire, then joined the railway on the buffet at GWR Paddington Station, but bombing very dangerous. Left to become a nippy briefly at Lyons Corner House. then became a GWR stewardess on trains, for six months, the first one locally. Married a Canadian pilot in 1941 and left to follow him around his postings.

Florence Brinklow 33, 58, 81, 119, 132

Born 1924. Railway work 1940-44, 1973-84. Worked in a warehouse, then joined LNER at King's Cross in 1940 on parcels delivery with horses. Left in 1944 and had son in 1945. Later worked at Ilford Car Sheds, cleaning trains in a gang.

Mary Buist 32, 74, 153

Railway work 1940-44. Married with children when war broke out. Started in munitions. Passenger guard, LNER Musselburgh.

Marjorie Cawthray 92

Born 1910. Railway work for around ten years before and during wartime. Worked as a waitress in the LNER tea room at Selby Station.

Betty Chalmers

121

Born 1921. Railway work 1937-44. Railway family. Worked on teleprinters and switchboard at LNER York Station. Married Army Officer in 1944, left York and worked in Cambridge Goods Office, near her husband for a year. Then left and came home when her husband went to Europe for the invasion.

Joan Cox

34, 93, 143

Born 1925. Railway work 1943-47. Worked in a shoe repairer's in Chichester at 14, then as a pantry maid at a hospital. Had to move with family to Croydon, and worked at an industrial firm. Then employed in 1943 at a mobile canteen presented by the Buenos Aires Railway to the railwaymen of Southern Railways, at Redhill. Left when she married in 1947 and became pregnant.

Dorothy Crawford

91, 118, 143

Born 1913. Railway work 1937-75. Housekeeper railway hotels, Glasgow, then Adelphi Hotel, Liverpool. Took up role in staff welfare in 1942 at LMS Watford HQ, then after the war was involved in managing the refurbishment of the twenty-six LMS hotels after bomb damage etc. Had a long career in hotel management until she retired in 1975.

Doreen Dickenson

38, 51, 61, 105, 123, 140, 147, 155

Born 1923. Railway work 1940-61. Started as a railway clerk at Canada Dock Goods Station, Liverpool in 1940. Worked in railway carriages when offices were bombed, then in Accounts at Aintree Station, before returning to Canada Dock. After four years she moved to LMS Great Howard St Office, where she worked for seventeen years, charging out for invoices. Married in 1951.

Maureen Evans

36, 50, 61, 102, 120, 135, 139

Born 1929. Railway family. Railway work 1932-53. Joined the railway at 14 as a junior messenger at Railway Carriage and Wagon Department in Gresty Road, Crewe. At 16 moved into the General Offices, doing wages. Married in 1953 and then left the following year when she was pregnant.

Betty Forrester née Ross

47, 93, 133 see also plate section

Born 1921. Railway work 1944-47. Telegraph Office, Thornton Station. Worked for four years in Women Auxiliary Territorial Service first, in Pay

Corps, then Signals on intercepts. Later became an ATS instructor. Joined railways after she broke her leg and ATS cohort had moved on without her. Left on marriage.

Gladys Garlick   40, 54, 83, 108, 127, 136, 148, 155 see also plate section.

Born 1922. Railway family. Railway work 1940-46. Worked in a shop until she joined the railways in 1940, as a porter at Bowes Park Station, in 1942 when she was 20 she became a senior porter, moving to Grange Park. In 1942 she trained at Hatfield as a guard, one of the first two on LNER, stationed at Gordon Hill. Met husband in 1945 and left in 1946, but did not marry until 1949. Shift work caused problems so she went to work in a draper's shop at Southgate. Later worked for London Underground.

Dulcible Haines   115, 157

Born 1912. Railway family. Railway work 1928-33, 1939-72. Joined the railway at 16 in 1928, as a shorthand typist, worked in the Continental Department. Married and resigned but rejoined as a widow just before the war, in February 1939, working in the LMS Establishment (Staff) Office, which transferred from Euston to the Grove at Watford. After the war she went back to Euston, in the Estate Dept, as supervisor of a small typing bureau.

Mary Hodgson   32, 49, 58, 96, 134, 142, 153

Born 1924. Railway work 1941-50. Started work in a shop in 1940, then moved to LMS in Chesterfield Goods Depot as a clerk in 1941 for four years. Became a station relief. Moved on to deliveries and shipping, Freight Rolling Stock, then Accounts Office. Had to leave in 1950 on marriage. Became a school secretary for thirty-nine years.

Georgina Huber   136

Born 1904. Railway work 1926-40. Employed at LMS Crewe Arms Hotel at Crewe. Sacked instantaneously as an alien in 1940 (although Georgina was born in Liverpool, her father was Austrian). Subsequently worked in catering and as a youth hostel warden.

Vera Jones   43, 67, 88, 150

Born 1925. Railway work 1941-46. Worked as an apprentice fitter in the LMS Crewe Works from 1941. Met husband there, married at 21 in 1946 and left.

Annie Lageu   35, 49, 95

Born 1918. Railway family. Railway work 1935-42, 1961-73. Shorthand typist, clerk. LMS Leeds. Called up to ATS Pay Office Nottingham in 1942 (with 'make-up' pay). Served there three years, then returned to railways briefly until 1946. Married that year then left when pregnant in October 1946. Rejoined railway in 1961 as shorthand typist Holbeck Motive Power in Leeds. Later moved to Stourton Area Office in Leeds until it closed when she was 55.

Violet Lee née Ridler   46, 73, 157

Born 1923. Railway work 1940-47. Railway family. Started work at a printer's in Gloucester. Joined GWR at 17 in 1940 as a passenger guard in the Cheltenham/ Gloucester area. Married at 19 but husband died in service in France at 22. Had a child but returned to GWR work with help from family. Left railway in 1947 when the Essential Works Order finished. Violet later researched the role of Second World War railway women, taking part in an NRM exhibition in 1995/6.

Doris Maley   36, 98, 122

Born 1913. Railway work 1929-68. Started as a relief clerk at LMS Euston in 1929, then became a typist at Broad St Goods Depot, London. Later became a relief clerk at Southend Central. Volunteered with Red Cross in the war, later with Girl Guides for over thirty years.

Nellie Nelson   57, 73, 126, 153

Born 1918. Railway work 1940-48. Started work in a market garden near York at 16, then worked at Rowntree's packing. When work stopped she joined LNER York as a porter in 1940. Left in 1948 when she had a family (husband a prisoner of war). Only railway jobs left for women then were carriage cleaning or refreshment rooms, so went back to Rowntree's eventually.

Marjorie Pateman   33, 58, 80, 132

Born 1925. Railway work 1942-48. Railway family. Worked in laundry in Stony Stratford, then started training on lathes in preparation for job at LMS Wolverton works. Married at 23 (awarded a chiming clock and a bread knife), then after the war looked after children and family members with ill health.

Christina Pettigrew later Mitchell   36, 96

Born 1923. Railway family. Railway work 1939-40, 1945-48. Started as a shop assistant then became a shorthand typist at LMS College Goods Station, Glasgow. Called up into the ATS in 1940 in Shropshire. Became a sergeant. After war returned to Glasgow Central station as a shorthand typist in LMS claims dept. Had to leave in 1948 on marriage, and went to work for Black & Decker.

Mary Purell   113

Born 1927. Railway family. Railway work 1941-? Started work as a clerk at Murrow Station in Cambridgeshire in 1941, later went to work in Peterborough.

Joan Richards   60, 99, 135, 154

Born 1923. Railway work 1941-48. Railway family. Worked in retail shop initially then became a GWR parcels clerk at Hartlebury Station. In 1945 when men were demobbed she had to move to Kidderminster. Married then left in 1948 when her daughter was born.

Laura Scott   33, 58, 79, 153

Born 1911. Railway work during wartime. Worked at Terry's Factory in York, packing chocolates, then as a sawdust bagger at York Carriage and Wagon Works until redundant. Later worked as a carriage cleaner at York LNER for two years.

Betty Spiller   32, 76, 130, 147, 152 see also plate section

Born 1924. Railway family. Railway work 1940-46. Joined Somerset & Dorset Railway as a porter at Evercreech Junction in 1940. At 17 became a lampman in that area. Wanted to join ATS at 18 but her job was 'reserved'. Had to leave in 1946 when men returned and she married. Later trained as a nurse, did ambulance work, lastly car maintenance work in a garage.

Edith Stretch   42, 54, 67, 131, 142, 150

Born 1920. Railway work 1937-42. Initially worked as a clerk in a wholesale grocers. Started work with LMS in 1937 as a booking office clerk at Hanley (an experimental move pre-war). In 1942 called up for war work, became a work taker at Swynnerton munitions factory. Married a signalman in 1943.

Mary Woodfield née Gunter   **40, 65, 86, 109, 141, 149**

Born 1919. Railway family. Railway work 1942-46. Started working in a factory in Birmingham at 14 in 1933, worked there for eight years; eventually trained in acetylene welding. Joined her family in Wales and started working as a GWR linesman's assistant at Undy, just before she married.

Somerset & Dorset Railway

Joyce Bell née Pearce   **86, 144, 156**

Railway family. Worked as a lengthwoman on the line from Highbridge to Evercreech. Redundant when men were demobbed at end of war. Then worked in shop in Burnham-on-Sea, later as cashier at ROF Puriton. Married in 1955.

Freda Box   **87, 109**

Worked as a crossing keeper with husband at Bruton Crossing from 1938. Husband was called up in 1940, so they left, but returned in 1947, until the crossing closed in 1964.

Norah Cook   **109, 128**

Railway family. Started working for the railway in 1942, as a passenger clerk at Highbridge Station. Had to move on in 1946 when men came back, but got a similar job at Shapwick. Then transferred to Highbridge Goods Office. Had married a driver by this time. Eventually had to leave as cattle cake dust gave her asthma.

Betty Cox née Simms   **87, 144, 156**

Railway family. Started at Evercreech Junction as a 'porteress', the first girl porter there in 1940. Later two more joined – Betty Lambert and Joyce Reakes. She left when the men came back.

Doris Dunning   **86**

First husband was a ganger who was killed. She later married another railway worker. She worked as an oiler and greaser around Highbridge.

Phyllis Parsons née Abbott   **130**

Worked as a passenger guard at Templecombe, joining in 1944. Left on her 20th birthday when she was called up after less than two years on the railway.

Emily Poole   **110, 141**

She started as a booking clerk at Evercreech New in 1941, then moved to Shepton Mallet in 1942, first as a goods clerk, later as a booking and parcels clerk. She left in 1952.

Theresa Roberts   **42, 66, 112, 141, 156**

Joined as a booking clerk in 1942 at Midsomer Norton and Welton Station. Worked for six years until the work started to clash with her social life, so she took another job with regular hours.

Edna Simms née Parsons   **113, 128, 149**

Railway family. Started in 1940 as a booking office clerk at Evercreech New Station. Married in 1942.

Abbreviations

GWR	Great Western Railway
LMS	London, Midland & Scottish Railway
LNER	London & North Eastern Railway
NUR	National Union of Railwaymen
RCA	Railway Clerks Association
REC	Railway Executive Committee
SR	Southern Railway

Notes

"I Cannot Offer Them a Delightful Life"

1. *Newcastle Journal*, 10 Mar 1941.
2. *Gloucester Citizen*, 29 June 1943; Penny Summerfield, *Reconstructing Women's Wartime Lives* (Manchester, 1998), p.126; Dorothy Sheridan (ed.), *Wartime Women: a Mass Observation Anthology* (London, 1990), pp.127-34.
3. *Railway Gazette*, 26 July 1940.
4. Jane Waller and Michael Vaughan-Rees, *Women in Wartime: The Role of Women's Magazines 1939-1945* (London, 1987), p.58.
5. *Ibid.*, pp.61-7.
6. Helena Wojtczak, *Railwaywomen: Exploitation, Betrayal and Triumph in the Workplace* (Hastings, 2005), pp.1, 4, 5,12, 20-26, 27, 31; Rosa Matheson, *The Fair Sex: Women and the Great Western Railway* (Stroud, 2007), pp.88,108.
7. *Southern Railway Magazine*, Nov/Dec 1942 20/225 115; *Morning Post*, 23 Feb 1877; Wojtczak, *Railwaywomen*, p.29.
8. *Southern Railway Magazine*, Jan/Feb 1943 21/226, p.16; Mar/Apr 1943 21/227.
9. Wojtczak, *Railwaywomen*, p.19; Matheson, *The Fair Sex*, pp.8,11,27, 37,51,53-55.
10. Wojtczak, *Railwaywomen*, p.48.
11. Matheson, *The Fair Sex*, pp.123-5.
12. Wojtczak, *Railwaywomen*, p.46.
13. Wojtczak, *Railwaywomen*, pp.120,172.
14. Michael Williams, *Steaming to Victory: How Britain's Railways Won the War* (London, 2014) p.248; Matheson, *The Fair Sex*, p.18.
15. David Wragg, *Wartime on the Railways* (Stroud, 2006), p.87.
16. The National Archives: ZLIB 15/35/13 *Facts about British Railways in Wartime* (London, 1943); *Yorkshire Post*, 26 January 1939.
17. *Yorkshire Post*, 26 January 1939.
18. Wojtczak, *Railwaywomen*, pp.202-4.
19. *Liverpool Evening Press*, 2 December 1939.
20. Williams, *Steaming to Victory*, pp.244-5.

21. *Liverpool Evening Press*, 2 December 1939.
22. *Daily Herald*, 4 December 1939.
23. Tom Harrisson, *Mass Observation file reports, 1937–1949* (Brighton, 1981): *Appeals to Women*, 1st draft 1 May 1942 (Ref 1238).
24. This is reflected to some extent in the experiences of Kathleen Church-Bliss and Elsie Whiteman working in a munitions factory in Croydon, as recalled in Sue Bruley (ed.), *Working for Victory: a Diary of Life in a Second World War Factory* (Stroud, 2001).
25. *Railway Gazette*, 28 March 1941.
26. International Labour Office, *The War and Women's Employment: The Experience of the United Kingdom and the United States*, (Montreal, 1946), pp.19,139; *Liverpool Daily Post*, 18 March 1941; Roger Broad, *Conscription in Britain, 1939–1964: The Militarisation of a Generation* (London, 2006), pp.36–55.
27. ILO, *The War and Women's Employment*, pp.15–22.
28. Carol Harris, *Women at War 1939–1945: The Home Front* (Stroud, 2000), p.11.
29. Broad, *Conscription in Britain*, pp.36–55.
30. *Schedule of Reserved Occupations (Provisional)* January 1939 Cmd. 5926.
31. Alan Earnshaw, *Britain's Railway at War, 1939–1945* (Penryn, 1989).
32. Jack Simmons and Gordon Biddle (eds.), *The Oxford Companion to British Railway History, from 1603 to the 1990s* (Oxford, 1991), p.557.
33. *Great Western Railway Magazine*, 52/4 Apr 1940 120.
34. *Great Western Railway Magazine*, 51/9 Sept 1939 385-6.
35. *Great Western Railway Magazine*, 51/11 Nov 1939 446.
36. LMS Magazine April 1939 XVI 4.
37. LMS Magazine April 1939 XVI 4 159, 201.
38. *London & North Eastern Railway Magazine*, Sep 1939 29 9 503-549.
39. *London & North Eastern Railway Magazine*, Feb 1939 79 2 76.
40. *London & North Eastern Railway Magazine*, Sep 1939 29 9 552.
41. *Ballyhoo Review*, 16 Jan 1940.
42. *Daily Mirror*, 18 Jul 1940.
43. *Hull Daily Mail*, 1 Oct 1940.
44. The National Archives: RAIL 1172/2121 *Railway Staff Conference*.
45. Wojtczak, *Railwaywomen*, p.178.
46. Tim Bryan, *The Great Western at War, 1939–1945* (Sparkford, 1995), pp.127-9.
47. The National Archives London, AN 2/1085 REC Railway Publicity.
48. *Carry On: LMS Wartime Newsletter*, Jan 1940 1/4.
49. *Carry On: LMS Wartime Newsletter*, Aug 1940 1/11
50. *Perthshire Advertiser*, 17 August 1940; *Aberdeen Journal*, 26 September 1940.

51. *Manchester Guardian,* 26 September 1940; *Carry On: LMS Wartime Newsletter,* October 1940 1/12

52. *Daily Mirror,* 25 September 1940.

53. *Times,* 2 October 1940; *Carry On: LMS Wartime Newsletter,* November 1940 1/13

54. *Manchester Guardian,* 16 November 1940.

55. *Manchester Guardian,* 27 November 1940.

56. *Carry On: LMS Wartime Newsletter,* Dec 1940 1/14.

57. *Great Western Railway Magazine,* June 1940 52 6 230.

58. Wojtczak, *Railwaywomen,* pp.185-7.

59. The National Archives: RAIL/1172/2117 *Railway Staff Conference: Correspondence and papers* Ministry of Labour and National Service, *The Employment of Women: Suggestions to Employers* (24 March 1941).

60. *Manchester Guardian,* 1 February 1941; *Lancashire Evening Post,* 31 January 1941.

61. The National Archives: RAIL/1172/2117 *Railway Staff Conference: Correspondence and papers.*

62. *Nottingham Evening Post,* 20 February 1941; *Chester Chronicle,* 22 February 1941.

63. *Carry On: LMS Wartime Newsletter,* Jan 1941 2/15.

64. J. White, *London in the Twentieth Century* (London, 2008), p.195; Judith Walkowitz, *Nights Out: Life in Cosmopolitan London* (New Haven, 2012), pp.201-7.

65. *London & North Eastern Railway Magazine,* Jan 1941 31/1 9, Sep 1941 31/9 222-3, Dec 1941 31/12 297, Feb 1942 21/2 28, Jul 1942 32/7 125, Aug 1942 32/8 149, Nov 1942 32/11 210, Dec 1942 32/12 228, Jan 1943 33/1 5, Feb 1943 33/2 28, Aug 1943 33/8 144, Sept 1943 33/9 164, Oct 1943 33/10 183, Nov 1943 33/11 206, Dec 1943 33/12 223, Jan 1944 35/1 8, Feb 1944 35/2 28, Oct 1944 35/10

66. *London & North Eastern Railway Magazine,* Jan 1941 31/1 9.

67. *Gloucester Journal,* 22 February 1941.

68. *Carry On: LMS Wartime Newsletter,* Jul 1943 4/33.

69. *London & North Eastern Railway Magazine,* Nov 1943 33/11 220.

70. Bernard Darwin, *War on the Line: the Story of Southern Railway in War-Time* (London, 1946), pp.179-180.

71. *Railway Gazette,* 27 September 1946.

72. *Chester Chronicle,* 22 February 1941.

73. *Birmingham Mail,* 3 November 1941; *Western Times,* 19 December 1941; *Marylebone Mercury,* 30 May 1942.

74. *Birmingham Daily Gazette*, 28 November 1941.

75. *Portsmouth Evening News*, 26 April 1944.

76. *Western Daily Press*, 27 February 1941.

77. *Great Western Railway Magazine*, Mar 1941 53 3 73.

78. *Great Western Railway Magazine*, May 1941 53 5 126, 132.

79. *Yorkshire Evening Post*, 5 February 1941.

80. *Dundee Evening Telegraph*, 15 March 1941.

81. *Lincolnshire Echo*, 2 April 1941.

82. *Railway Gazette*, 16 July 1943.

83. *Railway Gazette*, 7 January 1944.

84. *Hawick News*, 25 April 1941.

85. *London & North Eastern Railway Magazine*, May 1941 31/5 114, Sept 1941 31/9 216.

86. *Marylebone Mercury*, 8 March 1941.

87. *Walsall Observer*, 1 March 1941.

88. *Coventry Evening Telegraph*, 12 March 1941; *Nottingham Evening Post*, 23 May 1941.

89. *Southern Railway Magazine*, Mar/Apr 1941 19/215 32.

90. *Southern Railway Magazine*, Mar/Apr 1941 19/215 35.

91. Matheson, *The Fair Sex*, p.25.

92. *London & North Eastern Railway Magazine*, Sept 1941 31/9 222-3, Dec 31/12 297.

93. *Carry On: LMS Wartime Newsletter*, May 1941 2/19; *Perthshire Advertiser*, 31 May 1941.

94. Matheson, *The Fair Sex*, p.23.

95. Norman Crump, *By Rail to Victory: The Story of the LNER in Wartime*, p.110.

96. *Perthshire Advertiser*, 31 May 1941.

97. *Southern Railway Magazine*, May/Jun 1941 19/216 53.

98. *Southern Railway Magazine*, May/Jun 1941 19/216 56.

99. *Carry On: LMS Wartime Newsletter*, Jun 1941 2/20.

100. Waller and Vaughan-Rees, *Women in Wartime*, p.58.

101. For example, *Lichfield Mercury*, 23 May 1941.

102. For example, *Hull Daily Mail*, 18 July 1941, *Tamworth Herald*, 9 August 141; *Portsmouth Evening News*, 20 November 1941.

103. *Manchester Evening News*, 5 July 1941.

104. *Liverpool Daily Post*, 17 July 1941.

105. *Great Western Railway Magazine*, Aug 1941 53 8 233.

106. *London & North Eastern Railway Magazine*, Jan 1941 31 1 4-6.

107. *Daily Mirror*, 1 August 1941, *Newcastle Evening Chronicle*, 5 July 1941, *Daily Herald*, 5 July 1941.
108. *Daily Mirror*, 15 September 1941.
109. *Great Western Railway Magazine*, Oct 1941 53 10 264.
110. *Carry On: LMS Wartime Newsletter*, Dec 1941 2/23.
111. *Hartlepool Northern Daily Mail*, 29 November 1941.
112. *London & North Eastern Railway Magazine*, Oct 1944 34/10 192.
113. *Southern Railway Magazine*, Jul/Aug 1942 20/223 80-81.
114. *Lincolnshire Echo*, 5 January 1942.
115. *The Times*, 10 January 1942.
116. Matheson, *The Fair Sex*, p.22.
117. *Yorkshire Post*, 15 January 1942.
118. *London & North Eastern Railway Magazine*, Jan 1945 35/1 8, Feb 1945 35/2 28, Oct 35/10 186, 220.
119. *Hull Daily Mail*, 5 February 1942.
120. *London & North Eastern Railway Magazine*, Jan 1942 32/1 3; *Staffordshire Advertiser*, 14 February 1942.
121. *London & North Eastern Railway Magazine*, Feb 1942 21/2 28, Jul 1942 32/7 125, Aug 1942 32/8 149, Nov 1942 32/11 210, Dec 1942 32/12 228.
122. *London & North Eastern Railway Magazine*, Dec 1942 32/12 227.
123. *Southern Railway Magazine*, Mar/Apr 1942 20/221 32.
124. *Southern Railway Magazine*, Mar/Apr 1942 20/221 52.
125. *Southern Railway Magazine*, May/Jun 1942 20/222 6.9
126. *Evening Despatch*, 10 April 1942.
127. *Carry On: LMS Wartime Newsletter*, Apr 1942 3/25.
128. *Carry On: LMS Wartime Newsletter*, Aug 1942 3/27.
129. *Yorkshire Evening Post*, 10 September 1942.
130. *Daily Mirror*, 13 March 1942.
131. *Nottingham Evening Post*, 27 May 1942.
132. *Yorkshire Evening Post*, 6 July 1942; *Western Morning News*, 13 October 1942.
133. The National Archives: RAIL/1172/2117 *Railway Staff Conference: Correspondence and papers*.
134. *Dundee Courier*, 5 June 1942.
135. *Yorkshire Evening Post*, 30 October 1942.
136. *London & North Eastern Railway Magazine*, Oct 1942 32/10 186.
137. *Western Daily Press*, 21 November 1942; *Monmouthshire Beacon*, 18 December 1942.
138. *Carry On: LMS Wartime Newsletter*, Jan 1944 6/51.
139. *Birmingham Daily Gazette*, 25 November 1942.

140. Huntley Film Archives, *Women Work on World War Two Railways*. Film 90741. The date is recorded in this archive as 1940, but it may have been produced later in the war, from the range of jobs depicted.

141. *London & North Eastern Railway Magazine*, Feb 1945 35/2 39/40.

142. *Manchester Guardian*, 28 November 1942.

143. *Perthshire Advertiser*, 21 November 1942.

144. The National Archives: LAB8/777 Oct/Nov 1942. Ministry of Labour *Railway running sheds: vacancies for workshop grades.*

145. Bryan, *The Great Western at War*, p.128.

146. *Southern Railway Magazine*, Nov/Dec 1942 20/224 115.

147. *Railway Gazette*, 4 December 1942.

148. *Mid Sussex Times*, 8 July 1942.

149. *Whitstable Times*, 19 December 1942.

150. *Carry On: LMS Wartime Newsletter*, Dec 1942 3/29.

151. *Great Western Railway Magazine*, Jun 1942 54/6 109.

152. Matheson, *The Fair Sex*, pp.72–86.

153. *Great Western Railway Magazine*, Nov 1942 54/11 187.

154. The National Archives: ZLIB 15/35/13 *Facts about British Railways in Wartime* (London, 1943), p.56.

155. *Chester Chronicle*, 16 January 1943.

156. *Western Daily Press*, 15 January 1943; *Portsmouth Evening News*, 20 January 1943; *The Scotsman*, 27 January 1943; *Dundee Evening Telegraph*, 29 January 1943.

157. *Manchester Evening News*, 27 January 1943.

158. *Western Daily Press*, 13 February 1943; *Great Western Railway Magazine*, Apr 1943 55/4 56.

159. *Sunday Post*, 21 March 1943; *Birmingham Daily Post*, 31 March 1943; *Chelmsford Chronicle*, 22 October 1943; *London & North Eastern Railway Magazine*, Jan 1943 33/1 5, Feb 33/2 28, Aug 33/8 144, Sept 33/9 164, Oct 33/10 183, Nov 1943 33/11 206, Dec 33/12 223.

160. *Railway Gazette*, 24 April 1942.

161. *Carry On: LMS Wartime Newsletter*, Feb 1943 4/30, Apr 1943 3/31, Jun 1943 4/32.

162. *Carry On: LMS Wartime Newsletter*, Sep 1944 5/47.

163. *Leamington Spa Courier*, 11 June 1943.

164. *Great Western Railway Magazine*, May 1943 55/5 70-71.

165. *London & North Eastern Railway Magazine*, Jun 1943 33/6 106.

166. The National Archives: AN 2/187 Railway Executive Committee (REC) 1940–47 Employment of women. Collapsible seats and steps for female vanguards March 1943.

167. *Cheltenham Chronicle*, 24 July 1943, 25 September 1943.

168. *Yorkshire Evening Post*, 10 September 1942.

169. *Yorkshire Post*, 20 July 1943.

170. *Southern Railway Magazine*, Nov/Dec 1943 21/232 112.

171. *Southern Railway Magazine*, Nov/Dec 1943 21/232 114; Wojtczak, *Railwaywomen*, p.6.

172. *Mid Sussex Times*, 8 March 1944.

173. *Great Western Railway Magazine*, Jul 1943 55/7 102-3.

174. *Great Western Railway Magazine*, Mar 1943 55/3 36-7.

175. *Gloucester Citizen*, 25 September 1943.

176. *Nottingham Evening Post*, 8 October 1943.

177. *Hull Daily Mail*, 20 October 1943.

178. The National Archives: AN 2/187 Railway Executive Committee (REC) 1940–47 30 March 1943.

179. *Hartlepool Northern Daily Mail*, 3 March 1944.

180. *The Scotsman*, 15 April 1944; *Derby Daily Telegraph*, 30 August 1944.

181. *Yorkshire Post*, 30 August 1944.

182. *Walsall Observer*, 11 March 1944.

183. *Carry On: LMS Wartime Newsletter*, Feb 1944 5/40.

184. *Carry On: LMS Wartime Newsletter*, Apr 1944 5/41, May 1944 5/42.

185. *Carry On: LMS Wartime Newsletter*, Feb 1945 6/52.

186. *Carry On: LMS Wartime Newsletter*, May 1944 5/42.

187. *Carry On: LMS Wartime Newsletter*, Jun 1944 5/44.

188. *Carry On: LMS Wartime Newsletter*, Nov 1944 5/49.

189. *Carry On: LMS Wartime Newsletter*, Oct 1944 5/48.

190. George C. Nash, *The LMS at War* (Euston, 1946), p.80.

191. *Liverpool Daily Post*, 14 March 1944.

192. *Great Western Railway Magazine*, Nov 1944 56/11 170-171.

193. *Great Western Railway Magazine*, Feb 1946 58/2 29.

194. *Great Western Railway Magazine*, Oct 1946 58/10 223.

195. *London & North Eastern Railway Magazine*, Jul 1945 35/7 128.

196. *London & North Eastern Railway Magazine*, Sept 1945 35/9 179.

197. *London & North Eastern Railway Magazine*, Oct 1945 35/10 187-188.

198. *Carry On: LMS Wartime Newsletter*, Jan 1946 6/53.

199. *Southern Railway Magazine*, Feb 1946 24/251 26.

200. The National Archives: AN2/187 *Railway Executive Committee.* Reference to Staff Committee minute of 3 May 1945.

201. The National Archives: AN2/187 *Railway Executive Committee.* 2 December 1946.

202. *Great Western Railway Magazine,* Dec 1946 58/12 278; *London & North Eastern Railway Magazine,* Jan 1946 36/1 11.

203. *London & North Eastern Railway Magazine,* Apr 1946 36/4 99.

204. Matheson, *The Fair Sex,* p.25.

205. Southern Railway Magazine, May 1945 23 242 p.84

206. *Carry On: LMS Wartime Newsletter,* Mar 1945 6/53.

207. *Carry On: LMS Wartime Newsletter,* Jun 1946 6/68.

208. George C. Nash, *The LMS at War,* p.80.

209. *Carry On: LMS Wartime Newsletter,* Dec 1946 7/74.

210. The National Archives: AN2/187 *Railway Executive Committee Staff Committee.* 23 October 1946.

211. The National Archives: AN2/187 *Railway Executive Committee Staff Committee* 23 Sep 1947.

212. *Railway Gazette,* 15 March 1946.

213. Wojtczak, *Railwaywomen,* p.208.

Getting in

1. *Great Western Railway Magazine,* Nov 1941 53 10 264.

2. *Southern Railway Magazine,* Sep/Oct 1941 20/224 95.

3. *Southern Railway Magazine,* Sep/Oct 1942 20/224 95.

4. Wojtczak, *Railwaywomen,* pp.190-1; Matheson, *The Fair Sex,* pp.14-5.

5. *Chester Chronicle,* 16 January 1943.

Learning the Job

1. *Carry On: LMS Wartime Newsletter,* Apr 1941 2/18; *Southern Railway Magazine,* Mar/Apr 1941 19/215 35; *The Scotsman,* 9 December 1943; *London & North Eastern Railway Magazine,* Apr 1943 33/4 68-69.

2. *Daily Mirror,* 19 July 1943.

3. *Carry On: LMS Wartime Newsletter,* Mar 1944 5/41, Sept 1944 5/47.

4. Crump, *By Rail to Victory,* p.108.

5. *Yorkshire Evening Post,* 10 February 1943; *Yorkshire Post,* 12 March 1943.

6. *Great Western Railway Magazine,* Nov 1944 56/11 170-171.

7. *Carry On: LMS Wartime Newsletter,* Oct 1944 5/48.

8. For a fuller description see Robin Nelson, 'What's New in Text Messaging', *NRM Review*, Winter 2002/3, pp.22-3. Betty took part in a NAROH film in 2002, demonstrating the old telegraphy system.
9. Letter to the author, 7 August 2017.

Working with Men

1. *Railway Gazette*, 28 July 1944.
2. Crump, *By Rail to Victory*, p.107.
3. Bruley, *Working for Victory*.
4. Summerfield, *Reconstructing Women's Wartime Lives*, p.132.
5. A donkey box was a horse box. These were used to move horses and grooms by rail, as Southern Railway had a large number of racecourses and stables.
6. Connie-onnie was Liverpool slang for condensed milk.

Doing a Man's Job

1. *Liverpool Evening Press*, 2 December 1939; *Edinburgh Evening News*, 2 December 1939; *Liverpool Daily Post*, 15 February 1941; *Liverpool Daily Post*, 20 February 1941.
2. *Perthshire Advertiser*, 8 March 1941.
3. *Perthshire Advertiser*, 12 March 1941, 19 March 1941, 26 March 1941.
4. *Great Western Railway Magazine*, Jul 1942 54/7 123-4; Matheson, *The Fair Sex*, pp.29,34,70.
5. The National Archives: RAIL 1172/2131/2117/2118 *Railway Staff Conference*.
6. *Daily Herald* 4 October 1941; *Aberdeen Journal* 9 October 1941; *Derby Daily Telegraph* 29 January 1942, 2 February 1942; ILO, *The War and Women's Employment*, p.96.
7. Matheson, *The Fair Sex*, p.14.
8. *London & North Eastern Railway Magazine*, May 1941 31/5 133, Sept 1941 31/9 238.
9. *Yorkshire Evening Post*, 10 September 1942.
10. *Yorkshire Evening Post*, 3 June 1942; *Daily Herald*, 8 July 1942.
11. *Newcastle Journal*, 10 July 1943.
12. *Carry On: LMS Wartime Newsletter*, Jun 1941 2/20.
13. Matheson, *The Fair Sex*.
14. *London & North Eastern Railway Magazine*, Dec 1942 32/12 224-225.
15. *Carry On: LMS Wartime Newsletter*, Apr 1945 6/53.
16. *Coventry Standard*, 11 September 1943.

17. From a note by NAROH interviewer Nick Alexander.
18. A phrase which refers to train staff travelling out or back to their home depot.

Surviving Air Raids

1. The National Archives: ZLIB 15/35/13 *Facts about British Railways in Wartime* (London, 1943), pp.52-3.
2. *Carry On: LMS Wartime Newsletter*, Jul 1943 4/33.
3. *Great Western Railway Magazine*, Nov 1944 56/11 170-171.
4. *Liverpool Evening Express*, 24 March 1943.
5. *Carry On: LMS Wartime Newsletter*, Jun 1941 2/20.
6. *Sussex Agricultural Express*, 23 December 1942.
7. *Great Western Railway Magazine*, Mar 1942 54/3 58.

Tricky Situations

1. *Yorkshire Post*, 26 August 1944.
2. *Southern Railway Magazine*, Nov 1945 23/248 170.
3. National Railway Museum Search Engine Archive: Alan Hammond collection.

Yanks, Canadians and Italians

1. Waller and Vaughan-Rees, *Women in Wartime*, p.117.
2. *London & North Eastern Railway Magazine*, Oct 1945 35/10 186, 220.

The Railway Family

1. Hannah Reeves, 'Railway Families', *Local History News*, 122 (Winter 2017), pp.8-9.
2. *Carry On: LMS Wartime Newsletter*, Nov 1944 5/49.
3. *London & North Eastern Railway Magazine*, Aug 1939 29 8 481.
4. *Southern Railway Magazine*, Jan 1945 23/238 3; *Grantham Journal*, 16 March 1945.
5. *Grantham Journal*, 16 March 1945.
6. *Great Western Railway Magazine*, Mar 1946 58/3 62.
7. *Great Western Railway Magazine*, Jun 1946 58/6 132.

And Then the Men Came Back

1. *Great Western Railway Magazine*, Feb 1946 58/2 3.7
2. Matheson, *The Fair Sex*, p.26.
3. *Gloucester Journal*, 23 November 1946.
4. *Western Daily Press*, 23 May 1946.

5. *Staffordshire Advertiser,* 1 June 1946.

6. *Motherwell Times,* 12 April 1946.

7. Mrs Ada Bamber, one of the last batch of seven women ticket collectors at Preston, now redundant (*Lancashire Evening Post,* 30 October 1946); three women porter guards – Annie, Pat and Mrs Mac – said their farewells at the Central Station, Glasgow (*Sunday Post,* 3 November 1946).

8. *Hastings and St Leonards Observer,* 3 February 1945.

9. Wojtczak, *Railwaywomen,* p.205.

Epilogue

1. *Railway Gazette,* 20 October 1939, 30 October 1942, 9 August 1946, 8 November 1946

2. The National Archives: RAIL 1172/2121 *Railway Staff Conference;* AN 2/1085 *Railway Executive Committee* Railway Publicity; *Lincolnshire Echo,* 2 April 1941; Bryan, *The Great Western at War,* pp.127-9.

3. Matheson, *The Fair Sex,* p.22; The National Archives: RAIL 1172/2131/2117/2118 *Railway Staff Conference; Liverpool Evening Press,* 2 December 1939; *Edinburgh Evening News,* 2 December 1939; *Liverpool Daily Post,* 15 February 1941; *Liverpool Daily Post,* 20 February 1941.

Bibliography

National Railway Museum Search Engine

NATIONAL ARCHIVE OF RAILWAY ORAL HISTORY

NAROH2001 – 126	Irene Adgie
NAROH2002 – 98	Irene Barrett-Locke
NAROH2001 – 174	Florence Brinklow
NAROH2001 – 81	Mary Buist
NAROH2002 – 66	Marjorie Cawthray
NAROH2000 – 40	Betty Chalmers
NAROH2001 – 120	Joan Cox
NAROH2001 – 99	Dorothy Crawford
NAROH2003 – 14	Doreen Dickenson
NAROH2000 – 32	Maureen Evans
NAROH2001 – 94	Betty Forrester
NAROH2003 – 23	Gladys Garlick
NAROH2003 – 03	Dulcible Haines
NAROH2002 – 38	Mary Hodgson
NAROH2003 – 32	Georgina Huber
NAROH2003 – 35	Vera Jones
NAROH2001 – 69	Annie Lageu
NAROH2000 – 51	Violet Lee
NAROH2002 – 76	Doris Maley
NAROH2001 – 50	Nellie Nelson
NAROH2002 – 134	Marjorie Pateman
NAROH2002 – 07	Christina Pettigrew
NAROH2002 – 61	Mary Purell
NAROH2002 – 122	Joan Richards
NAROH2002 – 85	Laura Scott
NAROH2002 – 62	Betty Spiller
NAROH2003 – 15	Edith Stretch
NAROH2002 – 160	Mary Woodfield

SOMERSET & DORSET RAILWAY

Questionnaires collated in the Alan Hammond collection

Joyce Bell (née Pearce)
Freda Box
Norah Cook
Betty Cox (née Simms)
Doris Dunning
Phyllis Parsons (née Abbott)
Emily Poole
Theresa Roberts
Edna Simms (née Parsons)

Great Western Railway Magazine
London & North Eastern Railway Magazine
LMS Magazine
Railway Gazette
Southern Railway Magazine

The National Archives

AN 2/1085 Railway Executive Committee (REC) 1941-43. Railway Publicity.
AN 2/187 Railway Executive Committee (REC) 1940-47 Employment of women.
LAB 8/777 Ministry of Labour 1943-45. Scheme of training of women as fitters in railway running sheds.
RAIL 1172/2121 Railway Staff Conference: correspondence and papers, 1939-42. Employment of women.
RAIL 1172/2117 Railway Staff Conference: correspondence and papers, 1941-42. Employment of women.
ZLIB 15/35/13 *Facts about British Railways in Wartime* (London, 1943).
ZPER 132 *Ballyhoo Review*
ZPER 15/1 *Carry On: LMS wartime Newsletter*

Other sources

The British Newspaper Archive: www.britishnewspaperarchive.co.uk
Broad, Roger, *Conscription in Britain, 1939-1964: The Militarisation of a Generation* (London, 2006).
Bruley, Sue (ed.) *Working for Victory: a Diary of Life in a Second World War Factory* (Stroud, 2001).
Bryan, Tim *The Great Western at War, 1939-1945* (Sparkford, 1995).

Crump, Norman, *By Rail to Victory: the Story of the LNER in Wartime* ([London], 1947).

Darwin, Bernard, *War on the Line: the Story of Southern Railway in War-Time* (London,1946).

Earnshaw, Alan, *Britain's Railway at War, 1939-1945* (Penryn,1989).

Harris, Carol, *Women at War 1939-1945: The Home Front* (Stroud, 2000).

Harrisson, Tom, *Mass Observation file reports, 1937-1949* (Brighton, 1981).

Huntley Film Archives, *Women Work on World War Two Railways*. Film 90741 (1940).

International Labour Office, *The War and Women's Employment: The Experience of the United Kingdom and the United States* (Montreal, 1946).

Matheson, Rosa, *The Fair Sex: Women and the Great Western Railway* (Stroud, 2007).

Nash, George C., *The LMS at War* (Euston,1946).

Nelson, Robin, 'What's New in Text Messaging', *NRM Review*, Winter 2002/3, pp. 22-3.

Reeves, Hannah, 'Railway Families', *Local History News*, 122 (Winter 2017), pp. 8-9.

Schedule of Reserved Occupations (Provisional), January 1939, Cmd. 5926.

Sheridan, Dorothy (ed.), *Wartime women: a Mass Observation Anthology* (London, 1990).

Simmons, Jack and Biddle, Gordon (eds.), *The Oxford Companion to British Railway History from 1603 to the 1990s* (Oxford, 1991).

Summerfield, Penny, *Reconstructing Women's Wartime Lives* (Manchester, 1998).

Walkowitz, Judith, *Nights Out: Life in Cosmopolitan London* (New Haven, 2012).

Waller, Jane and Vaughan-Rees, Michael, *Women in Wartime: The Role of Women's Magazines 1939-1945* (London, 1987).

Warburton, L.G., *Wartime LMS* (Southampton, 2012).

Westwood, J.N., *Railways at War* (London, 1980).

White, J., *London in the Twentieth Century* (London, 2008).

Williams, Michael, *Steaming to Victory: How Britain's Railways Won the War* (London, 2014).

Wojtczak, Helena, *Railwaywomen: Exploitation, Betrayal and Triumph in the Workplace* (Hastings, 2005).

Wragg, David W. *Wartime on the Railways* (Stroud, 2006).

Index